To our dear Sammy
love to you
　　　　　Joanna & Royce xx
taken for us on Jean's visit Sept.-Oct 2004

KEEP OFF
THE SKYLINE

The story of

RON CASHMAN
and the Diggers in Korea

D1740102

KEEP OFF THE SKYLINE

The story of

RON CASHMAN
and the Diggers in Korea

PETER THOMPSON *and* ROBERT MACKLIN

WILEY
John Wiley & Sons Australia, Ltd

First published 2004 by
John Wiley & Sons Australia, Ltd
33 Park Road, Milton, Qld 4064

Offices also in Sydney and Melbourne

Typeset in 11/15 pt Berkeley Light

National Library of Australia
Cataloguing-in-Publication data:

Thompson, Peter Alexander.
  Keep off the skyline: the story of Ron Cashman and the
  diggers in Korea.

  Includes index.
  ISBN 1 74031 083 7.

  1. Cashman, Ron. 2. Australia. Army. Royal Australian
  Regiment. Battalion, 3rd. 3. Korean War, 1950–1953 —
  Participation, Australian. I. Macklin, Robert, 1941– . II. Title.

951.904240994

Front cover photo courtesy of Ron Cashman.

Back cover photos supplied by the authors, the Peter Thompson
image courtesy of photographer David Koppel.

Internal images supplied and reproduced courtesy of Australian
War Memorial, Olwyn Green and Ron Cashman.

Cartography by MAPgraphics

Printed in Australia by
Ligare Book Printer

10 9 8 7 6 5 4 3 2 1

For Olwyn Green

ACKNOWLEDGEMENTS

The authors are indebted to Dr Robert O'Neill, author of the two-volume official history *Australia in the Korean War 1950–53*, for reading our work and offering constructive comments on several matters of fact and interpretation. We would also like to thank General Sir Francis Hassett, who commanded 3 Battalion Royal Australian Regiment in Korea, for answering our questions about the fighting and generously giving us access to his written reminiscences. Our special thanks also go to (in alphabetical order): Betty Cashman, Ronald Cashman, Olwyn Green, Tim Holt, Clem Kealy, John Kennedy, Maurie Pears and William Ryan. Finally, the staff of the Australian War Memorial, Canberra, and the Imperial War Museum, London, are to be warmly congratulated on their sterling efforts as keepers of our sacred military archives.

Peter Thompson and Robert Macklin
January 2004

CONTENTS

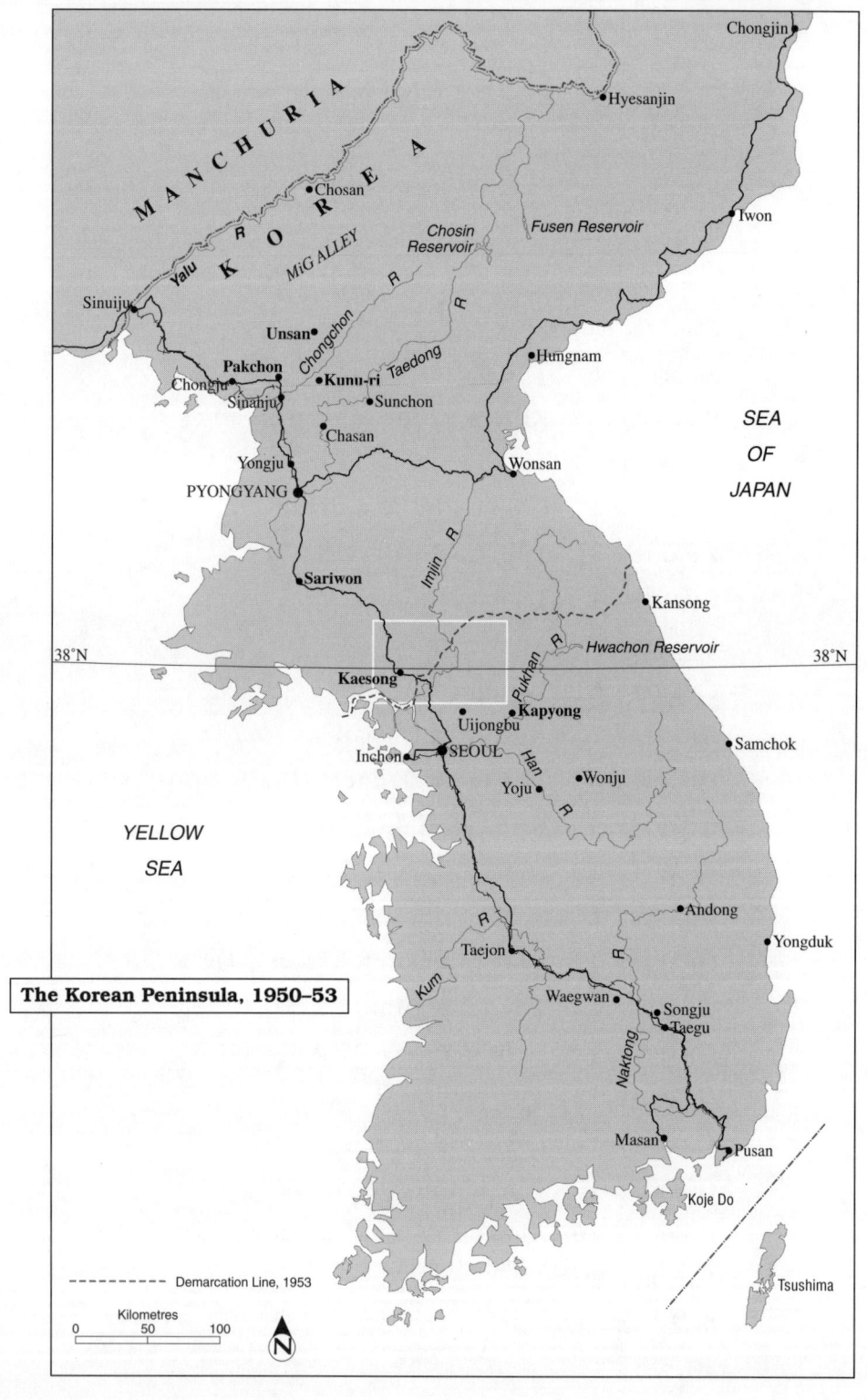

The Korean Peninsula, 1950–53

MANCHURIA

KOREA

Chongjin

Hyesanjin

Chosan

Iwon

Yalu

MiG ALLEY

Chongchon

Chosin Reservoir

Fusen Reservoir

Sinuiju

Unsan

Pakchon

Taedong

Kunu-ri

Chongju

Sinahju

Sunchon

Chasan

Hungnam

Yongju

PYONGYANG

Wonsan

SEA OF JAPAN

Sariwon

Imjin R

Kansong

38°N

38°N

Kaesong

Pukhan R

Hwachon Reservoir

Kapyong

Uijongbu

SEOUL

Inchon

Han R

Yoju

Wonju

Samchok

YELLOW SEA

Andong

Yongduk

Taejon

Kum R

Waegwan

Songju

Taegu

Naktong

Masan

Pusan

Koje Do

Tsushima

- - - - - - Demarcation Line, 1953

Kilometres

0   50   100

N

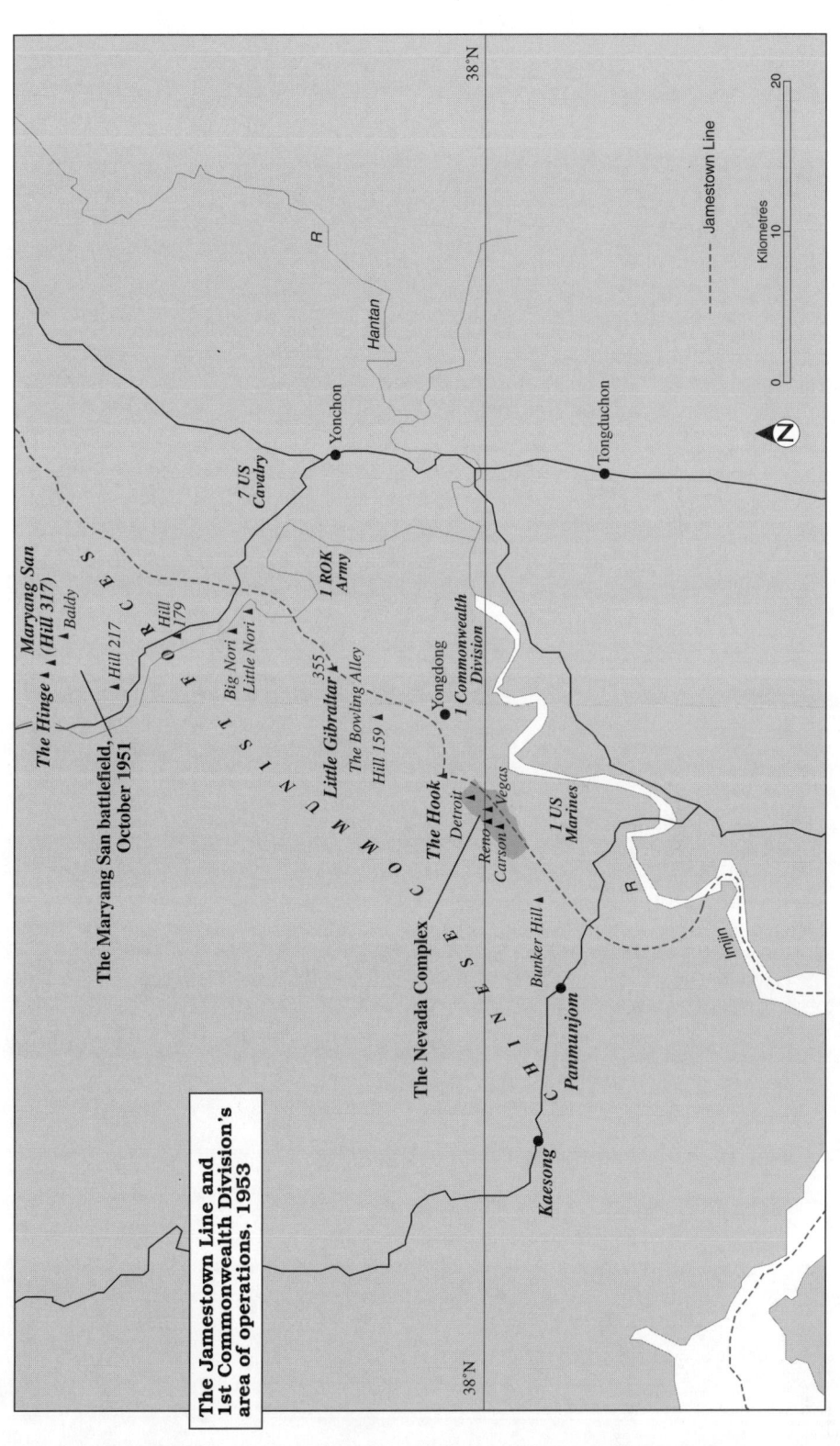

The Jamestown Line and
1st Commonwealth Division's
area of operations, 1953

The Maryang San battlefield,
October 1951

The Maryang San
(Hill 317)

The Hinge

Baldy

Hill 217

Hill 179

Hill

Big Nori

Little Nori

355

Little Gibraltar

The Bowling Alley

Hill 159

The Hook

Detroit

Reno

Carson

Vegas

The Nevada Complex

Bunker Hill

Kaesong

Panmunjom

Yongdong

1 Commonwealth
Division

1 US
Marines

7 US
Cavalry

1 ROK
Army

Yonchon

Tongduchon

Hantan R

Imjin R

C H I N E S E   C O M M U N I S T   F O R C E S

38°N

38°N

Kilometres

0   10   20

Jamestown Line

N

About the Authors

Australian-born Peter Thompson lives in London, where he worked as a Fleet Street journalist for 20 years, rising to deputy editor of the *Daily Mirror* and editor of the *Sunday Mirror*. He has written biographies of Robert Maxwell, Princess Diana, the Duchess of York, Aristotle Onassis and Jack Nicholson. He is co-author, with Robert Macklin, of *The Battle of Brisbane*, *Kill the Tiger* and *The Man Who Died Twice*.

In addition to his work with Peter Thompson, Robert Macklin is the author of three novels, *The Queenslander*, *The Paper Castle* and *Juryman*, and the nonfiction works *100 Great Australians* and *The Secret Life of Jesus*. He has written for *The Age* and the *Bulletin* and was previously associate editor of *The Canberra Times*. He lives and works in Canberra.

Authors' note
The secret war

'Keep off the skyline' was Ron Cashman's watchword in wartime Korea, where showing a silhouette on the horizon drew sudden death at the hands of a Chinese sniper. It helped keep him alive through almost two years of armed conflict against a vigilant and dangerous enemy. And it is an injunction he has applied ever since, through another fifty turbulent years.

'If you knew what this man has been through,' says Olwyn Green, widow of Lieutenant Colonel Charles Green, commanding officer of Cashman's battalion in Korea, 'you would be amazed. He is a hero ... in more ways than one.'

We first encountered Ron Cashman through his youngest daughter, Lyndie. She had read our two World War II books, *The Battle of Brisbane* and *Kill the Tiger*, and decided to tell us about her father's exploits in the Korean War.

'His adventures are so varied,' she wrote. 'I know he's my father, but he's an amazing man. As children we were in awe of him.'

Ronald Cashman is a man of great natural dignity and gravitas. He is not uneducated, although much of his wide knowledge is self-acquired. He is not particularly big, but at age seventy-one he still exudes strength and purpose. He has a finely tuned sense of humour. He seems to belong to an earlier time, or to no time at all. His hard life has chiselled and weathered his face into a map of Australia.

The Korean War has been central to Ron Cashman's life. When still a teenager he sought it out as an escape and an adventure, yet it magnified his problems a thousandfold. He won a medal for heroism but his main wartime legacy was combat stress. Undiagnosed and untreated, it wreaked havoc on the lives of his wife and their four daughters.

But foremost in this story is the conflict itself. Although it is ritually referred to in the Australian media as 'the Forgotten War', the truth is it was never well enough known to be forgotten. How many Australians have heard of the Kapyong Valley, Little Gibraltar, Maryang San or The Hook? These were scenes of Australian heroism and sacrifice that deserve their place in the public mind alongside the more easily recognisable battlegrounds of the two world wars and Long Tan in Vietnam. Lieutenant Colonel Maurie Pears, who won a medal for bravery as a young officer in the Battle of Maryang San, says, 'We went up to Korea in secret and we came home in secret.'[1]

With the Korean War (1950–1953), Australia's security role in the Cold War shifted from plugging a gap in Western defences in the Middle East to the battle against Communism in Asia. The war also confirmed the shift in Australia's primary defence allegiance from Great Britain to the United States, a process that began under Labor prime minister John Curtin during World War II and culminated in the South East Asia Treaty Organisation (SEATO). It irrevocably made Australia part of the bigger Asian picture.

The first, and only, war fought by the United Nations, the conflict in Korea was one of the key events of the twentieth century. Until 1950 the main belligerents in the Cold War had been the United States and the Soviet Union, with the other Big Four democratic powers, Great Britain and France, invariably aligning with the US. Korea knocked this balance of power off its axis. It became a test of wills between America, the world's only nuclear superpower, and the People's Republic of China, the world's most populous nation and a western ally in World War II.

Moreover, Korea provided the matrix for the wars of liberation in Laos, Vietnam and Cambodia, and its shadow has fallen across every other conflict that has bedevilled the region ever since.

The war began on 25 June 1950 when the North Korean leader, Kim Il Sung, launched an invasion of the South. It ground to a halt three years and at least two million deaths later, on 27 July 1953, with the signing of a ceasefire agreement between the main combatants. No peace treaty, however, has ever been concluded between the two Koreas.

The tensions between the rigidly Communist North, now a nuclear power under Kim Il Sung's unstable son Kim Jong Il, and the American-backed South remain as sharp and intractable as ever. The Korean peninsula is a flashpoint that could tip the world into nuclear tragedy. For reasons of self-preservation alone, the origins of the conflict should no longer be ignored. History demands the nation's attention.

But there is another, more personal reason for airing these events. The sacrifice of the men who fought there should be honoured. The veterans should no longer be shunned, relegated to the margins of Australian military history. Old men now, and many of them infirm, they are entitled to our respect and support. They should not have to ask for it.

Following Ron Cashman's experiences on and off the battlefield has enabled us to tell this immensely powerful and important story. It is by any measure a fascinating tale of war and the chaos that followed it; a compelling narrative of frontline exposure to a seemingly indestructible enemy and a horrifying descent into psychological terror.

Above all it is the story of one rookie soldier who joined B Company, 3RAR, during the Battle of Maryang San; who was wounded in action three times in later operations; who killed men in hand-to-hand combat; and who, in a brief interlude between long periods of barbaric trench warfare, met and fell in love with the woman who would see him through not only the armed conflict but its unexpected aftermath.

The story of Ron Cashman and the diggers of 3RAR is one of mateship and shared danger, of triumph against great hardship, of hope in adversity. It is the intensely human story of how a man, rightly acknowledged by the media today as a war hero, survived a living nightmare.

Peter Thompson
Robert Macklin

PROLOGUE

Killers in the morning calm

The night was cold. He had never known such cold. There was no moon and the darkness deepened the chill, enveloping him so there was no escaping it. The only sound was the wind, a soft growl as it crested the mountaintop then faded to the other side, down the valley where the darkness was still deeper. It was bitter cold, but it was safe.

The first glimmer of dawn quickened his pulse. The rising sun slowly reached down into the valleys and lit the white mist far below. The wind died. They called this place the Land of the Morning Calm, but when he saw the mist even the terrible, aching cold in his limbs was forgotten as the fear shivered and thrashed in his gut.

He climbed out of the trench, spoke softly to his mates and walked behind the position to take a piss. It wouldn't come. He knew the mist was rising and the enemy would be rising with it, inside it. Soon he would hear them: '*Jiaoqiang busha!*' — 'Lay down your weapons, we will spare your life'.

It was a lie.

A bugle sounded in the valley. The mist was still far off but it was rising fast. Now there were whistles in the mist and more bugle cries, and shouts: 'Go back, GI. Afraid, GI?'

He felt rage. 'I'm not a fucking GI. I'm an Australian!' But he kept it inside with the fear.

He peered over the ledge to the saddleback. The first tendrils of mist were reaching the pommel at the end of the far ridge. The bugles were becoming a mad cacophony. He ran to the other side of the peak. It was the same there, the thick mist rising and inside it the enemy, armed and dangerous, taunting, bloodthirsty.

He ran back towards his trench but the mist was around him now and he couldn't find the opening, couldn't see the dark slit through the milky white mist that was wetting his face and blinding him. And now they were all around him, screaming and firing their rifles and mortars and he knew it would come, that little expulsion of air, that *tsssst!* you heard before the mortar hit and blew you to pieces and there it was now, and he screamed . . . and screamed . . . and punched the air and smashed the Chinese faces down, smashed them again and again and again . . .

'Aahhh!' The harsh sound woke him. In an instant he was fully awake, staring into the darkness. His hand was bleeding where he had bashed the metal bed. Korea dissolved into nothingness. He was home. He could taste the bile at the back of his throat and feel the headache stabbing his temples. The door opened and Betty stood silhouetted in the pale light. 'Are you all right?' she asked.

He opened his mouth to answer; no sound emerged. He wanted to say, 'Yes,' but inside his brain the screaming started. 'No, No, NO!'

CHAPTER 1

The boy from Swan Lake

The young boy with icy blue eyes and a mop of wavy black hair edged his canoe through the reeds cloaking the banks of the island in Albert Park Lake. It was chilly that morning and a mist had formed over the lake but he was determined to explore the island.

Seeking a spot to land, he parted the reeds with the end of his paddle. Suddenly a whirlwind erupted as a fully grown swan attacked him with beating wings and stabbing beak. He had unwittingly disturbed it on its nest at the water's edge, and the bird was protecting its young.

The boy escaped unharmed, but he was so shaken that the incident would remain vividly etched in his memory sixty years later. 'It frightened the living daylights out of me,' he recalls. The reasons were not hard to fathom: sudden danger rearing up through the mist would become the leitmotif of Ron Cashman's life.

The mist had cloaked Albert Park that morning in 1942, when the greater world around him was changing dramatically; it had shrouded the mountains of Korea, where as a teenage soldier he fought an illusive, implacable enemy who used its cover for human-wave attacks; and it returned to haunt him in lurid nightmares long after he had been demobbed as a decorated war hero.

Ronald Kenneth Cashman was a child of violent times, and violence shaped his character. In the twenty-one years between the two world wars, and more particularly between the seminal events at Gallipoli and Kokoda, many young Australians were raised on the belief that military service was the only honourable way to become a man, to be a hero. Ron Cashman was a true believer, but his need went deeper than most.

He was born in the Queen Victoria Hospital, Melbourne, on 23 September 1932. His mother, Edna, took him home to 49 Kerferd Road, Albert Park. 'It's a beautiful road, Kerferd Road, very wide with a huge nature strip down the middle,' Cashman says. 'It's become very upper-crust now, but when I lived there it was strictly workingman country.'[2]

At the northern end of the wide, tree-lined boulevard was Albert Park Lake, named after Queen Victoria's consort, and on its western shores stood the Lake Oval, home of the South Melbourne Football Club. Its colours were red and white and it had two nicknames: 'the Bloods', after the red V on its jersey, and 'the Swans', after the great black birds that ruled the lake.[3]

The first Cashman in Australia had been an Irish soldier, who married an 'assigned maid', a convict released on licence. Ron's father, Michael, was born in Mudgee, New South Wales. He was in the Royal Australian Navy when he met Edna Florence Neason while on leave in Melbourne. Her parents, Bert and Hilda Neason, of English stock, were opposed to her marrying a sailor, and a Catholic to boot, and to gain their consent Michael bought his way out of the service.

His ardour was not surprising. A honey blonde, Edna was as pretty as a picture on a chocolate box, and she made a stunning bride. Michael Cashman was the proudest young man in Albert Park. He became a boilermaker in the shipbuilding industry, working for Australian Iron & Steel; promoted to foreman, he was able to feed his family through the worst of the Depression years.

But there were more sinister emotions than pride stirring in the man's raw-boned frame. Anger was one. He rarely smiled, and when he did it was usually at the discomfort of others.

'I thought he hated me,' Ron Cashman says. 'Every time he saw me he belted me.'

The Cashmans' home was a brick cottage with a living room, two bedrooms, a kitchen/bathroom and an outdoor lavatory. Respectable on the outside, neat as a new pin within. Edna toiled to keep it so. Toiled and trembled. For the great open hands that Michael Cashman used to belt his son were also used on his wife. Not once but countless times.

And the little boy, his head ringing from yet another terrible slap across the ear, would cower in the corner, stark with terror, as his father slapped and bashed the beautiful woman who occupied the centre of the boy's young life.

He wanted to help. He wanted desperately to stand up for her, to protect her, to be her shield from the blows. But he was too small. The man's hands were too big, his arms too strong. And Ron hated it. It made him feel like a poor, weak thing — useless, worse than useless when his mother needed him. As he grew older the helplessness became more painful. A son was expected to take care of his mother, but there was nothing he could do.

'Come here, you!'

The backs of his legs would tingle in anticipation of the pain. Grabbed by the scruff of the neck, he would see the razor strop in the man's hand, then lose sight of it as it rose in the little bathroom before searing into his legs, the pain forcing the breath out of him ...

Albert Park's pride and joy was its generous stretch of parkland running parallel to Port Phillip Bay. In common with much of the Yarra delta, it had once been swampy and dotted with stagnant lagoons, but between 1873 and 1880 the lagoons were dredged to form the lake and a few years later it was linked to the fresh waters of the Yarra.

The Sea Scouts had set up a base on the lake shore, and as a seven-year-old Sea Cub Ron used it as a weekend haven from his violent home. He learned to tie knots, sail a dinghy, paddle a canoe and swim like a fish. Here he was free, and he came to identify freedom with the military emblems all around him. The black granite fortress of Victoria Barracks had been built on St Kilda Road in 1859 and the soldiers had set up a rifle range in Albert Park, while a shore battery was located at the end of Kerferd Road to defend Port Melbourne from seaborne invasion.

The year Ron was born, 1932, was a time of immense international upheaval. It was the year the Japanese set up a puppet state in Manchuria; the year Hitler's National Socialists became the biggest party in the Reichstag; the year Stalin's purges in the Soviet Union plunged to new depths of brutality with the induced famine directed against 'rich' peasants in the Ukraine; and, in the democratic world, the year Franklin D. Roosevelt was elected President of the United States.

Cultural relations between Australia and England, meanwhile, hit an all-time low when Jardine's touring MCC team subjected Australia's batsmen to the head-high thunderbolts of Larwood and Voce during the notorious Bodyline Series.

At the age of five Ron was sent to Middle Park Central School (later the alma mater of Simon Crean), just a few blocks from his home. Ron was tall for his age, bright and eager to learn. His home life remained an unspoken secret and he buried the shame deep inside. No one must know what happened at 49 Kerferd Road.

He soon made friends, though, and when he discovered that some of his mates also suffered beatings at the hands of violent fathers he knew he wasn't alone. That early identification with other males, mere boys of six or seven years, gave him strength.

School was a place of rules, where proper behaviour was valued. But while the teachers were free with 'the cuts' to his open palm whenever he played up, there was always a reason for it. Here when he was hit at least he knew he had done something to deserve it.

He was pretty good at maths, history, geography and science — all subjects he could learn in the classroom — but he would later struggle with Latin and French because they required home study, and during those long, fearful evenings in his father's company nothing seemed to penetrate.

Ron was happiest with his mates. Summer holidays were spent swimming at Middle Park Beach and fishing off Kerferd Road Pier. Waiting for the fish to bite, he would watch the great ocean liners nudged by tugboats into berths at Station and Princes Piers in bustling Port Melbourne.

When war broke out in Europe in September 1939 and Menzies pledged Australia's unstinting support to the mother country, he watched troopships loaded with members of the 2nd AIF leaving to fight the Nazis. The diggers cheered as the ships pulled away from the quayside and the traditional paper streamers linking them with their loved ones stretched and broke.

Michael Cashman tried to re-enlist in the navy but was turned down on the grounds that he worked in a protected industry. His job for the duration of the war was repairing damaged Australian warships — tough, hard, dirty work that required travelling to whichever port the ships had limped into.

He was now away from home for two or three months at a time, and these absences were a release for his wife and son. They should have brought Ron closer to his mother, and in a way they did. But to make extra cash Edna worked long hours in a South Melbourne laundry and Ron was often fostered out to his grandparents, Bert and Hilda Neason. Grandfather Neason ran a billiard saloon and barber's shop in the eastern suburb of Ivanhoe. He taught the boy to play billiards. 'He was a great fisherman and hunter,' Ron recalls, 'and he used to take me fishing, rabbiting and foxing with a 12-gauge shotgun.' The family also included his uncle Stan Neason, who served in the army in New Guinea and later in Borneo.

It was an exciting time for a boy. In March 1942, three months after the Japanese sneak attack on Pearl Harbor, American soldiers began to arrive in Melbourne in their thousands. Ron watched the doughboys come ashore from their troopships, rifles and kitbags slung across their shoulders. South Melbourne Football Ground was turned into an American army camp and Ron quickly became a regular visitor. He wore a leather cap with earflaps like a pilot's and the Americans asked him to pose while they snapped photographs of 'the little Aussie flier' to send home, and they gave him Hershey bars.

To the east of Albert Park, the bars and brothels of Fitzroy Street, St Kilda, and the bayside funfair of Luna Park attracted thousands of Australian and American servicemen. The artist Albert Tucker watched Australian girls carousing with soldiers and painted his memorable *Images of Modern Evil*.

Young Cashman was fascinated by the scandal of Edward J. Leonski, an American private who murdered at least three women and attacked many others during an eight-month reign of terror in Melbourne. His first known murder victim, Ivy McLeod, was attacked in May 1942 as she waited for a late-night tram in Victoria Avenue, around the corner from Kerferd Road. Leonski had been drinking heavily in Albert Park pubs and had simply attacked the first vulnerable woman he saw. The newspapers were soon running stories about 'the Brownout Strangler' and the residents of Albert Park lived in fear. As Ron remembers, 'You thought he might be there in the dark.' Like a fatherly presence.

Leonski was eventually caught and hanged at Pentridge Gaol, but there was no end to Ron's trial of pain. The leather strap was brought out whenever Michael Cashman came home. The cries and whimpering of his mother, the sound of the hard slaps against her bare skin were seared into the boy's psyche.

He was never sure what caused his father's violence. Michael's own father had, in his turn, beaten his son, but that made no sense to Ron. If *he* ever married and had kids, he swore he'd rather die than raise his hand to them. Or to his wife.

Maybe religion had something to do with it. Michael was a Catholic, Edna a Protestant. They sent the boy to the Church of Christ as a compromise. 'It was the neutral zone,' Cashman says. 'I quickly became an agnostic.'

As a boy he always had a paying job; his father insisted on that. 'In the morning I delivered newspapers on a bike,' he says. 'There were three papers in those days — *The Age, The Argus* and the *Sun News-Pictorial*. Pedalling around Albert Park when it was pelting down with rain was a hard way to earn a few bob. In the evening I sold *The Herald* on the trams and *The Globe* on Wednesdays and Saturdays.'

His father commandeered his wages, of course, handing back threepence pocket money for Ron to spend at the pictures on Saturday afternoons. 'He was the tightest man I ever met,' he says. 'Scrooge had nothing on him.' So Ron turned his hand to other ways of making money. He caught frogs in the swamps at Fishermen's Bend (before it became an industrial complex and home to Australia's Own

Car, the Holden) and sold them at a penny each to medical students for dissection. Empty beer bottles brought a halfpenny and old newspapers fetched a few more pence from the butcher's shop.

He longed to leave home and join the navy. 'We had family members in the Services going back to the Boer War,' he says. 'It was only a matter of time before I joined up.'

As soon as he turned fourteen Ron applied for a place at Flinders Naval College on the Mornington Peninsula. 'They discovered I had a plate in my mouth to straighten my teeth,' he says, 'and, of course, being slightly less than perfect, I was rejected.' He joined the school cadets at the South Melbourne Technical College. He liked the sense of order, of being a team player with other young men against an unseen foe. He liked it so much that he 'jockeyed up' his age and joined the Citizen Military Forces, the home army that was to defend Australia and its territories in time of war. He enlisted on 23 September 1948, his sixteenth birthday, giving his age as twenty. 'They weren't too fussy in those days.'

Like other teenagers in the neighbourhood, Ron would take the tram into the city to see films starring the Hollywood pin-ups of the period, Betty Grable and Veronica Lake. His black hair had retained its natural wave and he had strong features, straight teeth and an underslung jaw like Burt Lancaster. But he was painfully shy with the opposite sex, a legacy perhaps of the beatings that had so damaged his self-esteem. He had no steady girlfriend, although he learned to dance the bridal waltz 'for future use'. At heart, he reckons, he was more romantic than he wanted his mates to know.

He was still only sixteen when he applied to enter the officers' training course at the Royal Military College, Duntroon. It was a bold move that might have placed him among the rising stars of the military establishment if it had come off, but he failed the entrance exam. 'I could never master foreign languages,' he says.

Meanwhile he played ruck for Middle Park Rovers, the South Melbourne junior side, and cricket for South Melbourne Colts at the time Ian Johnson, Keith Miller and Lindsay Hassett were in the senior side. He had always been tall for his age, but at sixteen he stopped growing at five foot ten. He grew a moustache, which he darkened with his mother's eyebrow pencil, and instantly looked more mature than his years. 'I also started smoking,' he says, 'With a moustache and a cigarette in my mouth, I could pass for twenty-one.'

In the school holidays he got a job peeling spuds in the kitchen at Myers department store in the City. It was not a task he enjoyed. In a man's world, this was 'women's work'. But with a pay packet and a grown-up appearance, his luck with girls changed. He met Peggy Coventry, niece of former Collingwood footballer Gordon Coventry. Coventry was one of the gods of the code. His goal-kicking record of 1299 stood for sixty years until broken by Tony 'Plugger' Lockett in 2001. Ron fell in love with Peggy and was delighted when his feelings were reciprocated. They went on dates to the movies, the beach and to milk bars. 'There wasn't a lot of choice in those days,' he says.

Peggy, however, was twenty-two and she thought her ardent beau was of a similar age. When she discovered she was being romanced by a mere sixteen-year-old, she was outraged and immediately ended the relationship. 'It broke my heart,' Cashman says.

He started drinking, just a few beers now and then with his mates in the local pubs. The Six O'clock Swill was in force and Ron was too young to be served legally, but he easily passed for eighteen. 'When the pubs shut at 6 pm you could get beer from a sly grog shop in South Melbourne for six shillings a bottle.'

Inevitably there were fights with other local boys. Albert Park was a quiet spot, but there was violence whenever one of the gangs from Port Melbourne came looking for trouble. 'It was nothing serious,' Cashman says. 'Just a dust-up between young, red-blooded youths.'

Ron was still trapped in an emotional no-man's-land, unable to settle down at school and unable to live peacefully at home. He was a pupil at Melbourne Boys High School when the war in Korea broke out in June 1950. 'I decided that I wanted to be in that; I wasn't going to miss it,' he says. 'So I scratched from Melbourne High, tried to enlist under-age, got caught out and had to hang around until I reached eighteen.'

He found work with Kenworth Rubber in Richmond driving a truck to garages where he collected old tyres that were melted down to reclaim the rubber, which Kenworth then turned into mats. It was dirty, unsatisfying work.

The Cashman family fortunes had taken a turn for the better, however. After Michael Cashman started a steel construction business and won a contract for building work on the new Altona oil refinery, they moved to a bigger house at 8 Smith Street, Williamstown, a pleasant old village right next to Altona on Port Phillip Bay.

Ron spent hours at the seafront watching ships move slowly across the grey waters towards Queenscliff at the entrance to the bay on their way out to the open sea. 'I had one thought in mind — to join the army and get over to Korea.'

Chapter 2
Olwyn's broken dream

Among the leafy hills of Queenscliff, Olwyn Green, wife of Lieutenant Colonel Charles Green, followed the news of the North Korean invasion on the radio at her bayside home, a large, rambling house called The Hermitage. As an army wife of seven years standing, she was interested in the news but not particularly concerned. Charlie had been Australia's youngest commanding officer in World War II, but the chances of his being caught up in a new war thousands of miles away seemed remote.

Colonel Green was halfway through a year-long course at the Australian Staff College in the old fort overlooking the Heads. It was unthinkable that he would be ordered to Korea until he had graduated; that hadn't happened to any officer in the history of the Australian Army.

The Greens, both country people, enjoyed college life but were a little uncomfortable with its rigid caste system. 'I left school at thirteen with a mind no bigger than baby care and it was difficult keeping up with the sort of social round that prevailed in the army in those days,' Olwyn says. 'The pecking order extended to the wives of officers; some would call themselves by their husband's rank: for example, "Mrs. Brigadier". I was an uneducated, naive kid from the country and I was all at sea in this strange, rather false world.'

All her feelings of inadequacy vanished when Charlie came home from college in the evening to join her and their three-year-old daughter, Anthea, at The Hermitage. 'Charlie had spent a long time finding this house,' Olwyn says. 'It had a very special atmosphere and we had a room with big bay windows overlooking the water. I always found the bay so romantic with its changing moods.'

Olwyn was an unashamed romantic. Their marriage had been a love match from the beginning. They had first met when he was a nineteen-year-old lieutenant and she a nubile girl of sixteen summers.

Olwyn was born Edna Olwyn Warner on 21 September 1923 at Lidcombe, Sydney. Her father was a petty officer in the Royal Australian Navy who had seen action in the North Sea during World War I. When he retired from the navy, the family moved to Ulmarra in the Northern Rivers of New South Wales, where he opened a small barber's shop. Olwyn attended Ulmarra Public School and for a short period took the bus to Grafton to attend the local high school, but at thirteen she had to give up her studies to work for her father.

'He expanded his business by buying the local newsagency and added a barber's salon,' Olwyn says. 'I took care of the newsagency while he cut hair in the salon. One day late in 1939 this tall, very handsome man walked into the shop. He came from Swan Creek and I think he was visiting a family in Ulmarra on his final leave before being posted overseas. He was in his lieutenant's uniform, with a Sam Browne belt and pips in his cap; he looked distinctively different from the slouch-hatted figures I had formerly seen.

'I had no idea what all the insignia meant, but I have to say the glamour of him had a profound effect on me. He was what the boys call "a soldier's soldier". He had enormous presence. Men have told me they could not believe that his background was so simple, for he looked as though he came from the more educated background that officers most often had. I was a bit stunned when he walked in. He wanted to buy a fountain pen. He bought one and left — and there was a great gap. I cannot explain how I felt. Maybe the arrow had hit me.'[4]

Charles Hercules Green was born in Grafton on Boxing Day 1919 and raised on a dairy farm at nearby Swan Creek. He was a tall, dark and popular boy, but while harnessing a horse at the age of eleven he had been kicked in the face. The ferocious blow fractured his skull, smashed his nose, cheekbone and the roof of his mouth and shattered his teeth. He would have died if his father had not managed to keep him breathing on the long journey to hospital.

But young Charlie Green was made of stern stuff. He endured a series of operations to rebuild his face and after a year's convalescence was able to return to school with little to show for his ordeal except a slightly thicker nose, a scar across his mouth and a set of dentures.

His accident had done nothing to dampen his ambition to be a soldier. At sixteen, he joined the Citizen Military Forces and he was commissioned as a second lieutenant two years later. On 13 October 1939, the day recruiting opened, he joined the Second AIF as a lieutenant in the 2/2nd Infantry Battalion, 6th Division.

These were exciting days for Charlie Green, but he could not forget the young shopgirl with the smiling hazel eyes, even teeth and long dark brown hair he had met on his final leave. He remembered her when he shipped out of Australia for the Middle East in January 1940, and he thought about her during the year the 6th Division trained in Palestine. In the rough, stony desert, thinking about her probably helped remind him of the lush pastures and flowing waterways of home.

She was still on his mind when Churchill threw the division into Greece in 1941 in a desperate attempt to halt the German invasion of that country. But the Germans broke through and put the 6th Division to flight. Green showed great qualities of endurance and leadership in guiding a group of Australian survivors through enemy lines, over rugged, snow-capped mountains and across the sea in an open boat to safety in Turkey. The journey took twenty-five days and was an epic among escape stories.

'It was not until he escaped from Greece that he contacted me,' Olwyn says. 'On impulse, he wrote to me. He had managed to get out of Greece with the fountain pen I had sold him that day in the shop.'

Letters continued until Charlie returned to Australia from the Middle East in 1942. Now a major at the tender age of twenty-two, he headed for Swan Creek and Ulmarra. Olwyn had a new job in a butter factory when the ardent young soldier suddenly reappeared.

There was no stopping Charlie Green once his mind was made up: he proposed to her the very week he came home. 'We were married on 30 January 1943 in the little Anglican Church on the Pacific

Highway in Ulmarra, not far from the school and the butter factory,' she says.

In March 1945, aged twenty-five, Green became Australia's youngest commanding officer of World War II when he took over the 2/11th Infantry Battalion at Wewak, New Guinea. Yet he had no wish for personal glory and would speak little of himself. His voice was a deeply pitched monotone that carried the weight of vast experience learned at an early age. In the 2/11th he was known as Chuckles, because his men, all West Australians, claimed that the dour young New South Welshman never smiled. In fact, he had a delightful sense of humour, but the damage to his face showed more clearly when he laughed and, despite his valour, he was probably a bit self-conscious.

After the war, Charlie Green left the army and took Olwyn back to Grafton, where the only work he could find was as a clerk in a produce merchant's store. His wife gave birth to daughter Anthea on 1 August 1947. But civilian life, particularly in the tedious, undemanding world of grain dealing, failed to hold Charlie's attention and in 1949 he jumped at a chance to rejoin the army. The following year he was selected to attend Staff College at Queenscliff, where he was doing well despite his lack of formal education.

He was in the middle of his studies when the war in Korea began at 4 am on Sunday, 25 June 1950, after the North Korean People's Army — the *In Min Gun* — swarmed across the 38th parallel, the demarcation line between the communist North ruled by Stalin's protégé Kim Il Sung and the capitalist South controlled by the corrupt and brutal Syngman Rhee.

In 1950 the Korean peninsula was home to thirty million souls, one-third in the North and two-thirds in the South. Following thirty-five years of Japanese domination, neither regime could be termed democratic, but the South had benefited from American patronage since 1945, when US forces had accepted the Japanese surrender on one side of the 38th parallel while Soviet troops had accepted it on the other. From that moment on, the two Koreas had been increasingly antagonistic.

Once President Harry S. Truman had ordered the withdrawal of US forces from Korea after Syngman Rhee was elected president by the country's first legislature in 1948, an invasion from the north was on the cards. It became a near certainty when Truman's Secretary of State, Dean Acheson, in a speech to journalists at the Washington Press Club on 12 January 1950, omitted Korea and Taiwan from the American Far East security cordon. Kim Il Sung interpreted this omission to mean that the United States would not shed American blood to defend the South.

Despite these portents, and escalating border clashes, the invasion apparently came as a complete surprise to the ranking US military commander, General Douglas MacArthur, in Tokyo.

MacArthur, who had just turned seventy, had ruled as *shogun* of Japan since the end of World War II, living in isolated splendour at the American ambassador's stately home in Tokyo with his wife Jean and son Arthur. The general kept an active but modest court. None of his lunches or dinners were formally elaborate and few included Japanese guests. No alcohol was served and the food, according to journalist Joseph Alsop, was what you would expect from a good army mess.

The pattern rarely changed. The guests, sometimes as many as thirty, would gather in the entrance hall to await the viceroy. Then Jean (who privately called him 'Sir Boss') would announce brightly, 'Oh! I hear the General coming.' He would stride down the sweeping stairway from their quarters above and kiss Jean 'as though he hadn't seen her for 100 years', and after a short speech of greeting he would lead the assemblage in to dinner. Films, usually westerns, were shown every evening but Sunday.

MacArthur worked at the Dai Ichi ('Number One') building, a graceless concrete slab that had once housed an insurance company. At 10.30 each morning he would arrive in a convoy with radio staff cars at either end. At the entrance, white-gloved MPs restrained large crowds of Japanese onlookers while he walked inside, his hands clasped behind his back and his corncob pipe, unlit, between his teeth.

The atmosphere in MacArthur's office was reverential. Few aides broached his inner sanctum with its massive desk, which was clear apart from in- and out-trays that dealt only with his personal mail. The great issues of state were conducted in conference, beginning with briefings from the Bataan gang, members of his wartime entourage who still competed for his favour. These meetings ended in earnest and elevated colloquy with the supplicants and mendicants of his oriental milieu.

The presence of his old team from World War II, when MacArthur had suffered the humiliation of flight before the advancing Japanese forces down the Bataan peninsula, highlighted the parallels with the start of that war. In 1941, as a Field Marshal of the Philippine Army, he had been living the high life in a grand suite of the Manila Hotel. The pre-dawn call came from his Chief of Staff, George Marshall, in Washington. The US Pacific Fleet at Pearl Harbor, Hawaii, had been attacked. MacArthur was warned to take precautions and advised to move his air force from Clark Field — advice he failed to take. Nine hours later the Japanese wiped out half this force on the ground.

Dawn had yet to break on that Sunday morning in June 1950 when a duty officer telephoned from the Dai Ichi: 'General, we have received a dispatch from Seoul advising that the North Koreans have struck in great strength south across the 38th parallel.' Shortly afterwards Syngman Rhee was on the phone to MacArthur, screaming into the handset: 'Had your country been a little more concerned about us, we would not have come to this! We've warned you many times. Now you must save Korea!'

MacArthur had no authority to 'save Korea', but he promised to do what he could, and he began by dispatching a squadron of fighter planes. Shocked, he confided to his diary, 'I had an uncanny feeling of nightmare. It couldn't be, I told myself. Not again!'

With Stalin's tacit approval a force of 56000 North Korean soldiers, supported by four hundred Soviet-built T-34 tanks and 180 combat aircraft, brushed aside the Republic of Korea (ROK) Army and swept towards Seoul with the goal of 'liberating' the southern half of the peninsula and completing the Korean Revolution.

Only twenty-four hours earlier, the British minister in Seoul, Vyvyan Holt, had reported to Whitehall that trouble was unlikely to occur in the near future.[5] Four days later the South Korean capital was captured and Holt was taken prisoner. He spent the next three years in captivity.

President Truman, fearing that it presaged a Soviet threat to Japan and the rest of the region, described the invasion as 'unwarranted and unjustified'. Olwyn Green recalls, 'It came as a complete surprise to the world, but Truman had the quickness and the insight to go straight to the United Nations and get a resolution for the UN to stop the aggression.'

The President then ordered US forces to return to the peninsula. The American occupation army in Japan was totally unprepared, both psychologically or physically. The Commander of XXIV Corps, Lieutenant General John R. Hodge, commented: 'There are only three things the troops in Japan are afraid of — gonorrhoea, diarrhoea and Korea.' Nevertheless, the first contingent, 403 members of 1/24th Infantry Division, named Task Force Smith after its commanding officer, Lieutenant Colonel Brad Smith, arrived on 30 June. Even then it was expected that the very sight of American troops on the battlefield would end the North Korean advance. When the tiny US force confronted the North Korean People's Army (NKPA), however, they were beaten back with contemptible ease. Reinforcements suffered the same fate, until the Americans, along with the surviving remnants of the ROK Army, were pushed almost into the sea.

The Americans managed to set up a 230-kilometre-wide defensive arc just south of the Naktong River outside the port of Pusan in the peninsula's south-eastern corner. Meanwhile the United Nations Security Council, at America's behest, ordered the North Koreans to pull back to the 38th parallel. When they refused, the UN called upon all members 'to render every assistance in the execution of this resolution and to refrain from giving assistance to the North Korean authorities'.

The resolution passed in the Council without veto. Ironically, at the time Russia was boycotting the international body in support of

Mao's Communist China, which had been denied a place on the Council in favour of Chiang Kai-shek's rump government in Taiwan.

The UN invited the United States to take charge of military action in Korea on its behalf, to appoint a Commander in Chief UN Command and to set about raising an army, which would eventually comprise forces from the US and fifteen other countries, including Britain, France, Belgium, Turkey, Australia and New Zealand. As units of the US Eighth Army dashed to Pusan from Japan to add muscle to the defensive perimeter, Truman appointed MacArthur to command the UN forces. The UN's formal approval followed automatically.

Australia and New Zealand prepared to enter the Korean War in response to the call from the Security Council. Britain placed its Pacific Fleet at the disposal of the UN on 27 June, and the following day Australian Prime Minister Robert Menzies' Liberal–Country Party government, which had come to power in late 1949, placed HMAS *Shoalhaven*, then serving with the Occupation Force in Japan, and HMAS *Bataan*, on her way to Japan to relieve *Shoalhaven*, at the disposal of UN Command. The Australian Government also ordered RAAF No. 77 Fighter Squadron, based in Japan, into action in Korea.

Australia's first contact with the enemy was made by the F51 Mustangs of that squadron, which strafed North Korean troops and supply convoys as they pushed the South Korean Army, the *Hanguk Gun*, south in the first days of the conflict.

Korea was predominantly a ground war, however, and Menzies made no promises regarding Australian troops for the simple reason that the nation had precious few trained soldiers and even these were unprepared for war. In mid July, when UN Secretary-General Trygve Lie pleaded for member states to provide soldiers to fight under MacArthur's United Nations Command, there was an embarrassing silence from Canberra.

However, once Australia learned on the diplomatic grapevine that Britain intended to send troops to Korea, she deliberately jumped the gun and upstaged Britain in Washington by declaring that Australian troops would fight alongside the Americans. With Menzies absent on a trip to Britain and the United States, Acting Prime Minister Arthur

Fadden announced on 26 July that an Australian contingent would fight in Korea. Fadden did not reveal the size of the force, but it soon became known that it would consist of a single infantry unit — the 3rd Battalion, Royal Australian Regiment.

In the second year of the war, when the going got even tougher and Truman made a direct appeal for greater assistance, 3RAR was joined on the Korean battlefield by the 1st Battalion RAR and, later, by its replacement, the 2nd Battalion RAR. But initially it was the men of 3RAR who would fight alongside the British, Americans, Canadians, French, Turks and South Koreans; indeed, they would persevere for so long in their thankless task that their battalion earned the nickname 'Old Faithful'.

At the outbreak of hostilities, 3RAR was serving at Hiro, Japan, as part of the British Commonwealth Occupation Force, a severely depleted army consisting mainly of Australian servicemen under the command of Australia's most experienced soldier, Lieutenant General Horace Robertson, a Duntroon graduate who had served with the 10th Light Horse in World War I and at different times commanded no fewer than five divisions in World War II. Robertson wore so much generalissimo's red braid on his uniform that he was known in 3RAR as 'Red Robbie'.

The battalion, however, was at half strength and in no condition to fight. Army service in Japan consisted mainly of ceremonial duties and guarding installations at Tokyo and Kure against civil unrest or possible sabotage. The men spent their off-duty hours playing sport, drinking or fraternising with Japanese women — and, in some cases, marrying them.

Private Leonard Russell 'Tim' Holt of Newcastle was nineteen years old when he arrived in Japan in 1946 to serve with the 67th Battalion, later designated as 3RAR. 'If you were a private soldier in Japan, you shut your mouth and put your impressions away in the back of your mind,' he says. 'There was very little interaction between officers of field rank and the diggers. They weren't snobbish but they had subalterns to mix with us. This was a normal peacetime army and you just fell into a groove.'[6]

Holt had done what Ron Cashman had longed to do: he joined the army when he was just fourteen years and ten months old. That was in 1941, but he had been discharged after 177 days when the authorities discovered his real age. He rejoined the 2nd AIF at eighteen in February 1945 and during training at Cowra gained the nickname 'Tim', not after Tim Holt, a dashing Hollywood cowboy of the period, but after the great Russian general Timoschenko.[7] Holt had considered himself such a dab hand at fieldcraft that his mates started calling him 'Timoschenko', which was duly shortened to 'Timmo' and eventually to 'Tim'.

Holt found his duties in Japan monotonous and was always on the lookout for a game of rugby or some unauthorised fun. 'They had rules that you couldn't do anything nice and pleasurable, and if you did they would seek you out and punish you severely,' he says. One of his pals was Private Hughie Bridger, the battalion wag, who was in trouble more often than most. 3RAR was strict about personal appearance and Bridger was once put on a charge for failing to shave. Escorted in front of his commanding officer, Bernard 'Ben' O'Dowd, he explained: 'I went to the shower block to shave but there were so many fellows using the mirror that I must have shaved the wrong bloke.' He was punished all the same.[8]

Good discipline was of course essential to the efficient running of the battalion. Corporal Clem Kealy, a former World War II commando, recalls: 'My first platoon commander was Lieutenant Alan "Monkey House" Morrison. When he first came out of Duntroon he was posted to Japan and he told someone who had been playing up, "If you do that again, I'll put you in the monkey house", meaning the jail. It became his nickname. He went on to become a major general.'

In June 1950, 3RAR consisted of battalion headquarters, a headquarters company and three rifle companies, all of which were seriously undermanned. Before it would stand any chance against the triumphant NKPA, its commanding officer, Lieutenant Colonel Floyd Walsh, had to find a support company, a fourth rifle company and some trained signallers, and then mould the men into a cohesive fighting force through war games and other training manoeuvres.

Walsh's first task was to procure maps of the Korean terrain and to equip his men with battledress, equipment and weapons, notably Vickers machine guns, mortars, 3.5-inch rocket launchers, 17-pounder anti-tank guns, radios, Bren gun carriers, Harley-Davidson motorcycles and a large number of trucks. The main burden of procurement fell on the shoulders of Major Ian Bruce Ferguson, a World War II veteran known to officers and NCOs as 'IB' and to other ranks, though never to his face, as 'Fergie'.

Bruce Ferguson, as he preferred to be known, was a man of medium build with a clipped moustache and a brusque manner. Born of Australian parents in New Zealand in 1917, he had lived in London, where he had attended Westminster School (and sung in the choir at Westminster Abbey), and Paris, where he had attended school at Versailles, before settling in Sydney. He was working as a cadet journalist on *The Sun*, an afternoon tabloid, when World War II broke out. He fought with distinction in the Middle East and New Guinea.

Ferguson had had long experience of the wiles of the private soldier and he put it to good use in Japan. 'He had a sense of humour but was a bit warped when he was dealing out punishment,' Tim Holt says. 'When he smiled you knew some poor bastard was going to get it in the neck. You did what he said or else you finished up in the pokey. He was quite a martinet.' Clem Kealy, a good judge of an officer's worth, disagreed. 'Fergie was a good boss — hard, but he was good,' he says. 'He was hard on himself too.'

There were many uncertainties in those frantic last days of July, the primary one being the lack of a start date. If the North Koreans continued their headlong advance, the Australians might have to go in next week, or even the day after tomorrow. Otherwise the war could be over before they got there.

In Australia, men were transferred to 3RAR from other units of the regular army and a recruitment drive was launched for one thousand volunteers to form K (for Korea) Force. The aim was to double the battalion's size to 39 officers and 971 men, and to create a pool of reinforcements. Josh Francis, Minister for the Army and the Navy, stipulated that applicants had to be aged between twenty and forty and must have previously served in some section of the army, such as infantry, artillery or signals. The appeal was so popular that hopeful volunteers started queuing at the Royal Park Depot in Melbourne five hours before the doors opened at 10 am on 27 July. There were so many that three out of four were rejected.

Tim Holt had been demobbed in 1950 and had moved to Wellington, New Zealand, to play rugby league. He immediately returned to Australia and re-enlisted in K Force with the aim of rejoining 3RAR as a fighting soldier.

Clem Kealy, who came from a farm in a Victorian hamlet named Fumina (population: five), had just sold the logging business he had started in peacetime. He joined K Force during a holiday in Brisbane after a few drinks with some old AIF comrades who were anxious to re-enlist. After training at Ingleburn, he was selected for 3RAR as a Bren-gun carrier driver. 'I had a ticket home to Melbourne to see my girlfriend for the weekend but the next day I was on the aircraft,' he says, 'so I gave my ticket to a mate, Harold Giddins, and asked him to explain to her that I was off to Japan and to give her my belongings. The next time I saw him was in Korea.'

Meanwhile, back in Hiro, those considered too old, unfit or unsuitable for war service were left on guard duty at 3RAR's camp while the remainder were marched thirty kilometres to the British Commonwealth Battle School at Haramura to undergo their first training manoeuvre, Exercise Experimental, in the rolling hills to the north of Hiro. The results were reasonably encouraging and two further exercises were held later that month.

Weapons and transport flooded into Hiro, including fifty 3.5-inch rocket launchers from the American army and fifty-six jeeps and twenty-six trucks from other sources. On his way home from the US, Prime Minister Menzies dropped in to address the troops.

At sea, the Australian destroyers *Bataan* and *Warramunga* entered the war zone on 29 August as escorts to the first two British battalions to arrive in Korea, the 1st Middlesex and the 1st Argyll and Sutherland Highlanders, which had been shunted into the line from

Britain's huge military base in Hong Kong. Australia's only aircraft carrier, HMAS *Sydney*, would not arrive until October 1951, although Australia would maintain a destroyer and a frigate in the war zone throughout the hostilities.

Colonel Walsh had performed capably in preparing 3RAR for battle, but it was known to the men — and to his superiors back in Australia — that he had never commanded a battalion in action.

Olwyn Green knew something monumental had happened when Charlie, his face grave, walked into the big living room where they had spent so many happy hours. 'He had come home early from Staff College and I was in that room when he told me,' she says. 'We were looking at the bay and it was misty. His face was ashen. He had to break the news to me that he had one week's leave before he set off for the Korean War. He didn't mention the fact that he had been selected above all other COs for the task of commanding the Australians. I am not sure it wasn't then that we both had a premonition that he would not come back. I have not forgotten the shock of it. I remember he said, "What we do for King and country". He did not point out to me what an honour it was and later, as the news got out, I was astonished that people were congratulating him. What for? That was all I could think. The romantic girl who had fallen for a handsome soldier in a fine uniform had lost all that kind of thinking about honour and glory. The honour of getting the command was never, never a consideration. He did not mention it *ever*. Can you believe that?'

Green had been given the job because past command of a battalion in action was considered a prerequisite for the Korean campaign and he was the best tried-and-tested officer in the land. The army's man management techniques left a lot to be desired, however. Colonel Walsh received the news of his dismissal in a Radio Australia broadcast on a Sunday afternoon while he was relaxing in the officers' mess.

'During his final leave Charlie took me back to Grafton where my widowed mother and young brother were living in half of a house we owned,' Olwyn says. 'Before Charlie joined the regular army we had lived in the other half of that house. I was in a terrible state, fearing something would happen to him. I can't remember hearing much news of the war in Victoria or when I got to Grafton. I was concerned only with his safety; nothing else.'

Colonel Green flew to Japan on 10 September 1950 and took command of 3RAR at the regimental barracks at Hiro on 12 September, the day after the battalion had been brought up to full strength with the arrival of reinforcements from the regiment's first and second battalions in Australia and the new intake of recruits to K Force. It now numbered thirty-nine officers and 971 other ranks, every one of whom had volunteered for service in Korea. The K Forcers made up roughly 50 per cent of the battalion. These experienced volunteers would go on to put 3RAR on the map in the first months of the war, but at the time Charlie Green had just two weeks to turn the whole battalion into an integrated fighting force.

'I had served in the Second World War and didn't have much of a problem but some of the young soldiers weren't prepared for war,' Clem Kealy says. 'They were doing guard duty in Japan and as far as they knew they were going back to Australia. From the time we were notified we were going until we went was only about a month, contrary to what a lot of people say. Colonel Green was only with us for a couple of weeks from the time he was posted until we actually arrived in Korea, and he spent some of that time in Korea preparing for the battalion's arrival in Pusan.'[9]

Regimental Sergeant Major William 'Dusty' Ryan, a World War II veteran from Auburn, NSW, recalls: 'I met Colonel Green in Japan and he did a very good job preparing the battalion. We were fortunate that within the battalion we had the skeleton of all that was needed. For example, we had Lieutenant D'Arcy Laughlin, who was a mortar expert, and he formed the mortar platoon. We had a good cross-section of diggers, NCOs and warrant officers. There were some young lieutenants among the officers, but they had good sergeants who looked after them until they got to know what it was all about.'[10]

Over in the Dai Ichi building in Tokyo, meanwhile, MacArthur decided he was not impressed with the NKPA and announced he could handle the situation 'with one arm tied behind my back'.[11] As the enemy continued its spectacular advance, he would quickly change his mind.

Dressed in their distinctive mustard-coloured tunics, the *In Min Gun* pressed hard against the Pusan Perimeter, and only powerful reinforcements from the US Marine Corps and air attacks on the enemy's overstretched supply lines from the North saved the Americans from expulsion from the peninsula. But once the defensive line held MacArthur planned a strategic masterstroke.

His plan, drawing on the tactical genius of military giants through the ages from Hannibal to Napoleon, called for the double envelopment of the advancing enemy.[12] He would land units of the 1st Marine Division at Inchon, thirty kilometres south-west of Seoul on Korea's west coast and well to the enemy's rear. 'I will, on the rising tide of the fifteenth of September, land at Inchon,' he pledged, 'and between the hammer of this landing and the anvil of the Eighth Army, I will crush and destroy the army of North Korea.'[13]

On that auspicious date MacArthur was on board the USS *Mount McKinley* to witness the Marines' successful amphibious landing, the biggest such operation since D-Day at Normandy. According to British war correspondent James Cameron who accompanied the invasion fleet, Inchon was 'MacArthur's final argument in his personal one-man deal with destiny'.[14] But it was a brutal affair. The American forces bombed and shelled friend and foe alike before the Marines stormed ashore. Cameron saw South Korean soldiers shoot old men and women. Children were held at gunpoint, their little arms raised in the air: Communists had to be ferreted out whatever their age.

At 3RAR's camp in Hiro, Charlie Green retained Bruce Ferguson as his second-in-command. He knew Ferguson of old, had handed over B Company 2/2nd Battalion to him when he had gone on to greater things in World War II. The two veterans worked a minor miracle in knocking 3RAR into a state of battle readiness in the time available to them. It was a confident but untried force that embarked in the US Navy troopship *Aiken Victory* on 27 September 1950, just two weeks after Green's arrival, and headed for war.

The battalion consisted of four rifle companies (A, B, C and D), a headquarters company, a support company and F, A and B echelons.[15] Before each operation, the commanding officer would hold an 'O Group' to decide which companies or platoons and which support weapons would engage the enemy. Behind this force would be battalion headquarters, F Echelon, A Echelon and B Echelon.

Battalion headquarters comprised the commanding officer (CO) and his intelligence officer (IO), a battle 2IC, an RSM, a regimental police escort (RP), a signals section and support platoon commands that would have sections or platoons in action. As well as representing that part of the battalion directly engaged in the fighting, F Echelon included elements such as mortar or medium machine gun, and other sections that might be needed to support any operation, along with the regimental medical officer (RMO) and regimental aid post (RAP). A Echelon contained the men and vehicles who would not be required in an operation but would resupply F Echelon with ammunition, fuel, rations and water. B Echelon held the men and vehicles who would receive equipment and stores and deliver them forward to A Echelon and possibly F Echelon. It included the water wagon, the quartermaster (QM), the adjutant and the cooks.

Each of Charlie Green's four rifle companies included a company headquarters, with either a captain or a major in charge and a captain or lieutenant as 2IC, three platoons under a lieutenant and three sections under a corporal. Each section was armed with one .303-inch Bren light machine gun with a two-man crew. The soldiers were armed with either a .303 rifle and bayonet or a short-range 9 mm Owen gun. Three sections formed a platoon commanded by a lieutenant, while a platoon sergeant, a 2-inch mortar crew, orderlies and radio operator would be located at platoon headquarters.

At company headquarters there would be the company sergeant major, a medical orderly, stretcher bearers, runners, two radio operators (one working the radio forward to the platoons and one back to BHQ), and NCOs from the mortar and machine-gun platoons of Support Company when necessary. Support Company consisted of the signals platoon, the mortar platoon with six 3-inch mortars, the machine-gun platoon with six .303 Vickers machine guns, the anti-tank platoon with six 17-pounder anti-tank guns and the assault pioneer platoon who would clear minefields and lay booby traps.

Clem Kealy, who was in 4 Platoon, B Company, thought the soldiers were young and 'a bit shaky but quite good'. Very few of the officers, however, were from K Force. Despite a regular downpour of late summer rain, the men sweltered in their winter uniforms — the same uniforms that would prove entirely inadequate in the coming Korean winter. Their transport, consisting of jeeps, trucks and two Harley-Davidson motorbikes, would prove insufficient to shift the whole battalion and their equipment. Once 3RAR got to Korea, they would have to rely on the Americans for motorised transport for much of the campaign, and when that wasn't available they would have to walk.

Charlie Green and General Robertson had flown ahead to Pusan, and the following afternoon 3RAR marched ashore in the battered port to the stirring strains of the regimental band. Once the formalities were over each of the bandsmen packed away his instrument and assumed his combat role of stretcher bearer working for the RMO, Captain Bryan Gandevia. They boarded a train with the rest of the battalion for the 110-km trip north to Taegu, where the two British battalions of the 27th Brigade — the Middlesex and the Argylls — had already gone into action across the Naktong River. Menzies, often devious in his dealings with Britain despite an apparent subservience, had urged General Robertson to make sure that the Australians beat the British into action beside the Americans. He was to be disappointed.

The dangers of 'friendly fire' were horribly demonstrated in the Argylls' first action, when they were mistakenly attacked with napalm by American aircraft just before a North Korean assault on their position on an isolated hilltop on the road to Songju. The Argylls' second-in-command, Major Kenneth Muir, rallied thirty men and launched a counterattack that broke up the North Korean offensive, but he was killed in savage hand-to-hand fighting. Muir was awarded a posthumous Victoria Cross. The Argylls had lost thirteen dead and seventy-three wounded in their first engagement. It was a grim start to the brigade's campaign.

From Taegu, 3RAR travelled further north by truck to join their British comrades at Waegwan. In their honour, Brigadier Basil Coad, the 27th's commanding officer, renamed his brigade the 27th British Commonwealth Infantry Brigade. The Australians spent several days on mopping-up operations in the area, and although they encountered no enemy soldiers, the battalion suffered its first fatality when Captain Kenneth Hummerston of Melbourne was killed in an unmarked minefield.

Within two weeks of the Inchon landing Seoul had been recaptured and the Eighth Army, commanded by the portly little Texan Lieutenant General Walton H. Walker, had broken out of the Pusan Perimeter. The NKPA had been fatally crippled between MacArthur's hammer and anvil, the survivors chased back over the 38th parallel in complete disarray. MacArthur and the Bible-thumping Syngman Rhee entered the shattered South Korean capital on 29 September to savour the fruits of victory and, in President Rhee's case, to take revenge against Communist sympathisers.

With their supply lines shot to pieces, the North Koreans were in full retreat and it looked as though the war would soon be over. At MacArthur's urging, and with President Truman's reluctant acquiescence, the United Nations had taken the fateful step of granting permission for UN forces to cross the 38th parallel, annihilate the North Korean Army and reunite the country under the South Korean government. 'I regard all Korea as open for our military operations,' MacArthur declared in a belligerent statement of intent read with great interest in the Chinese capital of Beijing. On 5 October the men of 3RAR were airlifted to Kimpo airfield on the north-western outskirts of Seoul to take part in the great push northward.

Back in Melbourne, Ron Cashman had celebrated his eighteenth birthday four days before the Australians arrived in Korea. He was now old enough to join the regular army. The army would give him pride. He would go to Korea. He would become a man. Edna Cashman accepted her son's decision with quiet resignation. In the army he would be safe from his father. But she knew he would face far greater dangers in Korea.

CHAPTER 3

The dragon's teeth

While China might tolerate the presence of South Korean troops in the North, the Chinese premier, Chou En-lai, warned the United States that 'an American intrusion into North Korea will encounter Chinese resistance'. Any advance towards the Yalu River, the boundary between North Korea and Manchuria, would be taken very seriously indeed. Premier Chou told the Chinese People's Political Consultative Committee: 'The Chinese people love peace but they never have and never will be afraid to fight against aggression. The Chinese people will not tolerate foreign aggression and will not stand by while imperialists carry out wanton acts of aggression against China's neighbours.'[16]

But MacArthur was flushed with hubris after his Inchon triumph, and he longed to administer a spectacular *coup de grace* right on China's doorstep in front of the news cameras of the world. Ignoring Chou En-lai's warning, he urged the United Nations troops, led by the US 1st Cavalry Division, to press on. On 9 October the Australians and the Argylls crossed the 38th parallel in convoy, reaching the battered garrison town of Sariwon on the road to the North Korean capital of Pyongyang without serious mishap.

Outside Sariwon the Argylls set up a roadblock to control access to the town and suddenly found themselves in the middle of a retreating North Korean regiment. Mistaking the Argylls' woollen caps for Soviet headwear, the North Koreans inquired politely whether the strangers were '*Russkis*'. They mingled with the Scots soldiers until they realised their error. In the ensuing firefight a large number of enemy soldiers were reported killed without loss to the Scottish battalion.

At 5 o'clock that afternoon 3RAR's RSM, Dusty Ryan, was standing in the middle of the road just north of the town when hundreds more armed North Korean soldiers approached the Australian position.

'There was a hot meal coming up for our men and I had gone back along the road from BHQ, where Green and Ferguson were, to divert the food truck into an apple orchard,' he relates. 'There were two other soldiers with me when up the road marched these North Koreans. They saw us standing there and one of them had rank and he came forward thinking we were Russian troops. Things were very friendly for a while and I was able to get word back to Green and Ferguson that we had a problem. Green asked Ferguson to sort it out and he came up with a platoon from one of the companies. One knucklehead fired a burst out of an Owen gun and things didn't look too good for a while.'

A tense stand-off developed as news travelled around the *In Min Gun* that the interlopers were not friendly *Russkis* at all but enemy soldiers. Ferguson jumped onto the front deck of a Sherman tank to be seen and, through an interpreter, coolly informed the North Koreans that they were surrounded and should lay down their arms. 'They were the longest two minutes of my life,' he said later. 'A deathly hush fell over the area and you could hear your own heartbeats.' It was an audacious gamble but it worked: a total of 1982 enemy troops surrendered and went into captivity. The firm of Green and Ferguson had got off to a good start.

With 3RAR at the spearhead of the Argylls and the Middlesex, the Eighth Army thrust up the west coast, while X Corps moved in from the east after another of MacArthur's daring seaborne manoeuvres had landed US forces at Wonsan and Iwon. A revitalised ROK Army took up the mountainous middle ground between the two armies, although there were huge gaps through which the enemy could infiltrate guerrilla forces.

On 22 October 3RAR went into action against the NKPA in the picturesque setting of an apple orchard at Yongju, thirty kilometres north of Pyongyang. In a ferocious firefight in which Green himself played a leading role, the Australians killed 150 enemy, wounded 239 and captured 200 at a cost of seven Australian wounded. Ron Cashman says, 'The Battle of the Apple Orchard is still regarded by the military authorities as a classic infantry action.'

Autumn was the most pleasant season in Korea after the extreme heat of summer, but as the Australians drove north the days became shorter and the nights more inhospitable. During the day, however, stands of aspen, elm and maple turned glorious shades of scarlet and gold in the sunlight, while on the upper slopes they could make out the familiar Christmas tree outlines of pine, fir and spruce. The rice had been harvested and bundles of straw dotted the paddy fields to provide winter fodder for livestock. Brigadier Coad watched an Australian platoon walk through one field 'as though they were driving snipe. The soldiers, when they saw a pile of straw, kicked it and out would bolt a North Korean [soldier]. Up with a rifle, down with a North Korean, and the Australians thoroughly enjoyed it.'[17]

On 25 October the Australians approached the Chongchon River, where the brigade was given the task of securing a bridgehead at Sinanju and capturing the towns of Pakchon and Chongju. 3RAR went forward to the Taeryong River fifteen kilometres north, where they were stalled by a broken bridge near Pakchon. Only one span had been demolished, however, and although the bridge was closed to transport it was possible for 'Monkey House' Morrison and two sections of 4 Platoon, B Company, to clamber over the debris of the broken span across to the 20-metre-high west bank.

Reg Bandy, the company sergeant major (CSM) of C Company and commander of 8 Platoon, who watched the action, says: 'When they reached the other side they were surprised to see North Koreans surrendering as they neared the Australians. But then from a nearby hill the enemy opened up with heavy but inaccurate fire on both the Australians and the prisoners.'[18]

Morrison brought his men and ten prisoners back across the bridge to rejoin the battalion. Colonel Green called up US Shooting Star jets to strafe the North Koreans on the hill while D Company were sent to clear Pakchon. They returned that evening with 225 prisoners.

The engineers were unable to repair the bridge that night, and Green was worried that the enemy occupying the high ground would hamper his advance the following day, so he sent A and B Companies across the broken bridge to the west bank. 'It was very cold, with the freezing wind coming down from Manchuria,' Reg Bandy remembers. 'C Company remained on the east bank in support of A and B, who crossed without contact and dug in. The enemy discovered them and began to fire on the forward companies. My platoon was sent across at midnight to reinforce A Company. At 4 am a T-34 Russian tank, two Russian jeeps, a motorcycle and half a platoon of [NKPA] infantry arrived — we let them ride well into our trap before we opened up with Brens, Owens, mortars, grenades, rifles and medium machine guns. They scattered. The senior tank colonel was killed along with many others.

'Just before dawn another T-34 arrived with infantry and started firing. A bazooka team tried to engage it but was unsuccessful. The tank fired at the CSM of B Company, who took shelter behind a traditional Korean grave and headstone. They couldn't hit him, but they threw an awful lot of dirt over him. In the morning the jets returned and rained hell on the enemy with napalm and rockets.'

The battalion had won the Battle of the Broken Bridge at a cost of eight killed and twenty-two wounded. The RMO, Captain Gandevia, evacuated the wounded to the east bank using a small open boat to span the gap in the broken bridge. Sergeant Tom Murray, the battalion's drum major acting as stretcher bearer, lowered each wounded man into the boat, which was then hauled across the swift-flowing river by ropes.

Murray was shot at by snipers as he saved several wounded in this manner. The final casualty was unlucky: the boat was smashed into a pylon by the current and sank in two metres of freezing water. Murray stripped down to his underwear and dived in to rescue the wounded man and carry him to safety. He was awarded the George Medal for this feat.

Reg Bandy says: 'If the CO had not visualised and anticipated what the enemy might do, the battle would have had a very different outcome. His orders were clear, his foresight outstanding. The battalion was used to quick decisions from the CO; we were trained this way, so were prepared for the consequences and were winning every battle. The CO was an outstanding leader, one the soldiers loved working for. He ruled with a firm, fair hand and was well backed up by his 2IC, Bruce Ferguson. This was the first time we were confronted by enemy tanks and we acquitted ourselves well.'

Colonel Green's men surged forward until they encountered a battalion-sized enemy force at Chongju. Both Pakchon and Chongju were on the main route between Pyongyang and the Manchurian border, and were thus of vital strategic importance to the North Koreans.

During a ferocious, day-long battle the Australians led a UN force that destroyed ten enemy tanks with rocket launchers, air strikes and US tank fire. Green expected a counterattack and it came at 7 pm, with up to 500 North Koreans assailing his position under heavy tank and artillery fire. The forward Australian platoon, which had sustained casualties in the earlier battle and was short on numbers, held its ground but was bypassed. The enemy's momentum carried them up to battalion headquarters, where Green and his command team came under fire at close range. The Australians fought back tenaciously and the attackers were thrown back, suffering heavy losses. The battleground was illuminated by searchlights from the American tanks as two platoons fought their way to relieve their besieged comrades in the bypassed platoon. Fighting continued around the perimeter until 10.15 pm, when the North Koreans broke off contact.

Dawn revealed the extent of the carnage. More than 150 enemy dead and twenty destroyed tanks and self-propelled guns littered the ground. The Australians had lost nine men dead and thirty wounded.

It was here that the battalion acquired its youngest recruit. Yung Kil Choi was a 15-year-old schoolboy who was fleeing south to escape the North Korean draft. While scavenging for food on the battlefield he was spotted by an Australian patrol from their vantage point on a hill. The soldiers fired a shot to attract his attention, then told him to approach them with his hands up. He remembers these 'strange men with the funny hats'. They took him back to camp where, he says, it was early in the morning because 'everyone was shaving'. He was still in his school uniform.

The soldiers handed him over to one of 3RAR's chaplains, Padre E. B. Phillips, who passed him on to Captain Gandevia, at the regimental aid post, a tent with six beds. Yung Kil was fed and given a place to rest under an ambulance truck used to transport the tent and medical gear to other sites. Over the next few weeks he was taught to make beds with folded blankets ('there were no sleeping bags at this stage,' he says) and made himself useful setting fires, sterilising instruments, making coffee for the wounded and replacing soiled bandages.[19] He would become a hard-working member of 3RAR's auxiliary staff for the rest of the war.

The Australians engaged the enemy again on 30 October. Colonel Green visited the forward platoons before they successfully assaulted an enemy hill. The road to Chongju was now open and the Argylls secured the town that afternoon.

Charlie Green had not slept for forty-eight hours and, after speaking in turn to each of his rifle companies, he ordered his tent pitched in the lee of the captured hill and turned in, knowing that the battalion's *esprit de corps* had never been higher.

Dusty Ryan was 150 yards downhill from his commander's tent when he heard the sound of an explosive shell hitting a tree. 'The North Koreans had fired a self-propelled gun three or four times during the day without success,' he says. 'Then one shell cleared the brow of the hill and hit that tree.'

It was 6.10 pm and Charlie Green was asleep when the shell exploded into hundreds of pieces of shrapnel. One piece slashed down through the tent's canvas and struck Green in the stomach. He was the only man in the battalion to be touched; his batman, who was standing in the tent at the time, was uninjured. 'Colonel Green was badly wounded and the RMO and the stretcher bearers got him to hospital as quickly as possible,' Ryan says.

Back in Grafton, Olwyn Green received a telegram saying her husband had been wounded in action. 'I swear I saw the telegram boy in my mind before he actually appeared,' she says. 'I had had a strong feeling earlier in the day that something had happened to him. The telegram was simply the confirmation.'

Charlie Green, who had had a premonition he would never see Australia again, was rushed to an American Mobile Army Surgical Hospital (MASH) unit, where he died of his wounds on 1 November. He was just thirty years old.

'It was the second night after the telegram had arrived that the news of his death was delivered,' Olwyn says. 'I was in bed trying to sleep. I heard a noise and saw a torch and a couple of figures on the footpath. One of them was Charlie's best friend from the time he had worked as a civilian in Grafton. The other was our GP, who had served in Charlie's original AIF battalion, the 2/2nd. They told me that Charlie had died of his wounds.

'Soldiers think that they have only so much luck before it runs out. Charlie had had six years of active service in World War II and was stretching his luck. He had had a premonition of death and the heroic thing is that this did not impede him. Yet it was such an unbelievable way in which he was killed. It was absolutely freakish — he was in a place where he shouldn't have been killed. He'd just been through a terrible battle, he had been in danger right in the front line and, when the battle was over, he had gone to his tent to have a rest and a shell had hit that tree and a fragment had ploughed through his stomach without hitting anybody else. I had to deal with that; that's what I had to deal with — why?'

For a time the question seemed unanswerable. Something of Olwyn herself also died that day. But paradoxically, the inexplicable nature of Charlie's death sparked in his widow a quest for knowledge that became a mission. It would lead her down unexpected paths to academic distinction as both a researcher and a military historian. She would collect the stories of as many of the eight thousand Australians who fought on the ground in Korea as her strength permitted, and would record their memories in her vast archive at the Australian War Memorial and in her academic theses.

Charlie Green was given a Christian burial in a churchyard at Pakchon on 2 November; his body was later moved to the war cemetery at Pusan. His death was a huge military blow to 3RAR. He was also deeply mourned as a humane and compassionate man. Major

General Hobart Gay, commanding officer of the 1st US Cavalry Division, who had worked with Green during the first phase of the advance, rated him as the best battalion commander in Korea.

Olwyn says: 'Charlie had had a fortnight to get the battalion ready for war and that was a remarkable feat on his part, and on their part too, because they fought three important battles in the six weeks he led them.'

Green had the common touch, which the men appreciated. Clem Kealy, a farm boy like his commanding officer, was B Company's jeep driver for a few days and Green had once hitched a lift with him. 'He always recognised me whenever I saw him after that,' says Kealy, not one to hobnob with officers. 'I knew him better than most.'

Some members of the battalion were appalled when General Robertson decided that Green's replacement would be not Bruce Ferguson, the man already fighting with them, but their previous CO in Japan, Lieutenant Colonel Floyd Walsh, who had been attached to the headquarters of the Eighth Army as an observer.

As far as MacArthur was concerned, the offensive was going well. His forces had pushed north to his main objective, the banks of the mighty Yalu. The first to arrive on its cratered shores were units of the ROK 6th Division, who sent bottles of the muddy water to Syngman Rhee in Seoul as a symbol of victory over their Communist foe. The President was otherwise occupied. His murder squads had taken the opportunity presented by the UN invasion of North Korea to eliminate 150 000 Communist officials and their sympathisers in Pyongyang and other Northern centres, just as the North Koreans had murdered thousands of his civil servants and supporters during their occupation of the South.

MacArthur turned a blind eye to the massacres and concentrated on winning a stunning military victory against the NKPA. He remained confident he had nothing to fear from the Chinese; they would not dare to join the war without the Kremlin's blessing, and to date Stalin's only discernible involvement in Korea was as Kim Il Sung's arms dealer. He also believed that only a few thousand Chinese soldiers could be infiltrated across the bridges over the Yalu without being spotted by American spy planes. If there were any signs of mass movement, he intended to bomb the bridges and put an end to it.

His intelligence chief, General Charles Willoughby, who had a reputation in the US Army for perfect hindsight, assured him there were only 16 500 Chinese troops in Korea. This numerical exactitude was presumably intended to convey the impression that Willoughby knew what he was talking about. He did not, and his figures, as usual, were spectacularly wide of the mark. Since their time together in Bataan during the fall of the Philippines, Willoughby's role at MacArthur's court had been to provide statistics to support his boss's grandiose schemes.

There was something else his agents had failed to discover: Mao Tse-tung, the former Beijing university librarian who had driven the Nationalist forces of Chiang Kai-shek out of mainland China, planned to unleash the greatest guerrilla war in history against America and her UN allies if they violated the banks of the Yalu and threatened Manchuria. Nor were his fears of an American invasion groundless: MacArthur was hell-bent on deposing Mao, whom he loathed, and replacing him with the favoured American puppet Chiang.

During October the Chinese People's Volunteer Army (CPV) had smuggled 130 000 men from the XIII Army Group across the river under the cover of night to join the beleaguered North Koreans. The Chinese force consisted of four armies, each of three 10 000-man infantry divisions, a regiment of cavalry and five regiments of artillery. Large as this seemed, it was a small fraction of the five million soldiers of the People's Liberation Army (PLA) who could be summoned into action if the need arose. Armed with Soviet weapons or those captured from the Japanese or Chiang's Nationalists, the Chinese had marched from their Manchurian bases into North Korea, where they fanned out and concealed themselves in the mountainous terrain along the Yalu to await the arrival of the Americans and their allies.

Their first reprisal fell on the ROK 6th Division, which had so recently celebrated on the banks of the Yalu. At the end of October Marshal Peng De-huai, commander-in-chief of the CPV, ordered his men to attack. The South Korean division lost two-thirds of its force in two days and the rest were cut off with the river at their back. Stragglers making their way to the American lines reported that their attackers had been Chinese; indeed, they had taken several Chinese prisoners. This news did not unduly alarm General Walker. He thought it normal that a few Chinese would be found close to the border. Moreover, a number of Chinese soldiers were known to be guarding hydroelectric plants on the Yalu that provided power for Manchurian factories.

Marshal Peng now decided to test the mettle of American troops. The first US force on the receiving end of the dragon's wrath were three battalions of the 8th Regiment, 1st US Cavalry Division, who had gone to assist the withdrawal of the South Korean division. On 1 November, the day of Charlie Green's death, the cavalrymen set up camp at Unsan, a town seventy kilometres south of the Yalu. Most were in their sleeping bags that night when a human wave of unidentified troops swept down from the hills and fell upon them to the accompaniment of a crazed orchestra of bugles, gongs and whistles. Machine-gunners raked the American foxholes while grenadiers blew up arms dumps and set fire to buildings with incendiaries.

No one had ever experienced anything like it. South Koreans with the Americans said the invaders were speaking a foreign language: considering the location, it must have been Chinese. Taken by surprise and unsure of enemy numbers, the 1st and 2nd Battalions decided to cut their losses and make a run for it under cover of darkness in their armoured vehicles and trucks. It was the first case of 'bug-out' among the UN forces. The Chinese, however, had anticipated this move and had set an ambush on the road south.

The temperature in this northern fastness in the heart of the Korean peninsula had dropped below zero that night, but bright moonlight illuminated the scene as the leading vehicles in the American convoy exploded in flames under a hail of gunfire and explosives. This created a deadly bottleneck and, as vehicles concertinaed into one another, American soldiers jumped out to exchange fire with the Chinese. Salvaging many of their vehicles, they made a fighting retreat back to Unsan, still occupied by the 3rd Battalion. The

Americans redeemed their position but in subsequent battles six hundred members of the 8th Cavalry were either killed or captured.

Curiously the Chinese made no attempt to follow up this devastating victory. Having demonstrated their ability to strike without warning, they simply melted away into the snow-covered mountains while Beijing waited to see how MacArthur would react. Mounting his soapbox, the Supreme Commander indignantly claimed that China's intervention in the Korean War was 'outrageous international lawlessness'.[20]

He ordered a force of seventy-nine B-29 bombers and 300 fighter bombers to destroy the bridges over the Yalu linking North Korea to Manchuria. The raid was largely a failure. Such was the ferocity of the area's anti-aircraft defences that the huge air force managed to blow up only four of the twelve major bridges on a 330-kilometre stretch of the river and damage several others. Soon afterwards the Yalu froze over and the Chinese were able to supply their soldiers across the ice.

Despite hard evidence to the contrary, MacArthur claimed that he was 'sure the Chinese Communists had sent 25 000, and certainly no more than 30 000, soldiers across the border';[21] there was nothing to fear.

Peng De-huai's early strategy had been devised to test America's military strength and her will to fight. The verdict at his headquarters was that US troops lacked the political resolve to risk their lives fighting for Korea. General Walker seemed to endorse this thesis when he ordered all units of the Eighth Army to pull back to the Chongchon River.

The withdrawal was under way when, on 5 November, Brigadier Coad ordered Colonel Walsh and 3RAR to recapture a ridge overlooking the main road that had been lost in a skirmish with Chinese soldiers earlier that day. The battalion's position was 1.5 kilometres west of Pakchon, but to reach the ridge they had to ford the Taeryong River, cross five hundred metres of paddy field and climb fifty metres under enemy fire.

'Walsh had dug us in on the wrong side of the river to defend ourselves against thousands of Chinese,' says Clem Kealy, who was with 4 Platoon, B Company. 'We were well dug in too, with overhead cover, gallons of water and stacks of ammunition. Walsh came up to us and asked if we had any questions. I said, "Yes, sir, why are we dug in on this side of the river? Shouldn't we be on the other side where we can defend the river? If we get pushed off here, it's 150 foot straight down into the water". About two hours later we were ordered to move across the river.'

Later that day A and B Companies, supported by mortar and machine-gun fire, stormed the ridge with fixed bayonets and succeeded in driving off the Chinese occupiers after a two-hour fight, much of it hand-to-hand. It was the sort of thing that Coad, whom the Australians referred to as 'the grey-headed old bastard', had come to expect of them and they did not let him down.

The position was consolidated by D Company, with C Company and battalion HQ holding the road. With the ridge secure, the road was now safe and the 27th Brigade was able to move south while 3RAR held the rearguard position.

During the night A, B and C Companies came under machine-gun and mortar fire, which caused Colonel Walsh to make a number of tactical blunders. First he moved C Company and BHQ about a kilometre further south along the road. Then, without taking the time to consult Brigadier Coad and in the absence of Bruce Ferguson, who was with the battalion's supply force somewhere south of the Chongchon River, he ordered the three rifle companies, A, B and D, to abandon the ridgeline.

A and B Companies were clear of the ridge and D Company was halfway down when Brigadier Coad learned over the rear radio link what was happening. He immediately ordered the Australians to hold their ground. It was too late to recall A and B Companies, so Walsh ordered D Company to return to the ridge.

Meanwhile, Chinese patrols had infiltrated the road and, as a heavy firefight broke out on the flat ground, the new CO was faced with the horrifying prospect of losing his entire battalion. The heaviest losses fell on A Company, which had to fight its way back to the battalion's lines. By the time D Company had extricated itself from the ridge without actually having made contact with the enemy, twelve diggers had been killed and sixty-four wounded in other companies.

At first light Coad drove to battalion headquarters and sacked Walsh, who was in an emotional state and clearly suffering from stress. The more phlegmatic Bruce Ferguson was appointed commanding officer of 3RAR. One of his first acts would lead to controversy. Clem Kealy recalls that Ferguson relieved a number of his junior officers, mainly lieutenants who had come out of Duntroon, and sent them back 'because he had all these K Force officers in Japan — young fellows of twenty-eight or thirty who had been in the Second World War — and he got them over'.

The Australians' first sight of the Chinese soldier, in early November, had revealed a short, bulky figure in a brown quilted winter uniform topped by a peaked cap surmounted by a red star badge. He was either firing a Soviet-made burp gun or hurling grenades shaped like a potato masher, all the while producing bloodcurdling screams. Before going into battle, he had been harangued by political commissars into a state of patriotic rage against imperialist American aggressors and their running-dog allies who were threatening the People's Revolution. The accompanying bugles, whistles and gongs were intended not only to terrify the enemy but also to coordinate various units during the attack.

On 1 November United Nations Command faced a disturbing escalation of the war when the first Soviet-built MiG-15 jet fighter suddenly made its appearance in the skies over North Korea. It attacked American warplanes bombing targets near the Yalu. Seven days later an American F-80 Shooting Star jet fighter shot down a MiG-15 in the first all-jet dogfight in military history. American pilots soon reported that they were sighting Caucasian pilots in the cockpits of the MiGs and intercepting a new language on their radios — Russian.

It was decided to withdraw the obsolete Mustangs of No. 77 Squadron and train the pilots to fly Gloster Meteor Mk 8 jet fighters. But the changeover took months to accomplish, and the Australian pilots found that the British-built aircraft had cramped cockpits and were somewhat limited in high-altitude combat. They envied the

Americans their freewheeling Sabres, which were more than a match for the enemy in MiG Alley. The UN forces never lost air superiority, a vital factor in beating off many Chinese attacks and disrupting enemy supply lines.

Thanksgiving fell on 23 November and the traditional fare of roast turkey dinners and mince pies was airlifted to the American, British and Australian forces now dug in on the Chongchon River. The following day the Eighth Army gunned its engines and headed north again to turn MacArthur's vision of a unified Korea into a reality. The official diary of 27th Brigade reads: 'Today has marked the opening of the offensive which it is hoped would reach the Manchurian border and finish the Korean War.'

MacArthur conceded that there were now between 40 000 and 80 000 Chinese troops in North Korea, a margin for error indicating that Willoughby was no longer taking any chances. (This estimate soon escalated to 180 000 but was still woefully short of the actual figure.) The Supreme Commander, who had flown to Korea to watch the offensive begin, was in an ebullient mood when he assured the troops of victory and promised they would be home by Christmas.

By this time, however, the Chinese armies in North Korea had almost tripled to 380 000. Half a million Manchurian coolies with thousands of pack animals followed in their wake to dig trenches for both attack and defence and to carry supplies to the front.

In the daylight hours this huge force virtually disappeared, as though made invisible by an Oriental conjurer. To dodge US reconnaissance aircraft and thus avoid the air strikes that had caused such widespread destruction to the motorised North Korean People's Army, the Chinese hid in caves and under camouflaged tents in the valleys and rice paddies, in forests on the upper slopes of the mountains, in ravines and crevices and every other conceivable hiding place. They slept and ate and waited until darkness fell, whereupon they resumed their painstaking labours, inexorably closing the gap between themselves and MacArthur's invading forces.

MacArthur's battle plan in November was similar to the one that had failed in October. Its aim was to trap the NKPA in a giant vice on the banks of the Yalu after US warplanes had sealed off the Manchurian border as a means of escape or reinforcement. Units of the Eighth Army would advance northward up the west coast, while others moved inland to the north-east. The South Koreans would hold the central mountains and the north-eastern provinces closest to the Siberian border. X Corps, under MacArthur's favourite commander, General Edward Almond, would then move inland from the east coast to link up with the Eighth Army near the Yalu, destroying the enemy in the process.

Back in the US, Truman's administration had finally accepted the idea that China had intervened in the war because it genuinely feared an American invasion of Manchuria. As MacArthur advanced northward again with an even bigger army, Washington thought it prudent to assure Beijing that this was not the case. A US-sponsored resolution to the UN stated that 'it is the policy of the United Nations to hold the Chinese frontier with Korea inviolate and fully to protect legitimate Chinese and Korean interests in the frontier zone'. Beijing was unimpressed.

The men of 3RAR had travelled only a few kilometres north in their new US Army winter gear when Colonel Ferguson's forward patrols reported skirmishes with the enemy. The Australians were a short distance north of Pakchon, scene of two of their earlier battles, when the Chinese mounted a major offensive against the Eighth Army.

The first hammer blows in the Battle of Chongchon River, on 25 November, fell on the ROK II Corps and the US IX Corps, commanded by Major General John Coulter. Units of the US 25th Infantry Division were overwhelmed by human-wave attacks by thousands of Chinese soldiers and had to fight their way through roadblocks that the enveloping forces had set up behind them.

Simultaneously the enemy had broken through the ROKA line and opened a 25-kilometre gap in the Eighth Army's right flank, exposing the US 2nd Infantry Division, stretched across the Chongchon Valley, to immediate danger. Shortly before midnight six Chinese divisions attacked the 2nd head on, while six more divisions poured through the gap and started to encircle it.

One Chinese strike force forded the freezing Chongchon River to storm American gun emplacements and succeeded in overrunning them. Ferocious fighting continued throughout the night, with individual American regiments holding their ground and, in some cases, mounting counterattacks, but many units simply 'bugged out', escaping from the fighting by whatever means available — jeeps, trucks, armoured vehicles or on foot. Some swam the Chongchon River, the water so cold their dripping clothing turned to ice as they staggered ashore.

The 19th Infantry Regiment of the US 24th Division bugged out north of the river in the face of a surprise attack by the Chinese 39th Field Army, the same force that had put the 8th Cavalry Regiment to flight. The 19th's abrupt departure from the battlefield would have been even more humiliating had 3RAR, with other units of the 27th Commonwealth Brigade and the US 61st Field Artillery Regiment, not held their ground and fought back.

On the morning of the 26th, the 2nd Division was withdrawing along its only remaining escape route — south-west down the Chongchon River towards the village of Kunu-ri, where the main road led along the river to Anju. Looking at his map, 2nd Division's commander, Major General Laurence B. 'Dutch' Keiser, identified a winding secondary road offering escape through the Kunu-ri mountain pass to Sunchon.

The Chinese were breaking through everywhere and attacking at will, and General Walker ordered the US 2nd and 25th Divisions to leave the area as quickly as possible. With the 25th Division clogging the Anju road, Keiser decided to take the 2nd Division down the narrow mountain road from Kunu-ri to Sunchon. Brigadier Coad, whose brigade had abruptly been attached to IX Corps when the Chinese attacked, was ordered by General Coulter to cover Keiser's withdrawal with British and Commonwealth troops. Visiting Coulter's IX Corps headquarters at midday on the 27th, Coad was astonished at the behaviour of some of the senior officers. 'The hysteria was quite frightening,' he said later.

Thick black snow clouds and a biting wind provided ominous signs of impending doom as the men of 3RAR travelled from Pakchon to Kunu-ri on 27 November. 'We had to travel about 35 kilometres to get there and the Americans couldn't supply us with enough trucks,' Clem Kealy says. 'They gave us about fifteen trucks and we got Support Company and two of the other companies into them, but C Company and B Company had to march the full distance. It was the first time it had snowed. We dug in in the hills north of Kunu-ri. I was asleep at 2.10 am when my mate woke me up and said, "You hear that digging? It's the Chows digging in." They were digging in opposite us less than 150 metres away. Our command got us under way in the middle of the night and very quietly withdrew us to another position about four kilometres away at a road junction. My section took over from a couple of American machine guns.'

On 28 November Brigadier Coad was ordered to move the 27th Brigade thirty-eight kilometres south to Chasan, just south of Sunchon, to act as the IX Corps reserve. The shortage of trucks had become acute and many of the men set off on foot to the strains of Argyll pipers distributed through their ranks. Aware that the Chinese were moving in all around, they were vastly relieved to make it safely up the steep, winding road leading to the head of the pass through the mountains at Yongwon-ni.

'That afternoon it was snowing and I saw the Americans bring out a Chinese prisoner sitting on the front of a jeep,' says Clem Kealy. 'All he had on were a hat and boots — his bare bum was sitting on front of a jeep. It would have taken every bit of skin off his bum. Some of the Americans were just smart arses.'

A and C Companies of 3RAR had the luxury of motorised transport and reached Chasan at 10 o'clock that night, but most of the battalion walked up to thirty-five kilometres over rough roads in atrocious weather before being picked up and driven to Chasan. The last remnants of the brigade did not arrive until 3.15 am on 29 November.

Coad was ordered to keep the road open between Kunu-ri and Sunchon to enable the 2nd Division to make good its escape. He was also told to defend a vital ferry crossing on the Taedong River at Chasan. He decided to send the 1st Middlesex Battalion north again to the southern exit of the Kunu-ri pass while the Australians guarded the ferry crossing. The Argylls would be held in reserve.

The Middlesex, nicknamed 'the Diehards', arrived at their destination to discover that the Chinese had taken a firm grip on the foothills surrounding the exit to the pass. With no tank or artillery support, they had no chance of keeping the pass clear of enemy soldiers. After suffering one officer killed and twenty-five men wounded in fierce fighting, the Middlesex withdrew ten kilometres to the south and set up a base called Nottingham to await the arrival of the 2nd Division. Having seen the Chinese in action they feared the worst.

With the US 23rd Infantry Regiment guarding the rear, the 2nd Division set off from Kunu-ri along the twisting valley road leading to the mountain pass in the early afternoon of 30 November. It had travelled barely a mile when the huge column of troop carriers, trucks, tanks, jeeps and motorbikes was assailed by blistering volleys of mortar and machine-gun fire. An entire Chinese division had formed a gauntlet of steel for ten kilometres along both sides of the valley. The Americans were trapped.

With little room to manoeuvre, blazing vehicles crashed into one another, spewing men onto the roadway where they were easy targets for the marksmen on the snow-covered hillsides. Tanks tried to bulldoze their way past wrecked vehicles only to encounter more blistering fire and come to grief themselves. Meanwhile American jets screamed back and forth along the heights, machine-gunning Chinese positions and dropping napalm, some of which fell so close to American vehicles that they burst into flames.

When his bodyguard was killed, General Keiser leaped from his jeep and, shouting encouragement to his men, fired bursts from his rifle at the enemy. But as the early evening closed around the trapped division, the Chinese swarmed down the slopes and engaged the

American infantry battalions at close quarters. Some Americans were reported to have simply sat transfixed in their vehicles, waiting to die.

The 23rd Regiment had been given permission to evacuate Kunu-ri along the road to Anju, leaving the rear units unprotected. There were many casualties. Some Americans broke free and escaped on foot across the hills. Many were captured.

The air strikes had begun to loosen the enemy's grip on the heights and, despite its huge losses, the 2nd Division resumed its excruciating progress along the pass towards the southern exit. A number of jeeps and other smaller vehicles ran the gauntlet unscathed, but some of the occupants were still firing their weapons when they reached the 1st Middlesex at their Nottingham base. Several British soldiers were wounded.

Over the five days of battle, the US 2nd Division suffered 5000 casualties, 3000 of them on 30 November, and lost much of its equipment. Gunners dropped phosphorous grenades down the barrels of their howitzers to disable them before fighting their way out. The 2nd Engineer Battalion lost 711 of its original 977 men, along with 95 per cent of its equipment.

Keiser was relieved of his command.

The great Chongchon encirclement had sent MacArthur's forces into headlong retreat. Across the peninsula, thousands of American, South Korean and Turkish troops were killed or wounded, while hundreds more died from hypothermia and pneumonia in the next few days.

For the 27th Brigade, the vital point on the road south of Sunchon was a newly completed wooden bridge over the Taedong River at Yopa-ri. The Chinese had reached it first and, after shooting up the American engineers building the bridge, had occupied a hill on the far side. With the aid of US howitzers, the Australians charged through a curtain of falling snow to drive the Chinese off the high ground.

After consolidating the position, they expected to make a stand in this area while the Eighth Army regrouped after its recent defeats. So they were dismayed the following morning when they were ordered to blow up the bridge and continue their retreat a further 144 kilometres south through Pyongyang to Hayu-ri. There seemed no reason for abandoning so much hard-won territory, yet General Walker's orders were quite specific: all UN forces were to pull back south of the 38th parallel while the United Nations Command assessed the impact of the full-blooded Chinese intervention. This, MacArthur announced, was 'an entirely new war'.

Ferguson gathered the battalion together in the shelter of a slope and, moving from one platoon to the next, quietly informed each man of his orders. Then he watched the assault pioneers blow up the bridge over which American blood had so recently been spilt.

3RAR's withdrawal ground to a halt when the battalion reached Uijongbu, a village on the route to Seoul taken by invaders since Mongol times, and there the Australians remained for three weeks while Walker tried to figure out Marshal Peng's next move. This was to be his last act in the Korean tragedy. On the morning of 23 December Walker left Seoul to visit units around Uijongbu. His jeep was involved in a head-on collision with a South Korean truck. The commander of the Eighth Army was thrown from his open vehicle and sustained serious head injuries. He was dead on arrival at a 24th Infantry Division clearing station.

Since taking over command on 6 November, Colonel Ferguson had extricated his battalion from several dangerous situations. Usually he travelled in a jeep or the sidecar of a motorbike, but now that the pressure was off, however briefly, he decided he wanted the luxury of a mobile command post. Having acquired a $2\frac{1}{2}$-ton Russian flatbed truck, hardier than the British version, he sent a team of foragers into Seoul to obtain the necessary materials. The city was largely deserted and the men had no difficulty 'liberating' a basin from a barber's shop, a bed and mattress from a mental hospital and a desk from an office.

Back at battalion headquarters, the carpenter transformed the truck into a sort of battle bus with an enclosed canopy, complete with bed, basin, desk, maps, documents and heater. The whole contraption was painted in camouflage colours and nicknamed Pandora's Box.

It appeared around the same time that the 60th Indian Field Ambulance, commanded by Lieutenant Colonel A. G. Rangaraj, formally joined 27th Brigade on 14 December. 'Maybe IB got the idea of the "Box" from that unit,' Dusty Ryan says. 'Some say it was a gift from the Indian CO, but I doubt that as IB was always at odds with him because the ambulance group were always setting up on the battalion's tail and cramping our mobility. However, the Indians were a very dedicated service and the battalion and the RMO were glad to have them there.'

When intelligence reports reached United Nations Command that another massive Chinese offensive was in the offing, all UN forces were ordered to pull back over the Han River, just south of Seoul. 3RAR and the Argylls were the last units to leave the South Korean capital. They crossed the frozen river over a railway bridge just before it was blown up and took up defensive positions with the rest of the UN forces.

Only a month after telling the troops (and their families) that they would be home for Christmas, MacArthur had presided over a 440-kilometre retreat, the longest in US military history. The destruction of the 2nd Division was the country's worst disaster of the war.

MacArthur's reputation as a master strategist had been torn to shreds on the dragon's teeth. No wonder, as the New Year began, that he was itching to give hot pursuit to enemy aircraft over the Chinese border into their Manchurian sanctuaries. Given a chance, he would have used nuclear weapons to blow them to kingdom come.

CHAPTER 4
Teenage soldier

T he war that would make Ron Cashman a hero and blight most of his life was just six months old when he enlisted at Royal Park Depot, Melbourne. He became recruit number 3/2913 in the newly formed Australian Regular Army. At eighteen he was too young to qualify for K Force, but on 8 January 1951 he was accepted as an ordinary private. He was elated. Now he could begin to put the horror of Kerferd Road behind him. The army was all he had hoped for. He relished the camaraderie. He belonged. And he had a place to prove his manhood. He was sent to the sprawling, bushland camp at Puckapunyal, 100 kilometres north of Melbourne, for his basic training. 'My ambitions were very basic: all I wanted to be was a rifleman fighting the Communists in Korea.'

First, however, he had to convince the army that he was worthy of a place among the professionals. He had camped at Puckapunyal while in both the school cadets and the CMF, and he noted that its facilities had been upgraded since his last visit. 'It was far removed from the straw-palliasse-on-the-floor job that it had been.'

Thanks to his CMF training, he convinced his instructors that he had the makings of a first-rate soldier, but his induction was not altogether smooth sailing. Only a week after he joined up he cleared out for the day and, on his return, found he was charged with 'absenting himself without leave'. 'I had gone home to show my mother my new uniform,' he said. 'I hitchhiked down to Melbourne. She was surprised to see me, but I could see she was proud.'

A week later he was charged with disobeying a lawful command given by his superior officer 'in that he at Puckapunyal at approximately 1900 hours threw a dixie on the ground and said, "I'll not wash dixies" (or words to that effect)'.

It was more of that 'women's work' business. 'In fact, my "superior officer" was a private who said I hadn't washed my dixie up properly so I did it again and he still didn't like it so I told him what to do with it,' Cashman says. It was the sort of initiation into the services that rubbed many raw recruits up the wrong way. 'It took me a while to settle in,' he said. 'There were plenty of little Hitlers around.'

About this time Cashman had his first encounter with the world of psychology. The results of his IQ tests were unexpected. 'They had shrinks who delved into the mysteries of a recruit's mind,' he says. 'One of them decided I was too bright to be a rifleman — I had to be a specialist of some sort.'

To his intense annoyance, the eager young combatant found himself being trained as a radio operator. 'But they weren't content with making me an ordinary signaller,' he says. 'I had to do the full treatment.' This entailed learning to operate the army's huge radio transmitters and receivers, as well as the linesmen's equipment to set up a radio station. He was mastering frequencies and wavebands while the 3rd Battalion, Royal Australian Regiment, prepared to take its place in the line. 'It was hard yakka,' he says, 'and being a reluctant radioman from the beginning I was not overly pleased, but I took to it like a duck to water.'

As the weeks passed, though, he feared the war would be over before he had the chance to do his bit. 'The whole thing seemed to be getting away from me,' he says. He reacted by disappearing. On 6 July 1951 he was charged with going AWOL for four days. He was confined to barracks for seven days and fined three pounds. 'I have no memory of where I went,' he says. 'All I know is I wanted some action.'

By the beginning of 1951 the war had scythed up and down the Korean peninsula three times. On 4 January Seoul was retaken by the jubilant Communists, Kim Il Sung again unleashing a gruesome purge of anyone who had cooperated with the South Korean regime.

The refugee columns, stripped of everything but dignity, had shuffled south then north again in the crippling heat of summer and now, in the worst winter in living memory, they poured south once more.

But even that did not last. Disrupted by night-time attacks by the US Fifth Air Force, the Chinese supply lines from Manchuria had been stretched to breaking point. Peng's armies had to withdraw or perish in their winter positions. The first great Chinese offensive was at an end.

The 27th Brigade had become known at UN Command as the 'Cinderella Brigade' because of the lack of artillery support for its infantry. Towards the end of January the 27th received a much-needed addition to its strength with the arrival of the 16th New Zealand Field Regiment under the command of Lieutenant Colonel John Moodie, a 43-year-old World War II veteran from Dunedin. The Australians were particularly delighted by the prospect of fighting alongside the other half of the famous ANZAC coalition. They had endured several close shaves with American gunners who posted junior officers forward with the assaulting troops to direct fire on the enemy. The Kiwis followed the British system of using experienced troop commanders in the front line. This would give 3RAR just what its infantry needed: close and rapid support fire with their familiar 25-pounders.

Following General Walker's death, command of the Eighth Army had passed to General Matthew Bunker Ridgway. When Ridgway visited the 3RAR camp, the Australians could hardly fail to notice that while he was dressed in an ordinary field jacket, combat pants and jump boots, he carried two live hand grenades attached to his braces. After handing out cigars to members of Colonel Ferguson's staff, he offered the Australian CO the direct support of an American 105 mm howitzer battalion. He was somewhat mystified when Ferguson thanked him for the offer but opted to stay with the New Zealanders.

In February the UN forces once more edged tentatively forward across most of their front. After Seoul was recaptured for the second time, the refugees turned tail once more on the crumbling roads as 3-ton trucks and Centurion tanks thundered past. Syngman Rhee's murder squads returned to Seoul to resume their grisly task.

As followers of Confucius, the Korean people believed in filial piety and ancestor worship. They preferred to pass into the next life at home among their families, but that wish was to be denied to countless thousands during these terrible times. As one defensive line replaced another in the relentless tug-of-war, farmhouses and villages were cleared over massive tracts of the Korean countryside. With nowhere to go, their occupants simply joined the refugee stream. Famine and disease reached crisis proportions. In the words of one survivor, 'Happiness was a bowl of rice.'

In late March and early April the Eighth Army advanced again with the goal of moving the battle line a few kilometres north of the 38th parallel, although a short strip of the heavily occupied western sector would remain unchanged. The 27th Brigade went into action under a temporary commanding officer, Brigadier Brian Burke, the British deputy commander of the 29th Brigade. He had been promoted after Brigadier Coad was granted compassionate leave to be with his wife, who was dangerously ill in Hong Kong.

Coad remembered 3RAR as 'the finest fighting battalion I had ever seen'.[22] The Australians were as fond of him in their own way as protocol permitted and were sad to see him go. 'We went over to the Middlesex sergeants' mess one night when we were out of the line,' RSM Ryan says. 'We were having a conversation with them and, as usual, referred to Brigadier Coad as "the grey-headed old bastard". A couple of the young British lieutenants who were in the mess complained about it. Colonel Ferguson had to write a letter of explanation. He wrote a very nice letter telling them that "grey-headed old bastard" was, in fact, an Australian term of endearment.'

Brigadier Burke took the brigade up the deep, narrow valley of the Kapyong River to the key town of Kapyong, fifty kilometres north-east of the South Korean capital on the main road to the east coast. They encountered no enemy troops and continued to advance, much to MacArthur's satisfaction.

The Supreme Commander's adventurism had already cost America and her allies the chance of an honourable victory in Korea. From his Tokyo HQ he called on the Chinese to admit defeat or face military action in their own territory. Indeed, he chose this moment to suggest that nuclear weapons might be needed to bring them to heel.

Truman was incensed. The General's unauthorised statement had made it impossible for the President to get the Chinese to the negotiating table. On 11 April 1951 he dismissed MacArthur and appointed General Ridgway as his successor. General James Van Fleet assumed command of the Eighth Army.

The Japanese people were devastated by the fall of the great war hero who had become their champion. As chief suppliers to the American forces in Korea, the Japanese knew that the war on the peninsula had been responsible for a mighty surge in their own economic recovery. They also acknowledged that MacArthur had set them on the road to democracy. Emperor Hirohito dropped in to thank him for his services to Japan and his route to the airport was lined with hundreds of thousands of tearful well-wishers waving little paper American and Japanese flags.

MacArthur flew to Washington, where he gave a farewell speech to a joint session of Congress on 19 April that concluded, 'When I joined the army, even before the turn of the century [1899] it was the fulfilment of all my boyish hopes and dreams. The world has turned over many times since I took the oath on the Plain at West Point and the hopes and dreams have long since vanished. But I still remember the refrain of one of the most popular barracks ballads of that day, which proclaimed, most proudly, that "Old soldiers never die; they just fade away". And like the old soldier of that ballad, I now close my military career and just fade away — an old soldier who tried to do his duty as God gave him the light to see that duty. Goodbye.'[23]

At the Capitol, and around radios and television screens wherever the mesmerising address was heard, listeners were overcome and sobbed aloud. Some in the House chamber could be heard shouting, 'No! No!' Telephones began ringing at newspaper offices supporting the General. The White House switchboard was besieged, most of the callers hostile and many of them abusive. Had the speech been delivered at a Republican convention there is little doubt that MacArthur would have been nominated for the presidency.

But in Korea there was no time for sentiment. Three days later Marshal Peng launched China's massive spring offensive with ten

Chinese armies dressed in olive-green summer uniforms and heavily armed with small arms, grenades and mortars. The Chinese had been massed between the Imjin River and Hwachon Reservoir, north of Kapyong, with North Korean corps on their eastern and western flanks.

Peng's principal objective was Seoul, while a secondary thrust would be made in the direction of Kapyong, the most vital point in the central sector of the Korean front. Both British brigades — the 29th on the Imjin River and the 27th at Kapyong — were marked down for annihilation in Peng's orders to his commanders on 18 April.

Standing in the enemy's path at the northern end of the Kapyong River valley, however, was the 6th ROK Division, which had replaced the 27th Brigade that very day. The South Koreans advanced short distances on 21 and 22 April but had made little effort to dig in and were in trouble as soon as the Chinese smashed into their forward units.

The enemy's strength was now truly formidable. American estimates put the number of Chinese soldiers driving towards Seoul at 337 000, while 149 000 attacked the central sector. These armies were supported by an additional 214 000 Chinese reinforcements and NKPA troops, making a total of around 700 000 Communist troops facing a United Nations force of 418 000, including 245 000 Americans, 152 000 South Koreans, 11 500 Commonwealth soldiers and 10 000 from other UN countries.

If the enemy broke through the 6th ROK Division, they could swarm unchecked towards Kapyong, destroying the 27th Brigade on the way. From Kapyong, they could swing eastwards and isolate the US 3rd Division, 1st Marine Division and numerous ROK units, picking them off piecemeal. The potential for disaster was as great as on the Chongchon River the previous November.

The Communist advance had to be stopped somehow while the UN forces made an orderly retreat and reformed further south in safer positions. The task of blocking the Chinese fell to the 27th Brigade, which was still part of IX Corps, even though it was in reserve and undergoing reorganisation. The brigade's firepower had been seriously reduced by the absence of the 16th New Zealand Field Regiment, which had stayed behind at the front with a US field battery of 105-millimetre artillery in the hope that their guns would slow down an enemy attack and stiffen the resolve of the 6th ROK Division to stand and fight.

But at 10.30 pm on 22 April the Kiwis discovered that the South Korean right flank had collapsed, and soon afterwards they lost radio contact with the forward units that had been directing fire onto the enemy. As South Korean soldiers and civilians started streaming through the gun emplacements to the snap and crackle of Chinese small-arms fire, the Kiwis hooked up their 25-pounders and, at 4 am on 23 April, drove their carriers south to a new position on flat ground amid groves of chestnut trees six kilometres north of Kapyong.

The men of 3RAR were in no mood to give quarter. 'The soldiers had been together for a long time and their company commanders and battalion commander had got rid of the fellows who were not suitable,' Clem Kealy says. 'We were a pretty tight-knit group by then and the Chinese couldn't have met us at a worse time.'

The diggers had enjoyed their break in a rest area to the north-west of Kapyong known as 'Sherwood Forest' because of its rough-and-ready amenities. Films were shown in a makeshift cinema, there was a beer ration and the men were able to bathe for the first time in weeks. Colonel Ferguson had issued an invitation to the Turkish Brigade, which was fighting with another corps to the west of the Australians, to send representatives to an Anzac Day service on 25 April. There were also plans for an Anzacs versus Turks soccer match. More than one source claims that, in some cases, the Anzac Day celebrations started a day or so ahead of time.

The 27th Brigade had taken advantage of its time in reserve to replace two of its seasoned battalions, the 1st Battalion, Middlesex Regiment, and the 1st Battalion the Argyll and Sutherland Highlanders, which had reached the end of their duty in Korea after eight months of hard fighting. The Argylls held their farewell party to the accompaniment of pipes, drums and drams, and some units were already embarking in ships for Hong Kong at Inchon on the west coast, while the Middlesex were half packed and eager to take their leave of the war. But neither of the two replacement battalions, the 1st Battalion the King's Own Scottish Borderers (1KOSB) and the 1st Battalion the King's Shropshire Light Infantry (1KSLI), would reach the battlefield in time to join the fray. The Middlesex were ordered to fight one more battle.

Brigadier Burke had just three battalions to put into the field against the Chinese 60th Division of the 20th Army: 3RAR, the 2nd Battalion Princess Patricia's Canadian Light Infantry and the Middlesex. Even with the addition of some attached American units, the defenders were outnumbered at least three to one.

According to 3RAR's war diary, Burke ordered the brigade from its assembly area at 8.30 am on 23 April to reconnoitre and prepare to occupy its positions in the hills and ridges slightly north of Kapyong. All hills on UN maps were named after their height in metres. The Middlesex would dig in on Hill 794, the dominating massif known as Sudok San, and 3RAR would be deployed on and around Hill 504, while the Patricias and B Company of the US 2nd Chemical Mortar Battalion, hitherto attached to the Argylls, would occupy the western hills running up to Hill 677.

The war diary comments: 'The object was to form a line in rear of 6 ROK Division as the enemy had commenced a general offensive along the front of 6 ROK Division and 24 US Division at 1930 hours on 22 April.'[24] But the Middlesex never got to Sudok San, and their absence left an inviting gap in the centre of Burke's defences.

At 10 am on 23 April the situation at the front had deteriorated so badly that the Diehards were ordered to move forward to protect the New Zealand batteries, which had edged north again into the teeth of the battle to support the South Koreans. For the next twenty-four hours, it would be touch and go whether the Middlesex made it home at all.

Colonel Ferguson had set up battalion headquarters at the rear of 3RAR's main position in the valley north of Kapyong. His command post straddled the road leading to the surrounding hills, where his rifle companies would fire down on the advancing enemy. Pandora's Box was parked in a paddy field among chestnut trees at a tiny farming hamlet named Sokchang-ni.

The Australian official history records that Ferguson had been ordered by Brigadier Burke to site his headquarters in that spot so that the Australians would act as a check on the 6th ROK Division and prevent its withdrawal from turning into a stampede. 'IB met Brigadier Burke in the area that BHQ was to occupy,' says Dusty Ryan, who was assigned to headquarters. 'It was the logical place for BHQ to be sited after they had viewed the area that 3RAR was allocated to cover.'

General Sir Anthony Farrar-Hockley says in the British official history, however, that Ferguson was 'not pleased' with that order because his forces were already spread thinly.[25] He deployed a section of medium machine guns, two 17-pounder anti-tank guns, the Assault Pioneer Platoon, RSM Dusty Ryan and some regimental police to protect BHQ. The Pioneers were sited on high ground overlooking headquarters and the other units occupied ground a little to the rear. The mortar platoon was located slightly further north towards the Kapyong River along with elements of the anti-tank platoon.

Headquarters Company was under the command of Captain Jack Gerke, a 34-year-old West Australian veteran of World War II. 'Gerke was a head down, arse up kind of fellow,' says Tim Holt. 'Some of the soldiers were only nineteen and twenty years old and they thought he was ancient. He was never easy to talk to, but woe betide you if you decided to embroider something and he found out. He had a way of looking at you that made you feel as though you were lower than the lowest worm. You never tried it again.'

All was tranquil as Ferguson briefed his company commanders at 10.30 that morning and ordered his four rifle companies to head for the area around Hill 504. 'We got off to a bad start in my opinion because Anzac Day was coming up and it so happened the Turks and the Kiwis were right alongside us, which meant we would all be together for Anzac Day,' Clem Kealy says. 'Some of the boys started [celebrating] on the 23rd and we might have started too, except our company commander [D'Arcy Laughlin, of Port Kembla] had an inspection to check we had proper battle equipment. When we got the order to move forward we had just come off parade, so we didn't have time to get on the booze, which was a good thing. Some of the others ran out of water because their bodies were dehydrated; that was no one's fault — it was just a fact of life.'

Looking northwards up the valley, Kealy's 4 Platoon and the rest of B Company were situated on a low ridge on the left of the road beside a stream that ran into the Kapyong River, while A Company, C Company and D Company were located on the right on or around Hill 504. 'Monkey House' Morrison had returned to Australia with eye trouble and Lieutenant Leonard Montgomerie of Port Clinton, South Australia, was in charge of 4 Platoon.

'Len Montgomerie was an excellent platoon commander and he made sure we dug in,' Kealy says. 'A Company didn't arrive until about 4.30 in the afternoon, whereas we had got in about 1.30. We had dug in and had had tea when they arrived. When they got hit the first time, they hadn't dug in and one of the platoons got mauled quite a bit. As soon as the Chinese withdrew, you have never heard so much digging in your life.'

To make matters more difficult, the high ground was rock-hard compared with the softer soil closer to the stream. D Company, commanded by Captain William Gravener, occupied the summit of Hill 504, A Company (Major Ben O'Dowd) was on a spur-line that ran down to the north-west and C Company (Captain Reg Saunders) on the rear spur. On the heights and along the ridgeline the men built sangars: shelters constructed of rocks and covered with earth.

At dusk, the Australians in the hills saw small groups of retreating South Korean soldiers heading south along the road to Kapyong in drizzling rain. Soon afterwards, advance elements of 6th Division's headquarters arrived in the BHQ area and set up a tactical post in some deserted houses. 'Towards evening on the 23rd there was a trickle of South Koreans coming down the road,' Dusty Ryan says. 'This increased gradually during the night until it was a mass evacuation. Some shots were fired among them, which we believe were their officers trying to get them to go back to face the Chinese.'

Ferguson sent a man over to liaise with the South Korean HQ but, according to the war diary, 'no concrete information as to the ROK Army dispositions could be obtained'. As the exodus from the north began to swell, the South Korean officers and their American advisers jumped into their jeeps and disappeared south without bothering to inform Ferguson.[26]

The war diary records that between 8 o'clock and 11 o'clock small groups of South Korean stragglers had reached the battalion headquarters area. However, twenty minutes later there was a constant stream of ROK Army vehicles and personnel. 'They were obviously panic-stricken and completely uncontrolled,' the diary notes. 'Intermingled with the fleeing ROK Army troops were the enemy and confused fighting broke out in the headquarters area.'

That brief diary entry conveyed only a glimpse of the true horror further to the north of BHQ as thousands of South Korean soldiers and refugees were swept along in a human tide, mostly on foot but also in trucks, ox-carts and any other vehicle that could be coaxed into life. Many South Koreans died under the wheels of these vehicles as, horns blaring and lurching crazily on the slippery, rutted track, they drove southwards.

Many soldiers had retained their rifles — it was a capital offence in the ROK Army to lose one — but had thrown away their ammunition and indicated that they could not stand and fight. Others linked arms and jogged in lines, panting with exhaustion as they carried each other down the crowded road. Many tried to jump aboard the New Zealand gun carriages and had to be beaten off by members of the Middlesex Battalion who were already hitching a lift back to Kapyong after being ordered to withdraw once again.

And in the midst of this turmoil were the Chinese, no longer members of the 60th Division, which had swung to the south-west, but the 118th Division of the 40th Army, a new force of fresh troops that was swooping down unopposed from the north. Their first move against the Australians in the Battle of Kapyong was to surround B Company, separating it from the other three companies. 'They started with us — B Company. We were the first attacked,' Kealy says. 'They used machine guns and grenades but we fought them off. In our company that night and next morning two men won the Military Medal and Montgomerie won the Military Cross.'

In the absence of the New Zealand 25-pounders, Ferguson had the use of fifteen Sherman tanks of the US Army's A Company, 72nd Tank Battalion. The tanks were ably commanded by Lieutenant Kenneth W. Koch, but they had no infantry to prevent the enemy getting in close. 'We had five American tanks in our area but surprisingly they were still under American command,' Kealy says. 'They sited themselves and put three tanks below us down on the river and two behind us. But the Chinese were down in that area in the late afternoon, watching the tankies on the river. As soon as they took on the tanks, there was only one able-bodied man left in each of those three tanks — everyone else was either killed or wounded.'

By 8 pm Ferguson had abandoned any attempt to regulate the flood of South Korean traffic streaming through his checkpoint. The New Zealand gunners and the Middlesex Battalion passed through at that time and had only just taken up position just over a kilometre to the rear when the Chinese hit BHQ. Kealy says: 'All of Support Company were around Battalion HQ — all the mortars and Pioneer Platoon — but they weren't dug in; they had shell scrapes but they weren't dug in. The Chinese did what they weren't supposed to do — they bolted down the road and attacked BHQ.'

It had stopped raining by the time darkness fell at 7.40 pm, and at 9.15 an almost full moon rose over the battlefield. In bright moonlight, fighting broke out in the headquarters area involving headquarters personnel, the Assault Pioneer Platoon and the anti-tank and mortar platoons forward of the headquarters area.

The difficulties of Ferguson's command were manifest in that he had to direct two battles simultaneously — the one involving his rifle companies in the hills and the one that had erupted unexpectedly around his headquarters. He communicated with the rifle companies by radio but the undulating terrain had blocked signals to the three companies on Hill 504, whose messages had to be relayed through B Company. Field telephone lines had been mangled by tanks and gunfire, and all except the ones to B Company and the anti-tank platoon were out of action. For a time Ferguson lacked a clear picture of what was happening to three of the rifle companies in the hills.

Spring had been slow to arrive in the hills of the Kapyong Valley and it was a cold night, with snow still clinging to some of the higher slopes. A Company came under heavy attack at 9.30 pm when the Chinese rushed 1 Platoon, the lowest of the three platoons on the west flank of Hill 504, but were beaten off. Undaunted, over the next three hours they followed up with major assaults from three sides.

Private Tim Holt, who had reached Korea as a reinforcement the previous month, found himself in action as a rifleman in A Company. 'It was a bloody and interminable night,' he says. 'There were short periods when you were almost frightened to death and other periods when you thought you could relax for a little bit. The Chinese kept coming, blowing their little bugles, and it was nightmarish. Sometimes you could see them but oftentimes, if you weren't looking in the right direction, there would be loud cries of "They're coming from this way or that way" and you could direct fire where it was most wanted. The hitting power of the .303 was very effective. If you got a hit, it meant that the fellow usually stayed down, even if he wasn't dead — you didn't have to worry. The Brens were magnificent for close support. There was one Bren per section and one in platoon headquarters if you were clever enough to steal it. They worked wonders at Kapyong.'

At 12.50 am on the 24th the Chinese resumed their attack on B Company, singling out Len Montgomerie's 4 Platoon, but the riflemen and Owen gunners inflicted heavy casualties. The Chinese received the same hostile reception when they turned their attentions to B Company's other platoons and A, C and D Companies on and around Hill 504. Throughout the night the diggers were cut off by enemy fire from all sides and it seemed doubtful to Brigade HQ, situated south of Kapyong, that they would be able to hold on; they were some distance behind the Chinese advance units and were being attacked by hundreds of burp-gunners and grenadiers.

But the Australian company commanders were alert to the dangers and had arranged their platoons in clusters that could defend an attack from any side. Mindful that Anzac Day was coming up, every Australian fought with great spirit and tenacity. Despite repeated human-wave attacks, the Chinese failed to overrun their positions.

Meanwhile fighting around headquarters had increased in intensity and at 4 am the enemy attacked the Pioneer Platoon above BHQ. Colonel Ferguson informed brigade headquarters over his rear radio link that his men had suffered numerous casualties and that the situation was now critical. By this time some ROK soldiers had been forced to stay and fight with the Australians and Brigadier Burke ordered a company of Middlesex to go forward. When they arrived in the BHQ area, they found Ferguson 'as calm and unruffled as ever'.[27] The enemy had positioned themselves in some deserted houses and were using machine guns and mortars within the headquarters area. As soon as one machine gun was knocked out, another took its place.

Six hundred yards to the south, things had become too hot for the liking of B Company of the 2nd Chemical Mortar Battalion. The mortar men abandoned their position and headed for the hills to the south-east away from the advancing Chinese, leaving behind their 4.2-inch mortars, ammunition and trucks. This was discovered only when Jack Gerke sent two men from Headquarters Company to see why the American mortars had fallen silent. There were no signs of fighting in the area.

All fifty vehicles were recovered from the paddy fields the following day, Gerke even chauffeuring six stranded diggers to safety. Others were driven out by members of Headquarters and Support Companies and by members of B Company of the US 74th Engineer Battalion. However, the position of the forward companies was still desperate and would remain critical throughout the daylight hours of the 23rd. At 8 am B Company were ordered to leave their positions on the ridge and cross the road to join C Company at the base of Hill 504. Soon afterwards they were ordered to go back and drive off a large number of Chinese who had occupied trenches adjacent to their original position.

'We lost three men killed and two wounded, but we killed eighty-seven Chinese in what was known as The Honeycomb: trenches that were dug on the flat to look like a honeycomb or the grid for a crossword puzzle,' Clem Kealy says. 'I know eighty-seven were killed in it because I counted them. Monty skewered them — he bent a bloody big bayonet on them. He got every one except one bloke who got up and ran away but he didn't get far before he was shot dead.'

Throughout the mayhem Colonel Ferguson had attempted to overcome his signals difficulties by driving towards the company areas in his jeep with a wireless operator constantly trying to make contact with A, C and D Companies. But at dawn an intensified Chinese attack on the headquarters perimeter persuaded Ferguson that withdrawal to the Middlesex area was his only option. His men had suffered many casualties defending BHQ. Every member of the light machine-gun section had been either wounded or killed and the Assault Pioneer Platoon had been driven off the high ground, enabling the Chinese to fire directly onto the headquarters position.

The main body of Headquarters Company, including the regimental aid post under Captain Donald Beard of Brisbane, pulled out in small numbers between 5.15 and 6 am; because of the Chinese presence along the road they took a safer route along a winding riverbed.

'At first light IB was stationed on the road at the rear of BHQ,' Dusty Ryan says. 'He was with his jeep and [his intelligence officer] Alf Argent was with him. He'd come back into the BHQ area and ordered the RMO and his crew to withdraw to the Middlesex area behind us. He also spoke to his 2IC, who was looking after the A Echelon and the F Echelon units.

'As he was doing this, an enemy 2-inch mortar dropped alongside the front wheel of his jeep. He was on the other side of the vehicle when it exploded — he was stunned but carried on. I was walking towards the jeep and was about twenty yards behind it when this happened. There was no other damage, except the front wheel of the jeep needed replacing.

'IB was able to tell me to see that all personnel had been cleared from BHQ areas and told me to destroy his van if it was unable to get out of the paddy fields. He said, "If you can't get it out, burn it", so we burned it. His driver, Dusty Miller — another Dusty — and his batman, Eric Michels, tipped some petrol over it and that was that.'

Once Ferguson had re-established his headquarters within the Middlesex perimeter, he was able to plan his next move. When Ben O'Dowd radioed from A Company that he had been unable to evacuate fifty wounded men during the night and that the forward companies were running short of ammunition, Ferguson mounted one of the Sherman tanks with Don Beard and Alf Argent and set off for the front line. He sat in the gun-loader's seat and when the tank came under fire he supplied the American gunner with ammunition to return fire.

At 11 am the tank arrived unscathed on the hillside below the embattled forward companies. After delivering the ammunition and loading the tank decks with the most seriously wounded men, Ferguson ordered the rifle companies to withdraw later that day. He appointed O'Dowd as senior company commander to take charge of the operation. The withdrawal would begin with B Company in mid afternoon, enabling the rearguard to break contact with the Chinese under the cover of darkness.

On the summit of Hill 504, D Company had been under constant attack since 7 am as the Chinese made frantic efforts to capture the key position overlooking the other Australian companies. That afternoon Captain Gravener called in air strikes against the Chinese with disastrous results for one of his own platoons. Two men were killed when their position was accidentally attacked with napalm by US Marine Corsairs after a spotter aircraft dropped a marking flare in the wrong place. Clem Kealy's mate from Ingleburn, Lance Corporal Harold Giddins, was showered with blazing petroleum jelly, while ammunition exploded in the intense heat.

Soon after that disaster the battalion's withdrawal began. As the enemy held the ground immediately between the battalion and the Middlesex area, Ferguson instructed O'Dowd that the rifle companies would have to ford the river and withdraw via the high ground to the east of Hill 504. With a large force of Chinese attacking from the north, O'Dowd decided that B Company would pull out first at 3.30 pm, while C, A and D Companies held off the enemy and then withdrew in leap-frog fashion: one company would take up a blocking position, the second would prepare the next blocking position through which the first would withdraw, and the third would move on to the next stage.

Repeated Chinese attacks on D Company threatened to disrupt O'Dowd's plan, but Gravener ordered 10 Platoon to engage the enemy at close quarters while the rest of the company pulled out undetected. The last defenders then broke contact and slipped away in the dark, while the New Zealand gunners blasted the Chinese with accurate fire. D Company reported that shells exploded only fifty metres behind the rearguard.

Ferguson was waiting at a checkpoint on the road into the battalion's new position to count the companies home. 'We came out on the afternoon of the 24th down a spur-line at the back of Hill 504,' Clem Kealy says. 'I was the first person out — I was the forward scout. When I got down to the river I called Monty up and said, 'What do you want me to do?' He said, 'Take your section up the road and make contact with the CO.' This I did. When I got up to the CO, he gave me a drink of coffee. I'll never forget that. We got back to BHQ at night-time; that was between 10.30 and 11 pm on the 24th. B Company was first out and the last company was Don Company. The Chinese didn't follow us up; we expected them to but they didn't, so we virtually came out without firing a shot.'

Clem Kealy spotted Harold Giddins on a stretcher at the regimental aid post, awaiting evacuation. In 1941 Giddins had been working for the Red Cross in Crete when he was captured by the Germans after volunteering to stay behind with the wounded. He had spent the rest of the war in a concentration camp. Now he was a casualty himself. The napalm had burned the tips off his fingers, the tips off his ears, a chunk of his nose and some of his chin.

Kealy asked his mate if he wanted a smoke and gave him a couple of puffs on his cigarette.

Giddins sat up and said: 'Will you do me a favour, Clem? Lift up my shirt and see what the trouble is.'

Kealy did as requested and replied: 'Christ, mate, the hairs aren't even singed.'

Calmly Giddins replied, 'Well, it's worth living now, mate.'

Tim Holt describes A Company's withdrawal as 'quite slippery'. 'I hadn't had any alcohol to drink for months and I remember feeling as though I was half-whacked,' he says. 'No sleep and an awful amount of fear dulls the senses, but once I knew that we were travelling south I smiled for the first time in hours and hours and hours.'

The 27th Brigade had stopped the advance of an entire Chinese division, which had broken off its attack and withdrawn exhausted. On the 25th the latter-day Anzacs celebrated their deliverance with a double ration of beer and spirits.

Thirty-two Australians had been killed and fifty-nine wounded in the Battle of Kapyong. Brigadier Burke recommended Ferguson for a Distinguished Service Order for outstanding leadership. The entire battalion received a US Presidential Unit Citation and added the blue silk ribbon of this high award to its battle honours.

The entire brigade was saddened, however, to learn of the fate of the 1st Battalion the Gloucestershire Regiment, one of the key components of the 29th Brigade, which Marshal Peng had singled out for annihilation. The Glosters had been destroyed in the Battle of the Imjin River, which had taken place at the same time as the Australians were battling the Chinese in the Kapyong Valley. Survivors of the crack British battalion had made their valiant last stand on Hill 235, subsequently known as Gloster Hill, but were overlooked by Chinese gunners on two higher hills and were being cut to pieces when the 29th Brigade was ordered to withdraw during the night of 24–25 April. After several rescue attempts had failed, the Glosters' CO, Lieutenant Colonel James Carne, gave his company commanders permission to fight their way out. Only thirty-nine men made it back to the brigade; fifty-eight Glosters were killed and seventy-five wounded, while five hundred went into captivity.

At midnight on 25 April 1951, the 27th Brigade's operational tour in Korea formally ended and the 28th Commonwealth Infantry Brigade, codenamed 'Newcastle', came into being. As well as 3RAR, the new brigade comprised three other battalions: the 1st Battalion the King's Own Scottish Borderers, which had hurried to the front after landing at

Inchon but had missed the Battle of Kapyong; the 1st Battalion the King's Shropshire Light Infantry, which was still en route from Hong Kong and would arrive in Korea on 11 May; and the 2nd Battalion, Princess Patricia's Canadian Light Infantry, which would later form the nucleus of an entire Canadian Brigade. The 28th Brigade's commanding officer was Brigadier George Taylor, a former champion rugby player and veteran infantryman who had excelled as a battalion commander after the Normandy landings. Colonel Ferguson was presented with 27 Brigade's flag in recognition of 3RAR's fighting qualities.

The enemy's offensive had broken down at Kapyong, and for the first time large numbers of Chinese soldiers had come forward and surrendered. They were tired, dirty, dispirited and, above all, hungry. It was a telling omen and one that gave great heart to UN Command and their own battle-weary forces.

The Communists' difficulties were confirmed on 30 April when they were forced to pull back for resupply and reinforcements. Another glimmer of hope was offered when Yakov Malik, Russia's delegate at the United Nations, proposed a ceasefire in Korea that would lead to the withdrawal of all belligerent forces from the 38th parallel. The two Koreas would return to the status quo ante bellum. At the time, the UN forces were some distance north of the 38th parallel across the peninsula, except for the western strip above Seoul. The Truman administration, however, jumped at the chance to negotiate a settlement.

The Communists immediately nominated a site that was both symbolic and provocative: Kaesong, the old Korean capital, was in Communist-held territory just south of the 38th parallel. The Communist propaganda machine could make it appear that it was the UN Command that was suing for peace after losing the territorial battle.

Stoically ignoring the propaganda ploy, the United Nations accepted the site and the peace talks went into formal session in a converted teahouse on 8 July, with Vice Admiral C. Turner Joy leading the UN truce team. The Communists' nominal leader was the North Korean Vice Premier and Chief of Staff, General Nam Il. The real power in that camp, however, was Major General Hsieh Fang, a Chinese propaganda specialist.

It took two weeks of argument and obfuscation to get agreement on a four-point agenda: establishment of a military demarcation line and a demilitarised zone; arrangements to ensure that the truce terms were carried out; the release of prisoners of war; and recommendations to the governments of countries supporting either side. The propaganda battle commenced as soon as the two sides sat down at the table. When the United Nations delegates placed a UN flag on the table, the Communists trumped it with a larger North Korean one. The talks continued in this combative atmosphere until the Communists broke them off on 23 August. Apart from the agenda, nothing had been decided.

Meanwhile 3RAR had experienced a mystifying change of command. The first intimations of trouble came one afternoon in late June when a lieutenant colonel in the British Commonwealth Occupation Force flew into Korea from Japan. He asked the junior officer who had gone to meet him at the airport, 'Do you know why I am here?' When the young man replied that he had no idea, the colonel said, 'I've come to sack your CO.'[28]

It was a callous thing to say and a shocking breach of security. After leading 3RAR for nearly eight months, Colonel Ferguson was relieved of his command later that afternoon. The following morning he said goodbye to his companies beside the surging Imjin River and departed for Kimpo airport. The ham-fisted manner of his dismissal would have left a nasty taste in the mouths of his men except that most did not realise he had been relieved of his command. 'We thought he had served his eight months as commanding officer and was returning to Japan,' said one. 'He never said anything about being sacked, and nor did anyone else. I still find it hard to believe.'

Ferguson's apparent crime, it turned out, had nothing to do with his capacities in the field and everything to do with the self-image of his superior, 'Red Robbie' Robertson. A man of overweening vanity, Robertson reacted violently to anything that might reflect poorly on his public persona. Ferguson had allowed the exigencies of the battlefield to take precedence over the timing of leave due to some of the troops under his command. That in itself was no hanging offence; however, a new dimension was added when complaints reached the press in Australia. That engaged the politicians and gave the army — i.e. Robertson — an image problem. The GOC put him 'on notice' that no more public disquiet would be tolerated. When one final complaint surfaced, Robertson reacted.

A mythology grew that the cause of his dismissal had been a reluctance to replace Ferguson's K Force officers and men with regular army and Duntroon-trained reinforcements who were standing by in Japan. According to his supporters, however, Ferguson's motives were not to deny the chance of action to new blood, but rather 'to maintain the integrity of the unit'. Alf Argent, Ferguson's former personal staff officer, said any large-scale changeover during the constant action and movement of those months would have gravely affected 3RAR's fighting efficiency.[29]

Red Robbie had made a special visit to the headquarters of the 28th Brigade on 1 May to present Ferguson with his DSO after the Battle of Kapyong, yet a few weeks later — after the 'leave issue' surfaced — he presided over his dismissal. There was speculation that it might have been connected to the distance of Ferguson's headquarters from the rifle companies during the battle, but as he had been acting on orders from Brigadier Burke in siting BHQ at the rear of the battalion, that explanation was unsatisfactory.

Captain Reg Saunders, the first Aboriginal to be commissioned in the Australian Army and the commander of C Company at Kapyong, maintained: 'He always positioned his Battalion Headquarters in isolation from the companies and did this again at Kapyong. He liked a neatly sign-posted and well laid out HQ. There was no tactical or battle HQ inside the main battalion defensive position up with the forward companies.'[30]

Olwyn Green says: 'I feel very strongly about Bruce Ferguson. I think he has been very unfairly treated in history. Veterans remind me that he was a very, very brave man. He still commands fierce loyalty, and that kind of loyalty would not exist if he had not been there for his men at Kapyong.'

Ferguson was certainly greatly respected by the men of 3RAR. 'He had won the Military Cross on the Kokoda Track,' Ron Cashman says. 'But he got a very raw deal in Korea.'

RSM Ryan, who took part in the Battle of Kapyong and was a valuable eye-witness to the events of those hectic days, denied that Ferguson had lost touch with his rifle companies at all. Asked how the stories started that he was out of contact and had become disoriented by the mortar attack on his jeep, Ryan explains: 'The ultimate answer to all this is the difference between a field officer and an RMC graduate. Red Robbie was a staunch supporter of the college. He came out of the college himself. Green relieved Walsh. Green was a field promotion. He didn't come out of the college.

'Then when Green was killed Walsh was in Korea doing an observation job for Red Robbie with the 34th Brigade. The battalion was in a bit of a tight spot; there was plenty of enemy contact at the time. Walsh fouled up and Brigadier Coad relieved him of his position and appointed Ferguson to take over. I think this was the beginning. You could go back for recreation leave in Japan when you had been there for ten to twelve months in Korea. Ferguson went back and this was a golden opportunity and they had Frank Hassett lined up to take over the battalion in July 1951. Hassett said to me I could go back to Japan. His comment was there was still "too much Ferguson in the battalion"; that was praise as far as I was concerned. There was a big clearout of Ferguson men. He brought in a lot of men from Japan that Ferguson wouldn't even wear in a fit.'

Ferguson flew home to Australia on 25 June 1951. His Canadian wife, Betty, told a friend that he had been called in to army headquarters and told, 'You are not going anywhere, Ferguson.' Indeed, he did not. He was shattered by the experience, which reverberates in the army to this day. Although he remained in the army for another sixteen years until his retirement in 1967, he never rose above the rank of colonel — nor did he seek higher rank — but he did serve as head of instruction at Duntroon.

The shake-up in 3RAR personnel that followed Ferguson's departure created opportunities all the way down the line. Back in Australia

Ron Cashman had topped the radio course at Puckapunyal and come second in the linesmen's course. When he heard on the grapevine that there was a vacancy for a radio operator in Korea, he presented himself to the officer in charge of signals and told him that he was the man for the post because, according to his examination results, 'I was the best he had'.

The officer was amused by Ron's presumption but, as soldiers had to be nineteen years old before they could volunteer for overseas service and Cashman was still eighteen, he said: 'You're not old enough.'

'I will be by the time I get there,' Cashman replied.

CHAPTER 5

At the front

Private Ron Cashman was posted to 3RAR as a signaller and transferred from Puckapunyal to the Leave and Transit Depot (LTD) at Marrickville. At the age of nineteen, he had at last escaped his father's violence and was on his way to the war zone of Korea. At the time, he was unaware of the irony.

While he and his mates sank a few schooners in one of the Marrickville pubs, the Henson Park Hotel, word went around that their new CO in Korea — Francis George 'Frank' Hassett — was an old Marrickville boy; he had been born in the inner Sydney suburb on 11 April 1918 and had attended Marrickville Public School. 'To be born in Marrickville at the height of the Depression, you had to be able to talk or run or fight, or do all three, because it could get pretty tough,' Hassett says.[31]

The departure date of 3RAR's reinforcements for Korea was classified information, so there were no girlfriends or family members waving a tearful farewell at Mascot Airport. Not that Cashman minded. He was looking forward to doing his bit in Korea, and acquiring the skills and strength he needed to stand up to his father.

In jungle greens and with kitbags slung over their shoulders, the soldiers boarded trucks and were driven to the airport, where they were loaded into an unpressurised Qantas DC4. It was 14 September 1951 and the plane would take them to Japan via Darwin, Manila and Guam.

Manila was Dodge City with palm trees. Here the men were given twenty-four hours' leave and Cashman took the opportunity to enjoy his first 'grown-up sexual experience' with a local bar girl.

There was trouble, though, after the men had had a few drinks. Cashman and two mates found themselves in the slums and hailed a taxi to get them back to their hotel. Instead, the driver delivered them to an ambush point in a deserted lane, where they were set upon by a gang of thugs. 'We fought them off with our webbed belts, but one of my cobbers was decked by a thrown bottle,' he says. 'Luckily, an armed police patrol drove by, though there's no way those bastards would have beaten us as long as we had the belts.'

Without further incident, the men reached 3RAR's Reinforcement Holding Unit at Hiro, Japan, and were given a few days' leave to settle in. Cashman had had a sheltered upbringing, but he still considered himself a man of the world. 'I'd made a couple of conquests in Melbourne, and Manila was a bit of a starter on the way through,' he says. 'But I had no idea of the sort of things on offer in Kure. Nowadays they would be called "the depths of depravity".' Women would grab the Australian soldiers in the street and try to drag them off to drunken orgies; not all of them resisted. 'I never dreamed that anything like this went on,' he says. 'Apart from being shown some horror movies about venereal disease, we weren't warned about it at all.'

Cashman and two of his mates visited a bar opposite a traditional Japanese dance hall within walking distance of the barracks. The girls in the big front saloon bar were dressed in Western clothes and were roistering with the all-male clientele. But Cashman and his mates, who were quieter and more reserved than some of the Commonwealth troops, were escorted to a small private room at the back of the premises next to a little garden.

The girls in this room were dressed in geisha costumes and were more refined. One of them was named Keiko-san. She told Cashman that her husband had been a dentist in Hiroshima, and as the wife of a professional man she had been respected in society. But her husband had been killed in the atomic bomb blast and her world had been destroyed. 'She was a nice girl, and with my boyish outlook on life I fell in love with her,' Cashman says.

He visited her whenever he got the opportunity, and they would drink and dine together in the private room. One night the military police raided the bar and stormed into the room looking for

Australian soldiers. Keiko-san had the presence of mind to hide Cashman behind some palm trees in the little garden, saving him from trouble.

Shortly afterwards the army moved him and his unit to the battle school at Haramura. Cashman's signals expertise was conveniently forgotten and he was handed a Vickers machine gun. 'They had me running up hill and down dale with a Vickers on my shoulders,' he says, 'while this crazy English colonel ran around flogging people across the arse with a short swagger stick if they were too slow. Completely crazy he was — wore a monocle and all.'

Back at Hiro, Cashman found time to continue his relationship with his Japanese lover. 'Hiro and Kure opened up a new world for me,' he says. He made friends with Peter Cerdapavia, a private from Ivanhoe, but admits that he wasn't the friendliest man among the new intake. 'I was too busy trying to get to Korea, and mates got in the way.'

Cerdapavia was different from the other reinforcements. He had already completed one tour of duty in Korea as a staff sergeant with 3RAR's B Echelon, the supply company that stayed well behind the lines. As a result, Cerdapavia had seen no combat, so he had signed up for a second tour masquerading as a private in order to get into the action.

Since their successful engagement against the Chinese in the Kapyong Valley in April 1951, 3RAR had been caught up in another major reorganisation of UN forces. On 28 July the 1st Commonwealth Division, consisting of the 25th Canadian Brigade, 28th Commonwealth Brigade and 29th British Infantry Brigade, was formed as part of I Corps (pronounced *eye core*). Its first commanding officer was Major General James 'Gentleman Jim' Cassels.

Cassels was a popular choice with the Australians, having served the previous year as head of the United Kingdom Services Liaison Staff in Melbourne. A clubbable veteran of World War II, in which he had commanded the 51st Highland Division during the Rhine crossings, he was known and liked in Australian military circles. Moreover he knew and respected the fighting abilities of the Australian soldiers under his command.

3RAR was one of three battalions in the 28th Commonwealth Brigade, the other two being the Borderers (1KOSB) and the Shropshires (1KSLI). Britain supplied 58 per cent of the divisional manpower, Canada 22 per cent, Australia 14 per cent, New Zealand 5 per cent and India 1 per cent (the vital field ambulance to treat the wounded).

In September UN Command formulated plans to strike back at the enemy. General Van Fleet, head of the Eighth Army, ordered the Commonwealth Division to join Operation Commando, a massive offensive aimed at driving the Chinese from high ground on the Imjin salient just above the 38th parallel. The objective was two-fold: to deprive the enemy of the open route to Seoul, and to give the UN negotiators some leverage at the armistice talks. General Cassels decided to use the 28th Commonwealth Brigade and the 25th Canadian Brigade to seize Hill 355 and Hill 317, both vital components in the Communists' western defences.

Hill 355 was known to the Koreans as Kowang San, but its formidable sheer approaches had so impressed the Americans, who had already attacked it without success, that they called it Little Gibraltar. Hill 317, three kilometres to the north, was named Maryang San. Shaped like a pyramid, it was broader than Little Gibraltar, although it too had dishearteningly steep sides and deep crevices. Both hills were heavily defended.

As the Australians were considered by many senior officers to be one of the best, if not *the* best, fighting unit in the Eighth Army, Brigadier Taylor, commander of 28th Brigade, had given 3RAR the toughest assignments. It would be Frank Hassett's first test commanding the battalion in battle, a task made more difficult by the fact that the Australian companies would start the operation with only about ninety men each, fifteen below strength.

Although of humble Irish antecedents on his father's side, Hassett was a Duntroon graduate, having been accepted by the Royal Military College in 1935. 'Looking back, I am still amazed at the chain of circumstances that led to my soldiering career,' he says. He had left school at sixteen with only the Intermediate qualification.

'I was restless in my job as a clerk. I was looking through the daily paper when my eye lit on an advertisement for Duntroon. Just at that moment my brother passed through the room and I asked him about the College, which I knew nothing about. He knew something about Duntroon from his CMF experience and spoke well of it. I decided to apply for entrance.'

He failed the medical because of a 'minor ailment', and he was on the verge of abandoning the idea when he overheard two doctors discussing him: 'That young boy Hassett is the type we want. He'll develop well.'

'To a boy of sixteen who had just been rejected, this was a pleasant and encouraging observation,' he recalls. When he reapplied he was interviewed by the adjutant of the Corps, 'a kindly little captain named Cardale'.

'He told me in a sympathetic way that there was a problem in that I had only an Intermediate Certificate. As well, the Selection Board had disbanded and would not meet again until next year. Only a warm-hearted man like Cardale would have registered my disappointment and said, "Just a minute". He then went to Colonel Lavarack, who had been chairman of the Selection Board and had an office nearby.

'I was taken to Lavarack, who questioned me about my aspirations. With much older eyes, I can now picture the scene — a thinnish, somewhat nervous boy, obviously immature and naive. I have since been on numerous RMC Selection Boards, and clearly I lacked many of the qualifications usually sought. I had not been in the School Cadets, I was not overly prominent in sport and I was both immature and ignorant about the career I was seeking.

'Lavarack, later Chief of the General Staff, and later still Governor of Queensland, well known as an impatient man with a fiery temper, was kindness itself to me. But I left thinking, "Well, that's that". Two months later my mother handed me a letter, which she had received quite some time earlier, telling me to report to the College on a certain date.'

As it turned out, both the doctors and Lavarack were vindicated. In his four years at RMC Frank Hassett grew three inches, gained three stone and won both the infantry and physical training prizes.

During World War II Hassett fought in the Middle East with 2/3rd Battalion of the 6th Division while his 3RAR predecessors, Green and Ferguson, were with 2/2nd Battalion. Hassett and Ferguson came together in an incident that he remembered with great clarity more than sixty years later.

'The 2/3rd Battalion was to break into the Tobruk perimeter,' he recalls. 'The patrol to mark out the forming-up place and start line was under the command of Bob Knights, the brigade major, with myself assisting, as Bob's main chore was to do the marking out with his brigade party. This included Bruce Ferguson, the brigade intelligence officer. The escort patrol was from the battalion, under Harry Bamford, whose platoon had earlier reconnoitred and knew something of the area.

'It was a good, simple plan. The only catch was that a brilliant moon was due to rise at about 2300 hours, which would turn the flat desert into daylight, with no cover ... After a while at one of our check stops I said to Harry Bamford, "I think we're getting pretty close — less than a hundred yards or so". He and his scouts could not have gone more than about thirty yards when there was an explosion and his party was knocked down. They were in a minefield.

'Bob and I were together checking bearings and Bob dropped his compass and said, "My bloody arm's hit". A piece of mine had sliced through his forearm. I told him I would go forward and have a look.

'Harry and his scouts, all wounded, were lying in a small half circle. A very cool voice, either Harry's or one of the scouts, said, "Don't anybody move". But at the same time another mine went up and we were all wounded, the others for a second time.

'I was knocked down and a little dazed, with a number of small shrapnel wounds [in the back], but a piece had gone clean through my foot and I had difficulty in moving. My first clear memory was talking to Bruce Ferguson about sorting things out.'

In fact, Ferguson, who was relatively unhurt, assisted Hassett out of the danger area as the Italians opened fire.

On 6th Division's return to Australia, Hassett had been appointed lieutenant colonel at the age of twenty-three — the youngest officer of that rank in the Australian Army. For the remaining two and a half years of the war he served in Queensland, at Duntroon and in New Guinea, but always in headquarters, training or instructing capacities: despite several attempts, he had not been permitted to rejoin a fighting battalion. Instead he became a tactical expert, adept in jungle warfare and such techniques as 'running the ridges' to gain the high ground against the Japanese.

'My posting to 3RAR came through about May 1951,' he says. 'I was to relieve Bruce Ferguson, but there was to be no handover/takeover. Ferguson was to move out before I arrived. I was puzzled at this and was to find out later that Ferguson had been abruptly relieved because the GOC-in-C, Lieutenant General Sir Horace Robertson, was displeased with the leave and relief arrangements within 3RAR. The CO 3RAR appointments had not, to this point, had a good run — the first killed, the second sacked and the third summarily relieved, all within the space of a year.'

Hassett acknowledged there were big changes in the battalion after the Battle of Kapyong in April. He wrote later that 3RAR 'was not at this stage a highly cohesive unit of the type that came later to Korea. The recent enormous turnover of personnel meant that it was basically a collection of well-trained individuals that had been strung out in a defensive position for the past three months and was quite unpractised as a unit in the battle procedures and techniques required for a battalion in attack.'

However, he says, 'it was a very good battalion and looked it — not in the sense of being parade ground smart but in its fitness, its confidence, its air of knowing what this war was all about and feeling able to handle it. It looked tough and it was tough — mentally and physically robust.'

Hassett made sure that the rifle companies spent every waking hour for three weeks training in full battledress to develop cohesion and stamina for the rigours ahead in Operation Commando. Every man experienced the tension of coming under enemy fire in a preliminary operation named Mindon, which sharpened their reflexes for the testing time ahead.

As D-day — 3 October — drew near, Hassett was confident that his men were fit for the job. He also knew he could rely on his handful of battle-hardened officers. C Company's commander, Jack Gerke, now promoted to major, had served as an infantryman in World War II and seen action in Syria, North Africa, New Guinea and Borneo. He had fought in the Battle of Kapyong; he was tough as nails.

Hassett says: 'The battalion was a mixture of K Force volunteers and enthusiastic young regulars — just the right blend of experience, youth and dash. The battalion was keen to perform, in fact spoiling for a fight.'

The day before the attack began 3RAR moved to the forming-up place where, on the eve of battle, the great Gladys Moncrief stepped onto a makeshift stage and, accompanied by a pianist, sang to the Australian troops. It was a poignant reminder of home — 'like your mother singing to you,' says Maurie Pears, then a 21-year-old lieutenant.

The three battalions of the 28th Commonwealth Brigade, plus the Northumberland Fusiliers and the Centurion tanks of the 8th Royal Irish Hussars, were ordered to capture Hill 355 on the first day of Operation Commando. The Chinese, however, pinned down the main assault battalion, the King's Own Scottish Borderers (the Kosbies), which had attacked up the most predictable — and therefore the most heavily defended — southern route to the summit. Defensive fire was pouring down from two positions on Hill 220, a spur to the northeast of Hill 355. Casualties were light, however, and the Kosbies' commander, an abstemious Calvinist named John MacDonald, decided to dig in on the lower slopes of Hill 355 and resume his attack the following day.

Reluctant to see the offensive stall, Brigadier Taylor ordered Colonel Hassett to support the Kosbies by capturing the troublesome enemy positions on Hill 220. Late in the afternoon of 3 October Hassett summoned Jack Gerke to his side at Tactical Headquarters. C Company was delegated to flank Hill 355 and attack Hill 220.

At four o'clock the following morning the valley was enveloped in heavy mist when Gerke led C Company, accompanied by a section of Vickers machine gunners and a forward observation officer from the 16th New Zealand Field Regiment, towards the start line to attack the first of the two Chinese emplacements on Hill 220. They threaded their way through deserted rice paddies until they were six hundred metres short of the foot of the hill. There Gerke rested his men while the Vickers machine gunners set up their weapons to give covering fire to the assault.

To lead the attack, Gerke had chosen 7 Platoon, commanded by Maurie Pears of Paddington, NSW. Pears, a Duntroon graduate who had arrived in Korea in May as a reinforcement, had total faith in his commanding officer, describing him as 'a very strong and fearsome leader'.

At 6 am, as 7 Platoon set off across the valley, the first streaks of dawn lightened the sky and the great bulk of Little Gibraltar loomed in the background through the low-hanging mist. When Pears reached Hill 220 he ordered two of his three sections to edge up the steep slopes in single file, thus presenting the enemy with a one-man front to fire at. But the mist lifted as they climbed and almost immediately mortar bombs started exploding among the pine trees dotting the hillside. Several diggers suffered minor shrapnel wounds; some had their webbing cut from their bodies. But their rapid ascent saved them from a severe mauling. Most of the mortar bombs fell on the reserve section at the base of the hill, wounding the sergeant and all five of his men. 'I lost my reserve section to mortar fire and there were only the two sections left up there,' Pears says.

He found that the walkie-talkie with which he was to keep in touch with company headquarters down in the valley would not work at elevation. But he was still unaware that his reserve section was disabled as the two leading sections mounted the crest in narrow formation and ran at the enemy trenches. Encountering a fusillade of small-arms fire, they took shelter behind some large boulders.

While Pears and the first section held their position, the second section worked its way round the left flank but became bogged down on the slopes and lost contact with platoon headquarters and the enemy. Unable to make contact with Jack Gerke at company headquarters, Pears pondered his options.

The situation was confused and the attack seemed in danger of breaking down when Gerke dashed onto the crest with his radio operator, Jim McFadzean, to consult with Pears. But the inactivity did not suit Jimmy Burnett, a 27-year-old Bren gunner from Ayr, Queensland. 'While we were trying to work out where everyone was and what they were doing, Jim got fed up,' Pears says. 'He stood up with his bloody Bren, started to shoot and ran forward. Everyone went with him.'

Firing his heavy weapon from the hip, Burnett's courageous dash through the low scrub surprised the defenders and opened up a gap. The first section of 7 Platoon plus platoon headquarters — a total of eight men — stormed the breach with small arms and grenades, and in minutes the Chinese had broken. Leaving a large number of dead and wounded on the battlefield, they started scrambling off Hill 220 and running down the rear slopes of Hill 355 in a disorganised retreat. Five of the wounded were taken prisoner.

While 8 Platoon mopped up the bunkers and the Vickers machine gunners raked the escaping Chinese with fire from their positions on the valley floor, 7 Platoon regrouped and pushed ahead to the second enemy emplacement on Hill 220. Gerke sent a radio message to Hassett that the first Chinese position had fallen to the Australians at 9 am and that the second attack was in progress.

Frank Hassett says: 'All companies covered a lot of difficult ground, much of it under fire. From the beginning of the attack C Company fought and moved more than twelve kilometres as the crow flies. All supplies and casevac [casualty evacuation] had to be man-handled by porters or carrying parties from within the battalion, four men to a stretcher, a heavy commitment for understrength companies and platoons still engaged in battle.'

The second attack was a carbon copy of the first, with Jimmy Burnett once again firing his Bren gun from the hip and forcing the Chinese to keep their heads down while the grenade throwers lobbed their deadly missiles into the crowded trenches and bunkers. Attacking so soon after the first assault, the speed of the two forward sections of 7 Platoon had taken the Chinese by surprise. They fled down the rear slopes of Little Gibraltar, where they were shelled by the New Zealand gunners.

By now it was 11 am and Hill 220 had fallen to the Australians. While 9 Platoon moved forward to consolidate the second emplacement, all fifteen survivors of 7 Platoon continued to probe forward along the spur leading to Hill 355 to flush out the remaining enemy.

'Our main assault on Hill 355 was from the rear,' Maurie Pears says. 'We were badly mauled on the way up, but with the Kosbies at the front making a hell of a noise with their bagpipes and with us coming up the back, the Chinese thought we were in greater force than we were and actually withdrew.'

By 4 pm all of the enemy had been cleared from Little Gibraltar.

General Sir Anthony Farrar-Hockley would later write that 3RAR and the Borderers had each claimed the taking of the peak. The New Zealand official history says that the Australian platoon 'pushed forward on to the summit even before the Borderers reached it'.[32]

Maurie Pears says: 'Dr O'Neill's official history clearly puts us on there first, but the KOSB history and the British history don't. In fact, Hill 355 was taken jointly by both of us. The hill is a massive plateau and the Kosbies got to the top of the southern feature and we got to the top of the northern feature. The reports treated the pinnacle as one, whereas there are four pinnacles on top of the plateau. We've agreed [with the Kosbies] that everyone got there together and it's not a matter of dispute. It was a wonderful operation. 3RAR couldn't have got there without the Kosbies and the Kosbies couldn't have got there without 3RAR. We shouldn't be battling about something as unimportant as who got there first.'

Throughout the battle Colonel Hassett had moved around the battlefield on foot, leaving his adjutant, Captain (later Sir) William Keys, at BHQ to communicate with the forward companies on the radio or phone and to keep Brigade informed on the rear link. Travelling with a signaller and a three-man armed escort, the CO was exposed to enemy shellfire and sometimes small-arms fire, but the fighting men appreciated his presence in their midst.

On the evening of 4 October Gerke handed over 3RAR's positions on Hill 355 to the Kosbies but kept his men in position on Hill 220 to prepare for an enemy counterattack that did not eventuate. On the morning of 5 October the Kosbies relieved C Company of all their remaining positions and Gerke's men returned to their original defensive positions, where they had so recently enjoyed Gladys Moncrief's concert.

After shaving and washing, the men grabbed a few hours' sleep. Their next role in Operation Commando would be even more daunting than the first. 'We had a night in reserve,' Maurie Pears says, 'and then moved straight across the valley to support D Company on Hill 317.'

Hill 317, Maryang San, was the division's chief objective. As it had to be taken from behind enemy lines, it was also the most difficult on the entire I Corps front. Two American battalions had previously tried to take it and been repulsed. The hill was now swarming with two Chinese regiments of some 6000 men.

Hassett noted that the Americans had made two mistakes: they had moved their troops during daylight hours in full view of the enemy; and, failing to use the element of surprise, they had attacked only from the front.[33]

Knowing that Australian soldiers had been successful in 'running the ridges' when fighting the Japanese in New Guinea, Hassett decided to use the same manoeuvre after noticing that a wooded ridge ran from the eastern flank to the summit of Hill 317. Attacking through a blanket of thick mist with the support of the Kiwi gunners plus British and American tanks, at dawn on 5 October B and D Companies launched an assault on Hill 317 from the front and on the flanks. Captain K. Q. 'Haggis' Hunter, the New Zealand forward observation officer with B Company, watched the Australians take on some Chinese who had opened fire from a hilltop. 'The mist filled up suddenly with Chows and Diggers, all dashing north, south, east and west with bayonets,' he said. 'I retired quietly to the end of a ridge and had a smoke while waiting for the scuffle to die down. It ended with the Aussies snaffling some more Chows — caught them in their bunkers, too.'[34]

The Australian attack continued all day until the men were exhausted. 'D Company did a wonderful job on the foothills of Hill 317 and B Company was also involved in massive fighting there,' Maurie Pears says. 'But they were chopped around so much that the CO pushed C Company through them.'

Hassett ordered Gerke, although ten men short after the earlier battles, to move through D Company and capture Baldy, a feature immediately to the east of Hill 317, and then take Maryang San itself. Gerke raced his men through the Australian lines and, with the cheers of D Company ringing in their ears, they captured Baldy after a brief struggle. While artillery hammered the Chinese positions, Gerke and C Company advanced three hundred metres across a scrub-covered saddle to Hill 317.

'We came up the northern slope, but we couldn't walk — we climbed up on our hands and knees,' Pears says. 'Fortunately the Chinese strategy at the time was to withdraw in the face of what looked like overpowering opposition. They didn't have the communications that we had, and when they suffered casualties and it looked like they were starting to lose, they would invariably pull back and reorganise, so you would take the feature and then have to fight off a very severe counterattack.'

Once again the Chinese were surprised by the speed of the Australians' attack and at 5 pm the boulder-strewn summit fell to C Company without a fight. Those Chinese who hadn't fled down the slopes were taken prisoner. From the top of Maryang San, the Australians realised for the first time the strategic importance of their prize: Hill 317 commanded a panoramic view of the surrounding hills and valleys in three directions. It was not only a marvellous stronghold but also the perfect observation point.

For their heroism in the Battle of Maryang San, Jimmy Burnett was honoured with a Distinguished Conduct Medal, Jack Gerke got a Distinguished Service Order and Maurie Pears a Military Cross. Pears had been wounded but courageously opted to stay with his men.

The Chinese, however, true to form, were not about to surrender such a prize without a spirited counterattack. Throughout the day-light hours and into the night of 6 October the Australians on Hill 317 were subjected to a heavy Chinese bombardment that grew in fer-ocity until by dawn the following day it was almost continuous. Many men were wounded and Hassett knew that to hold Hill 317 it was vital for him to take The Hinge, a wooded knoll that dominated the ridgeline 900 metres to the north-west. He nominated B Company, led by Lieutenant Henry 'Wings' Nicholls of Sydney, to make the attack and moved his tactical headquarters onto Hill 317 to direct artillery fire against the target.

The start time of 8 am on the 7th allowed the fog to disperse suf-ficiently to enable the New Zealand gunners to give Nicholls close artil-lery support until his men had almost reached the Chinese trenches. After four hours of desperate fighting during which the Australians sus-tained twelve serious casualties, B Company overwhelmed the Chinese and occupied The Hinge. Hundreds of Chinese dead and wounded were left on the battlefield. The enemy still held a well-fortified spur known as Hill 217, and the Australians knuckled down to prepare for the inevitable counterattack. They were supplied with a generous ration of rum to warm them up for the difficult night ahead.

While these battles had been raging, Ron Cashman, Peter Cerdapavia and other reinforcements were bundled into RAAF DC3 'biscuit bombers' and flown to Kimpo airfield outside Seoul. From the air, Cashman noted, Korea looked like a vast uninhabited territory of mountainous terrain broken only by valleys and rice paddies and the occasional village. The people themselves seemed to be off limits, and Cashman met none of them before he and his mates were dispatched north to the battlefield, jolting over dirt roads and muddy tracks in the backs of open trucks. 'I finished up with a .303 rifle, which was all I'd wanted in the first place,' he says.

The success of Frank Hassett's mission depended on whether B Company could hold The Hinge on the night of 7–8 October. Given the exhausted condition of his men and the availability to the Chinese of a seemingly unlimited supply of reinforcements, it was a tall order. Hassett reinforced the defenders with fifteen men from C Company, but 3RAR was now seriously under strength and the force that would face hundreds of Chinese attackers on The Hinge numbered fewer than one hundred men.[35]

'There was a stream of wounded coming back and the situation looked grim,' Hassett says. 'I sent for one platoon commander, John McWilliam, and told him to take his platoon forward to strengthen the hard-fighting forward B Company. This platoon had already taken part in the capture of both Kowang San and Maryang San. It had fought and moved some ten kilometres in that difficult, mountainous terrain. It had taken casualties and was down in rations and ammunition. It was now under heavy shellfire and lying exhausted in what little cover it could find. I could hear the sounds of desperate fighting in the area to which it would be sent. I knew it could take further casualties and that it might or might not win the fight. That it would be isolated in such a forward position and that a counterattack was inevitable. That at best it would spend the coming freezing Korean night without packs or blankets.

'John McWilliam, sadly killed a short time later, accepted my orders calmly and I watched him walk to his platoon, speak briefly, and without hesitation his men picked up their gear and moved forward with him into the heavy fighting to their front. It takes good soldiers to do that.'

At 8 o'clock that night the Chinese laid down a merciless half-hour barrage of artillery and mortar fire on B Company. The bombardment was so intense that Frank Hassett compared it with the opening salvos of Montgomery's famous artillery blitz at El Alamein.

One of the biggest dangers was the shells and mortar bombs that exploded in the trees on the well-wooded summit. These airbursts caused many casualties from jagged splinters and shrapnel, like the shell fragment that killed Charlie Green in the Battle of Chongju. During the night a Chinese battalion launched three massive human-wave attacks on The Hinge from three directions, while an English-speaking Chinese called on the diggers to surrender. Every attack, however, was greeted with withering Australian gunfire.

Bugles sounded, whistles shrieked and white phosphorous flares illuminated the night sky as hundreds of Chinese soldiers launched themselves at the Australian defences. Many were cut down and others simply ran over their bodies. The Australians sustained further casualties but showed they were as capable of defending their positions as they were in taking them. Every Chinese attack ended in failure.

Maurie Pears had a ringside seat for the Battle of The Hinge, but found himself in a dangerously exposed position. 'I was sitting on the top of Hill 317 with the reserve platoon while 9 Platoon and 8 Platoon were forward of me, with B Company on the northern side of The Hinge,' he says. 'However, on top of 317 we were enfiladed by the Chinese artillery divisions on the west coast, so they were shooting into us from our rear, which caused enormous problems. But we held The Hinge throughout the night with massive casualties to the Chinese and severe casualties to us.'

In the early hours of 8 October the shooting ceased and an unnerving silence descended over the battlefield. Ammunition drops were made by South Korean porters and the Australian wounded were carried to safety. As dawn broke, the Chinese were permitted to come forward to carry away their dead. The battlefield was strewn with scores of Chinese corpses.

This was the moment that fate had chosen for Ron Cashman to go into the front line. 'I got shot into B Company and lobbed onto The Hinge, close to Hill 317,' he says. 'Exactly where we were I'm not sure. But there had been a hell of a barney that night and we went in with the supplies early on the morning of the 8th.'

His new comrades in 6 Platoon were a dirty, ragged, battle-weary bunch who had hardly washed, slept or changed clothes in six days. There was no time for anything more than grunted introductions. The new arrivals were handed over to Reg Saunders, who now commanded the battalion's Vickers and mortar platoons. He allocated a fighting pit to Cashman and Peter Cerdapavia and indicated three different directions from which the Chinese might attack.

The trenches abandoned by the Chinese were only chest high on the taller Australians, with shallow fighting pits in front in which to fire their weapons. 'We had to do some fancy digging to get a bit of cover,' Cashman says. 'I burrowed a coffin-shaped hole in the back wall of the trench and that's where I hid as long as I could. I covered the fighting pit with some rocks and branches to protect it from grenades and mortars.'

The Chinese gave up trying to reclaim The Hinge, however, and even abandoned Hill 217. 'We'd been on our feet for four days and four nights with very little sleep,' Maurie Pears says, 'and at that stage it was decided to relieve 3 Battalion with the KOSB.' C Company went into position on the flank of Hill 317 on the eastern side and B Company moved across the valley to take up a new position on a small feature just over two kilometres in front of the rest of the battalion.

The men of 3RAR had fired 900 000 rounds of small-arms ammunition and used 12 000 grenades and mortar bombs in the Battle of Maryang San. They had destroyed at least two Chinese battalions of some 2000 men at a cost of twenty men killed and eighty-nine wounded. It was Australia's most dramatic contribution of the Korean War.

Frank Hassett says: 'The soldiers at Maryang San were exceptional in their courage, their endurance and their intelligent recognition of what had to be done and the best way of doing it. I was proud to be a member of this team.' He adds: 'Maryang San is our biggest battle since World War II but has been the least publicised.'

Ron Cashman now had a chance to get to know his comrades in 6 Platoon. His experiences proved the army adage that it was much better to go on active service with a unit than to join it as a reinforcement.

'At first, I was the odd man out,' he says. 'Everybody else in the section knew each other and had been together for quite some time. The platoon sergeant, for instance, was a Second World War bloke, Joe Stuart. I was left to it. Nobody was really interested in what I did. I suppose they were all pretty bloody jumpy themselves, so I guess they were looking after number one. They could have given me the odd clue and helped me, but they didn't. I was left to it. I had to find my own feet.

But that was all right. That's what fighting men did. And he was now one of them.

CHAPTER 6

Wounded in action

L ieutenant 'Wings' Nicholls had earned his nickname as a paratrooper in 1 Australian Parachute Battalion during World War II. It was still daylight when he led the men of B Company into their exposed position in no-man's-land more than two kilometres to the north of their battalion. They worked quickly to dig foxholes and set up trip flares and booby traps before the autumn gloom enveloped them. Ron Cashman had acquired an Owen gun after the Battle of The Hinge and had decided to clean it.

'I was sitting there, right on dark, with my Owen gun totally dismantled down to the last spring, when the CSM came along. He called me all sorts of village idiot and ordered me to put it together quick. I saw his point.' The reprimand was like a greeting card. It told Cashman he was now accepted as a fully fledged member of the company. The men's original reserve had simply been their natural reluctance to accept that a mate had been killed or wounded by acknowledging the soldier who had taken his place.

It was a standing order in 3RAR that every man have a daily shave, but Cashman was permitted to keep his moustache, as was Wings Nicholls, who sported a handlebar model. 'We were the "poofters" in the company,' Cashman says. 'The fact is we depended on each other and became strong mates. Mateship bound the Australian infantry together. Somebody would look after you. If you ran out of cigarettes or rations, somebody would share theirs with you. Rank had little to do with it. A man was respected for his ability, not his rank. Mateship transcended rank in the front line.'

Frank Hassett defined mateship as 'concern for your fellow soldier'. Nobody mentioned the word love, but that is what it was — brotherly love. Cashman had no difficulty in recognising it. His own reserve vanished and he became a willing member of the team.

Peter Cerdapavia was not so fortunate. After two weeks in B Company, he was tracked down by his former comrades in B Echelon, who had gone looking for their missing staff sergeant. He was supposed to be in charge of the battalion's armoury thirty kilometres behind the lines, and that is where he ended up.

Cashman discovered that most of 3RAR's equipment was World War II vintage. In fact, the basic weapon issued to almost every man in his section was the Lee-Enfield .303 rifle with eighteen-inch sword bayonet, which had been standard issue as far back as World War I. 'It left a lot to be desired in a firefight,' Cashman says. 'Firing one bullet at a time at fast-moving targets when you were being rushed was not nearly enough.' Every section had one Bren gun ('a marvellous weapon that would chew through trees and hit the bloke standing behind them'), one Owen gun ('excellent at close quarters') and some 2-inch mortars ('handy for shooting up flares').

'Our support weapons were the ever-reliable Vickers medium machine gun and the 3-inch mortar, which wasn't all that reliable — we could never rely on their accuracy for close cover. You wouldn't call them in any closer than fifty yards unless you were in dire straits. Then we had the 25-pounders manned by our ever-loving Kiwis, who could usually drop one on a two-bob bit. And we had the 36 mm grenade, which was probably the most effective weapon of all. You could rely on it to operate almost every time.'

The Chinese infantry, on the other hand, were armed with a rifle with a fold-back bayonet ('most unattractive in close proximity') or a burp gun, a Chinese-made version of a Russian sub-machine gun with a circular, 75-round magazine. It could fire short, lethal bursts if a well-trained soldier was on the end of it.

'In my early days,' Cashman says, 'if a Chinese fired thirty bullets at somebody, twenty-nine of them would finish up in the wide blue yonder. But in time they improved their skills immeasurably. When I first arrived in Korea, the Chinese mortars and artillery were just coming into their own; they were just mastering them. They had a lot of good equipment because they had captured most of it off the Yanks. They were getting pretty good then, but not to the extent they did later. They were great ones for grenades. They had a concussion grenade that must have been designed to take prisoners. If they threw it into a fighting pit or bunker, it knocked everyone stupid. They had another one shaped like a potato masher that was a wooden handle with a grenade at the end of it. It had a fairly heavy shrapnel jacket around it and was quite effective. I have a friend who lost all of one leg and two-thirds of an arm to one of those grenades. It landed in the fighting pit with him and before he could get it out it messed him up considerably.

Finally they had a big, bell-shaped grenade that I've always wrongly called an anti-tank grenade — they tried to use them to knock the tracks off the tanks. They were real monstrosities. They were very good for taking out strong-posts and, of course, out in the open they threw a lot of shrapnel around. One of their favourite techniques was carrying grenades in a vine. They would have a vine around their shoulder like a bandolier with a dozen potato masher grenades hanging from it. Despite stories to the contrary, the Chinese soldier was well equipped.'

After an unnerving forty-eight hours in the wilderness, B Company was pulled back to The Hinge without further casualties and then went into reserve. This was the luck of the draw; there had been a brief lull in hostilities while the Chinese prepared a fresh attack. It soon came.

On the night of 19–20 October 3RAR was back at the front line and 6 Platoon was on patrol investigating a feature in front of The Hinge to see whether or not it had been occupied. Cashman had moved from the scrub-line onto a hillside when a grenade exploded in front of him, throwing him backwards. 'I didn't know I'd been hit because I got up and threw two grenades into an area where I thought I might find some customers,' he says. 'Then I heard two of our fellows yelling behind me and I quickly put two and two together that if these blokes had been hit, then so had I. I felt the blood and that's when it started to hurt.'

At that moment, a white phosphorous flare lit up the sky overhead as the Chinese gunners searched for targets. The Australians lay spread-eagled on the hillside and could see the flare starting to descend. Nobody dared move; they hardly breathed. Cashman admits he was petrified; it seemed to be coming straight at him.

'All these thoughts were rushing through my head: There's no way in the world it's not going to land on top of me. What do I do? Do I get up and run and get shot, or do I stay here and get barbecued?'

The flare landed too far away to harm him, and Joe Stuart, the platoon sergeant, immediately ordered his men under cover before mortar bombs started raining down on the hillside.

Cashman had been wounded in the shoulder and the other two men had been hit in the torso, but all three could still walk. Once they were patched up with field dressings to stop the bleeding, Stuart led them back along the valley to their camp. Cashman made it safely but started to lose consciousness. He woke up the following morning at the Indian Field Ambulance station.

'I was greeted by a grinning Indian orderly who handed me a bowl of curry. It was the first time I had come across curry and, strike me pink, it nearly lifted the palate out of my mouth. But they were terrific, the Indians.'

The wounded men were evacuated to an American MASH at Uijongbu, twenty-four kilometres north of Seoul, and from there they were flown to the British hospital at Kure, Japan. 'I was back where I had started from two weeks earlier,' Cashman says. 'It was a pretty quick round trip, but some of the blokes I had gone over with had been killed.'

At the hospital it was customary for the CO and the matron to inspect the wards every morning while patients stood to attention beside their beds — 'If you had both legs amputated, you were allowed to sit to attention'. The high point of the day was afternoon tea, when patients were given a bottle of 'absolutely marvellous' Guinness.

Cashman had a chunk of metal removed from his shoulder and a week later asked a doctor whether he could go back to his unit — the inactivity was driving him insane.

'Have you nearly finished your tour?' the doctor asked.

'No, I've just started the damn thing.'

Cashman was granted forty-eight hours' leave and then sent back to the front.

While he was in Japan there had been a big change at the top of 28 Brigade's command. Despite the success of Operation Commando, Brigadier Taylor had been sacked by General Cassels. The diggers heard that Taylor had fallen foul of some of his commanders, and a cabal of British officers including the 1KOSB commander, John Mac-Donald, had conspired to have him removed. As MacDonald succeeded Taylor as commanding officer of 28th Brigade, there were grounds for suspicion.

MacDonald disliked the Australians, but his attitude barely filtered through to the diggers on the line. 'We didn't much care who was paying the rent,' Cashman says, but they did prefer Taylor's gregarious style of command to that of the dour Scot, whom they saw as the embodiment of a Presbyterian wowser.

On the night of 4–5 November the Chinese attacked the Kosbies' positions on Hill 317, the adjacent Hill 217 and The Hinge after launching a murderous rocket and artillery barrage. The Kosbies suffered heavy casualties and were forced to withdraw, although one of their number, Bill Speakman, won the Victoria Cross in attempting to retake Hill 217 with repeated grenade attacks.

With their apparently unlimited supply of reinforcements, the Chinese continued to mount human-wave attacks against the Australians. 'The bugles and the whistles were psychological warfare,' Cashman says. 'You heard bugles to the left, bugles to the right and bugles in front. There was a crescendo of Chinese artillery fire and the bugles got louder and louder as they attacked. It was frightening but you got used to it after a while.'

Their favourite method of attack was called 'one point — two sides', which entailed a flying wedge attacking a particular point in a V formation and then enveloping the two sides. After one such attack ten bodies were found stacked in front of Bluey Drayson's Bren-gun pit.

'When the Chinese tried to take The Hinge back from us, their troops were probably the same ones who had been fighting for a number of days beforehand,' Cashman says. 'When they hit the Kosbies, they gave them a shower with Russian katyusha rockets, then blew the living daylights out of them with artillery. Then they swarmed over the hill en masse. Probably the weight of the rockets, the artillery and then the mass attack of very fresh troops would have shunted most units off.'

As far as B Company were concerned, the immediate effect of the loss of Hill 317 was that their new position was now overlooked by Chinese gunners. 'We were a fine body of shell-shocked lads,' Cashman says. 'Many of the men hadn't recovered from the thumping they'd received on The Hinge and we weren't greatly comforted when a Chinese shell hit a tree and gave us an airburst for our troubles. Fortunately no one was injured.'

As soon as Cashman returned to B Company the men were bundled into trucks and driven to the bottom of a heavily wooded mountain, Hill 264, now called Observation Post Typhoon, beside the Imjin River. Occupying the hill were the Seventh Cavalry, Custer's old regiment, many of them decked out in smart yellow scarves.

In the absence of Korean porters, Cashman and his mates made three trips up the hill with their supplies. No trenches had been prepared for them, so they set to work with combat shovels digging foxholes and making little tents with their ponchos. The ground was rock hard and the roots of the pine trees made digging even more difficult.

'It was getting cold. Sometimes it rained. Life was totally miserable. Then we settled in. I was intimately acquainted with 6 Platoon by this time, and there were fresher reos [reinforcements] than me. I was a wounded vet, so I was up the social ladder a little.'

The Imjin River ran in a straight line along the front of OP Typhoon from east to west and then took a ninety-degree turn to the north. The American defences followed the southern bank, while the Chinese were dug in on the opposite side. B Company was in the line protecting the eastern flank of Hill 317 (Maryang San), which was being defended by the Kosbies against sustained Chinese attacks.

Now attached to the Seventh Cavalry, B Company lived on American combat rations (C rations), and when Thanksgiving Day rolled around they got their share of roast turkey and all the trimmings, with ice-cream to follow.

The first snow of the encroaching winter fell on the night of 22–23 November. There was 16 degrees of frost the following night but the Imjin River had not yet frozen over. For the next week B Company's main duty was to send patrols across the river into a vast valley that ran directly north to investigate the enemy's strength and intentions. 'It was Charlie's country and we had a river between us and home,' Cashman says.

'By the time the Seventh Cavalry were replaced by the US 3rd Infantry Division (3ID) the task of patrolling the valley had become our regular job. This was no great drama except that it was necessary for us to cross the Imjin River and I was sick and tired of sloshing around with boots full of water. One night I decided to take them off and hang them around my neck. Once across the ford, I would put the boots on again. The Yanks had set up a .30 calibre machine gun on a bluff overlooking the ford. We said good night to them and crossed the river.

'We'd got part way up the valley when Charlie arrived on the scene, shooting and whistling and attacking in all directions. We headed for home across the river, shouting in Australian accents to let the Yanks know it was us. I had my dry boots on and was cursing about getting them wet. Halfway across the river that American machine gun opened up and proceeded to spray bullets left, right and centre. We dived under water and finished up about a hundred yards further downstream. Not a soul was hit but ten or twelve very cold, very wet and very annoyed diggers stormed back to the outpost and let our feelings be known to the Yanks. Then we went back up the hill. There were no dry clothes, of course. That was one of our more amusing nights.'

The Americans were anxious to drive the Chinese out of the valley, and their first move was to take a large, bald hill in a sweeping bend in the river directly in front of OP Typhoon. This feature was still on the southern side of the river but further to the north. To cover the US advance, it was decided that 6 Platoon should occupy a three-hilled feature across the Imjin in the right angle where it turned northward.

All three hills were joined by a ridgeline. The first hill had an ancient Korean graveyard, a minefield and a burned-out village. The second knoll, later dubbed Little Nori, was slightly higher and the third, Big Nori, was higher again. With Brian Falvey in charge, 6 Platoon occupied Little Nori, finding it unoccupied though pockmarked with old trenches and fighting pits. They soon discovered, however, that the knolls on either side of them were very much in Chinese hands and they had been lucky to choose the only unoccupied hill.

The platoon dug in and formed a barbed-wire perimeter. The Chinese were no more than 120 metres in either direction and they were soon under fire from snipers. The Americans, meanwhile, prepared to storm the bald feature.

'We were actually their insurance against a flank attack. We had to report in every hour by radio that we were still there. So what did Charlie do? He brought up this thundering great self-propelled gun and placed it at the base of our hill on the blind side to the Yanks. It was parked just below our barbed wire and fired a couple of shots at us to convince us to keep our heads down. Then it proceeded to hammer the living daylights out of the Yanks across the river for the rest of the night. By dawn it had disappeared.'

It was probably a Soviet-built SU-76 self-propelled gun. Around this time Stalin had sold the Chinese hundreds of these guns along with improved T-34 tanks, personnel carriers and heavy trucks to give their forces greater mobility on the battlefield.

The Chinese also stationed mortars on the eastern side of Little Nori and opened fire on the Americans, while a small number of infantry were sent to harass 6 Platoon 'to make sure we stayed at home'.

The Americans had spent much of that day attacking the large bald hill and with great bravery had dispossessed the Chinese. But now they were on the receiving end of fierce artillery and mortar fire, and when the Chinese mounted a human-wave attack they could not hold the position and were driven back. 'That began our less than happy few weeks on the middle knoll,' Cashman says. 'We became the ham in the sandwich.'

The Americans could do nothing to relieve the situation because the big Chinese gun was no more than thirty metres from 6 Platoon's position and opening fire with artillery or mortars to knock it out would have meant risking the lives of the Australian troops. Nor could 6 Platoon attack the Chinese gun — they had no bazookas and no one was going to risk attacking it with a Bren gun.

'So the poor bloody American infantry were taking then losing this damn hill and it was like being at the movies for us. We could sit and watch them charge up, get beaten back, then up again until they had it. Within a night or two, Charlie had the thing back again, compliments of their mortars and the SP gun.'

One morning 6 Platoon watched an American truck drive along the dirt track leading up to the bald hill. The next moment the front of the truck leapt into the air as though it was a toy. The Chinese had mined the track behind US lines.

'One thing I can be sure about is the guts of those fighting units, although I am not so sure about the brains that were ordering it,' Cashman says. 'You can send men to their doom only so often before they call it quits.'

One night Bluey Drayson hit one of the Chinese soldiers with a burst from his Bren gun, and in the morning when Cashman spotted footprints in the frost he followed them. They led him down to the base of Little Nori and along a track up to the first hill that contained the minefield, the graveyard and the burned-out village. At the edge of the minefield he found a stretcher made out of two barbed-wire fence pickets and some old blood-stained ponchos. On the ground he found a padded jacket with three bullet holes where the owner's navel would have been. The footprints disappeared into the minefield, heading straight towards the graveyard.

Cashman gave up the hunt. 'I was going to take the jacket back for Bluey as a trophy,' he said, 'but Brian Falvey was a very regimental man and pretty strict, so I left it behind.'

Later that evening he retraced his steps and booby-trapped the path where the footprints had been to disrupt further sallies. 'I put a phosphorus grenade and a 36 mm grenade in tins on either side of the track with a trip-wire between them. Next morning, the wire had been cut and neatly laid on either side of the footpath.'

With the self-propelled gun on one side of Little Nori and the mortars on the other side preventing an advance, the Americans decided to make an air strike on the main Chinese position on Big Nori. Four jet fighters were sent in, and as the first one swooped down and fired its rockets the Chinese opened fire with a .50-calibre machine gun and cut its tail clean off 'just like a knife'.

The plane was carrying napalm, which the pilot promptly dumped just in front of 6 Platoon's forward trench, the occupants of which had the air sucked away from them by the fireball. Luckily they were unhurt. The plane then dived straight into the ground in the hollow between Big and Little Nori and exploded in flames. The other US planes circled for a while and then flew off.

Later that day Cashman made his way down to the scene. All that remained of the plane was a lot of aluminium confetti, with the breach blocks of the cannons just showing at the bottom of the crater.

Meanwhile there was no respite for those in the ham sandwich deadlock. 'We were a bunch of nervous wrecks,' Cashman recalls. 'We had a 50 per cent stand-to every night, which more often than not became 100 per cent. I actually went to sleep standing up in my pit one night. We had the US Army radio checks on us every hour on the hour, to be sure we still owned the hill.

'Finally, after what seemed like an eternity, Centurion tanks rumbled across the Imjin at the ford and the Irish Hussars carried the exhausted members of 6 Platoon back to 3ID's camp at OP Typhoon. They were replaced by a company of Filipinos. The Chinese attacked in force before the new arrivals had time to settle in. The Filipinos were wiped out and, for the time being, the position was lost.'

On 25 October 1951, after an adjournment of two months, the peace negotiators had reconvened at the new site of Panmunjom, a village only a few kilometres from the Australian positions. Day after day until 17 November the two sides haggled over battlefield maps in search of a demarcation line acceptable to both sides. Then Washington instructed the UN delegation to reach agreement on a provisional line and Admiral Joy, stripped of his bargaining powers, was forced to propose that the present line of contact be recognised as the provisional line, provided an armistice agreement was signed within thirty days.

The issues still to be settled ranged from appointing an overseer to monitor the creation of the final demilitarised zone to the repatriation of prisoners of war. The Communist delegation prevaricated for another six days, then agreed that the line of contact should form a temporary demarcation line from which both sides would withdraw two kilometres to establish a demilitarised zone. If the armistice agreement was not signed in thirty days, both sides would return to the positions they had previously occupied. This agreement was ratified on 27 November.

General Van Fleet was delighted with the apparent breakthrough. Without consulting his Supreme Commander, General Ridgway, he instructed General Cassels and every other divisional commander that for the next thirty days all offensive action in enemy territory with the objective of securing new ground should cease. The commanders were told they could undertake operations only to retain their 'present positions' or to reclaim territory lost in fresh enemy attacks; in effect, Van Fleet had ordered a thirty-day ceasefire.

When he finally heard of it, Ridgway was furious. The Chinese, however, wasted no time in taking advantage of the thirty-day breathing space. Moving 850 000 troops and uncounted Chinese coolies and North Korean workers onto the 250-kilometre-long Main Line of Resistance (MLR), the enemy embarked on a massive building project to secure their existing territory. At the end of the period, the Chinese had burrowed, bulldozed and blasted communications tunnels through every strategic mountain and hill. They created deep tunnels from which their heavy artillery could fire its rounds and then retreat out of harm's way, and they constructed hundreds of cavernous galleries capable of holding entire divisions and their supplies.

The defence system in depth extended up to forty kilometres behind the MLR and involved a complicated layout of minefields, camouflaged redoubts and checkpoints. At its core, the tunnels were so deep they could probably have withstood a nuclear attack.

Mao's Christmas message to Washington was clear: We are now immovable.

CHAPTER 7

A Korean Christmas

After a lengthy separation from 3RAR during which B Company had won its spurs with the Seventh Cavalry and the 3rd Infantry Division, Ron Cashman's unit was reunited with their own battalion in time for Christmas 1951. This was spent under canvas at Castle Hill on the route that Genghis Khan had taken to Seoul. Icy winds swept across the mountains bringing snowstorms in their wake, and the troops experienced a white Christmas whether they wanted one or not.

'Before Korea, Melbourne was the coldest place I'd ever been in and that first winter was quite a shock,' Cashman says. 'During the autumn months cold winds blew in from Siberia and there was heavy frost, but in December it snowed and it was bone-searing cold.'

The tensions of frontline combat had taken their toll. In conversation many years later, Cashman affects the manner of the lively raconteur, but despite the bantering tone it is clear that his unit was showing unmistakable symptoms of deep strain.

That festive season brought a visit to the battalion by Josh Francis, the Minister for the Army and the Navy. 'We all took Josh as a bit of a joke, because nobody was all that impressed with politicians coming up and peacocking around the place,' Cashman says. Francis, however, took his duties seriously. While the battalion stood to attention on the freezing parade ground on Christmas Day, he took his place on the reviewing stand with an oversized army parka covering his suit, white shirt and tie. On his head was a black homburg, which he removed and clutched to his left breast when taking the salute.

The minister then made an excruciating speech, which started with the words, 'I have come a long way to see you. I left Australia quite some time ago to be here with you today.' At the end he said one of his purposes was to listen to any grievances that the men might have, and then he called for comments. Immediately a voice from the middle of D Company piped up: 'Sir, before we left Australia you promised that we would lack for nothing ... Well, that's what we bloody well got — nothing.' Attempts to find the ingrate failed and the parade ended in disarray.

Christmas dinner of roast turkey and all the trimmings, washed down with copious quantities of beer and with diced bananas and custard to follow, was served to one thousand men in large marquee tents. After his experiences on the parade ground, Francis was looking forward to a reviving tot of whisky, but unfortunately one of the officers had put the bottle of Scotch down for a few moments and it had disappeared. The minister had to settle for beer.

This mystery was later solved when a young soldier was heard shouting, 'I've come a long way to see you bastards!' while swigging from the missing Scotch bottle. He was promptly arrested and put on a charge. Francis was lucky to escape with nothing worse than a bruised ego. Another young soldier lurking at the entrance of the Support Company tent smashed a plateful of bananas and custard into the face of Major Archibald 'Daddy' Lukyn, the company's CO, in the mistaken belief that he was the minister. Lukyn was badly cut by broken china and his attacker was sentenced to a term of imprisonment.

Tim Holt says: 'Whoever did that to Daddy Lukyn was a complete and utter coward. Daddy was a little fat fellow and a hail fellow well met. He was everybody's friend and hitting him in the face was like kicking a dog.' Holt adds: 'Josh Francis was a politician through and through, but I found out later he had been a subaltern in World War I. He was a bit out of his depth in Korea and was just trying to be jolly and jovial at Christmas time.'[36]

On Christmas Day 3RAR's forward sentries were astonished to discover that the Chinese had crept up to the barbed wire overnight and decorated it with banners, cards and propaganda leaflets. Soon afterwards they opened up with an artillery barrage to show that their season of goodwill had ended.

Cashman was walking through a cemetery when an incoming shell exploded on a nearby grave. 'It must have been a fairly large projectile because it excavated the grave and, as lightning never strikes twice, I hopped in until the shelling stopped,' he says. 'In the bottom of that hole I found a very ancient coin — a big, thick, silver thing about two inches across and about three-sixteenths of an inch thick. Apparently Genghis Khan had a fortress on this site, hence the name Castle Hill. So maybe it came from that era. The Koreans attached to our camp as domestics knew nothing about it; they'd never seen anything like it.'

The new year arrived in a flurry of snowstorms as 3RAR trudged back to the Jamestown Line, the Commonwealth Division's section of the MLR that stretched across the Korean peninsula, and started digging. The mobile phase of the war had ground to a halt and the long, hard, static war of attrition was about to begin. That did not mean that the shooting had stopped; far from it — once Van Fleet's thirty-day ceasefire had lapsed on 27 December, artillery and mortar duels started with revitalised ferocity. The stonk, as an artillery bombardment was known, became an everyday fact of life. The big freeze, however, restricted hand-to-hand fighting with light machine guns, side-arms, grenades and bayonets. Men on ambush patrol were liable to freeze to death if they had to stay in one position for more than half an hour.

Winter bit deeply. The temperature frequently dropped to minus 20 degrees Centigrade. Cashman wrote to his mother about the Australian Army's winter wear. 'When we went out barbed wiring in the slush and snow, we were like drowned rats,' he says. 'We started to pirate from wherever we could — gear from the Yanks, gear from the Brits, whoever left anything lying around lost it.'

The men wore so many layers of clothes to ward off the cold that they lumbered around camp like abominable snowmen. First Cashman put on a string vest, a standard piece of kit in the British Army that puzzled the Australians until they learned its heat-saving properties. Then he donned a fleecy-lined singlet, a pair of fleecy-lined underpants, a shirt and several woollen jumpers and then a thick, hooded jacket.

As well as underpants, he wore a pair of long johns with a diagonal split in the rear and an opening at the front. On top of this went a very thick pair of olive-green long johns and a pair of three-layered, reasonably waterproof pants. On top of that, when occasion demanded that he blend in with the snow-covered scenery, he wore a very big white fur-lined parka and a pair of white canvas pants. The parka had a wire-framed visor that enabled him to see all round while affording some protection against the elements.

On his feet he wore three pairs of thick woollen socks, and his boots were at least one size too big to accommodate them. 'The first lot we were given had been made for the Norwegian campaign in World War II and the stitching rotted and the boots fell apart on everyone's feet,' Cashman says. 'But the next batch were especially designed for mountain terrain and cold weather and were very insulated.'

When the men were required to lay an ambush or spend any amount of time in one place in the open, they tied six empty sandbags around their feet and legs, 'otherwise your feet would just freeze'.

Frostbite and trenchfoot were a constant menace and both claimed casualties. Metal burn was another problem; the troops dared not touch the metal of their guns with bare hands. Cashman wore three pairs of gloves that came up to his elbows, one of which had a thumb piece and a trigger-finger piece so he could operate his weapon. On top of that he wore a huge pair of white waterproof mittens that were joined by a strap across his shoulders. 'During any action these could be shaken off and would hang there,' he says, 'and then you could just turf off one pair of gloves and handle your equipment without losing your fingers on the steel.' On his head Cashman wore an American pile cap and a balaclava, 'compliments of our womenfolk at home'.

It was physically impossible to sneak around quietly, so fighting patrols were kept to a minimum. 'We were so encumbered by all this gear that if we ran into someone, well, by the time we got undressed and ready to start fighting he would have disappeared. We concentrated on laying up ambush patrols at places where Charlie was known to visit, such as villages and creeks. Through winter it was pretty much an ambush-and-defend role. We weren't in a position to go running around annoying Charlie much.'

Cashman and his mates looked forward to their daily beer ration of one bottle of Japanese Asahi beer that never needed chilling. Sometimes the brand was Kirin or Nippon II. 'Korean grog could be acquired on the black market but it caused untold damage to those stupid enough to drink it,' he says. 'Officers had a spirits ration, which was quite often stolen.'

The men lived on American combat rations dating from World War II. They were packed in a small cardboard container the size of a shoebox. There were three main meals: ham and lima beans, baked beans or pork and baked beans, and hamburger patties in gravy. 'The most revolting was the ham and lima beans — none of us had ever heard of lima beans until we started to be force-fed them.' The box also contained salt biscuits and a small tin of jam, coffee, sugar, a little tin opener and some high-quality toilet paper. 'For a digger in the field it was good tucker. You were never going to get fat on it but there was enough to keep you going. It could be eaten hot or cold.'

To heat their food, the men placed a can on a little three-legged stand and lit a fuel pellet beneath it. The pellet looked like a giant mothball and burned with an unobtrusive blue flame. Eggs froze and had to be thawed out before they could be cooked. Water bottles were kept close to the body so that body heat would prevent the water from freezing. The men slept with their boots on and their weapons inside their sleeping bags to keep the mechanical parts operational. On patrol, Cashman cradled his Owen gun under his parka. 'The snow was sometimes up to the top of our thighs,' he says, 'or without warning you'd disappear into a four-foot-deep shell-hole covered with snow.'

The men lived in eight-foot-square hutchies lined with sandbags and covered with a tarpaulin to make them as waterproof as possible. The roof was then camouflaged with logs and soil, but as Chinese observers had been watching their construction through binoculars they knew just where to aim their guns.

Cashman often shared a hutchie with Private Eddie Wright. 'Eddie was an Englishman who came from the sticks — a village called Trench in Shropshire,' Cashman says. 'He had transferred from the Paras to join K Force in the UK and he became a good digger. He got the job as platoon radioman because Brian Falvey knew the Chinese would never understand his accent. We didn't ourselves most of the time.

'We hung a poncho over the doorway to keep the weather out and the light in after dark. The men were so attuned to reacting quickly that they would wake instantly when someone touched the poncho. This happened when it was their turn for picket duty at night. Outside the door a small tunnel turned sharply into the main trench and the fighting pit. We depended mostly on candles for lighting the hutchie, although some of the people higher up the social scale had lanterns. Bunks were always cut into the wall and a few beer boxes were scrounged for furniture. Pegs were driven into the wall and equipment hung on them, first to keep it out of the way and second to keep it dry if the hole was filling with water during rainy spells. Such times saw us sitting crouched on the bunk, watching the water level rise and cursing our ill fortune.'

Heating was provided by petrol burners made from ammunition cases with sand in the bottom and a drip feed fuel supply. Many casualties were caused by blazing petrol setting fire to a hutchie. Battalion HQ had pot-bellied stoves, which were effective and safe.

The diggers slept in blankets in the warmer weather and sleeping bags in winter. 'The early model of sleeping bag was dangerous in that getting out was a problem,' Cashman says. 'Many troops were caught and killed in them. The later models were much more efficient at keeping us warm and the zippers flew open if you belted both sides of the bag from the inside. As you slept with your weapon, you needed to get out quickly.'

The fighting pit was dug forward of the trench and measured two metres by one metre and up to two metres deep. One night there was an alert and Cashman scrambled out of his blankets and dashed to his pit. There was no sign of Dixon, the man with whom he was sharing

Left: Units of the 15th Chinese Field Army cross the frozen Yalu River, October 1950.

Below: Lt. Col. Charles Green (left) with Brigadier Basil Coad, commander of the British Commonwealth Brigade, near Chongju, 29 October, the day before Green's fatal injury. (AWM HOBJ1648)

Lt. Col. Bruce 'I.B.' Ferguson, CO 3RAR, Pakchon, 7 November 1951. (AWM 146990)

Men of 3RAR grab a few minutes' rest, 1951.

These diggers had to claw their way up an icy cliff before coming under deadly Chinese machine-gun fire, March 1951.

Lt. Col. Frank Hassett (left) shortly before taking command of 3RAR, with Maj. Gen. James 'Gentleman Jim' Cassells, GOC Commonwealth Division, July 1951. (AWM HOBJ2314)

A group portrait of 4 Platoon, B Company, 3RAR, 1951, with Lt. Len
Montgomerie (centre, front row) (AWM 147350)

Cashman and
Eddie Wright
inside 'our
foxhole' on the
Bowling Alley,
early 1952.

6 Platoon prepares for an 'ambush patrol'. This was the ill-fated assault on Cloncurry in which Cashman (third from left) was wounded for the third time, May 1953.

In the aftermath of Operation Buffalo, a wounded Max Wilson, on a stretcher in the back of a jeep, about to be evacuated, 14 August 1952. Cashman had just saved his life.

Cashman and KATCOM Kim Heung Koo enjoy the sun on The Hook, July 1953.

Corporal Cashman, summer 1953.

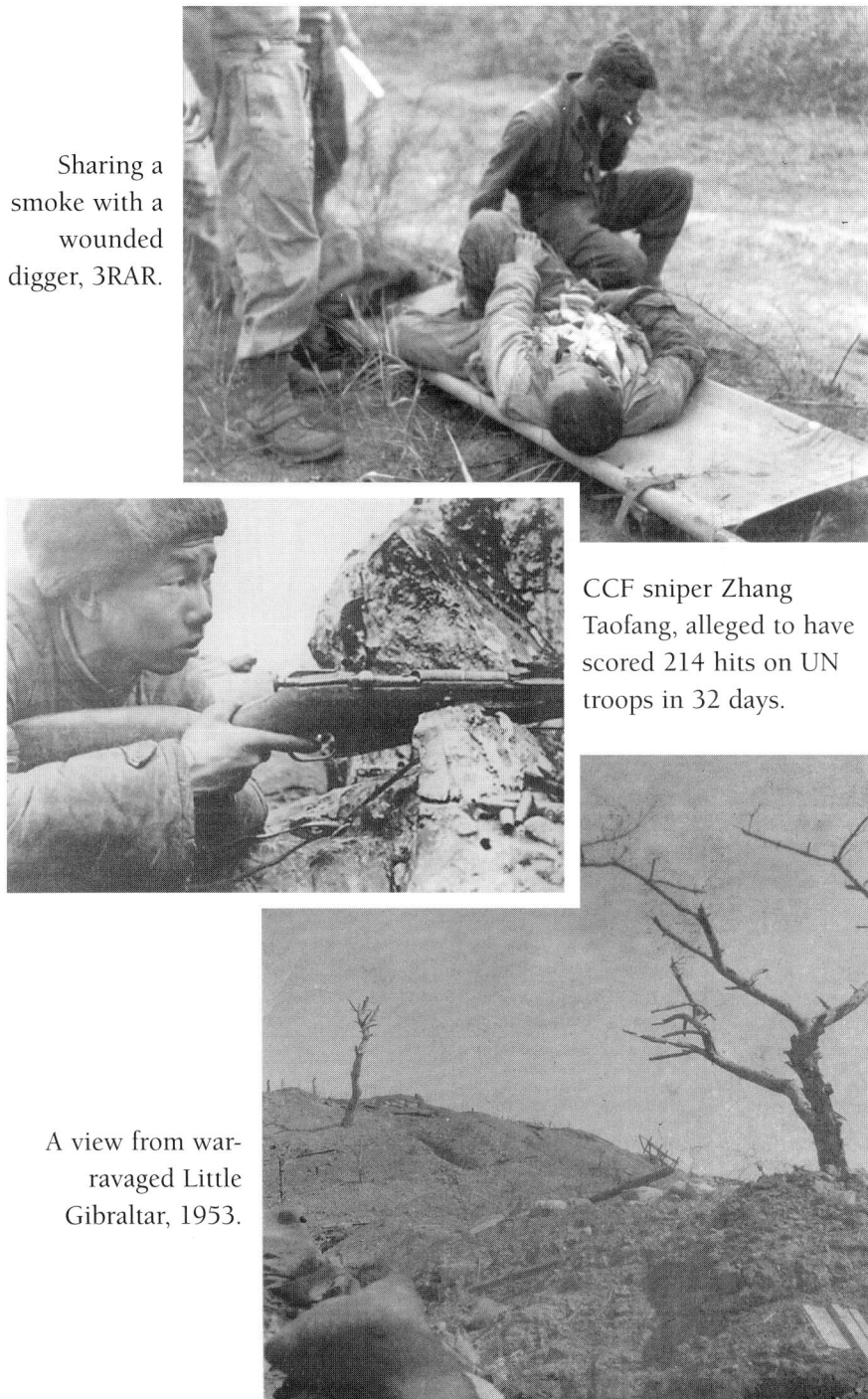

Sharing a smoke with a wounded digger, 3RAR.

CCF sniper Zhang Taofang, alleged to have scored 214 hits on UN troops in 32 days.

A view from war-ravaged Little Gibraltar, 1953.

US military attaché presents Olwyn Green with the Silver Star won by her husband for outstanding leadership and bravery during the Battle of the Apple Orchard.

Olwyn Green would become a tireless archivist and champion of the diggers in Korea.

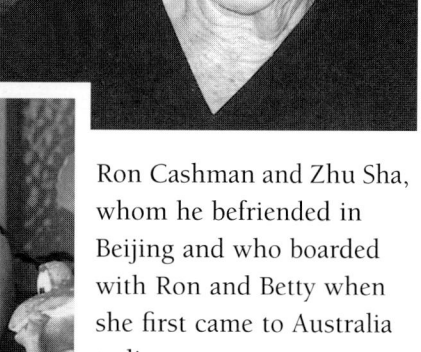

Ron Cashman and Zhu Sha, whom he befriended in Beijing and who boarded with Ron and Betty when she first came to Australia to live.

Betty Whipple, 'Sydney's Betty Grable'

a hutchie at the time. Dixon had taken his boots off to go to sleep and they had frozen solid. Cashman found him in the bunker holding one of his boots over a candle and trying to defrost it.

Apart from the enemy and the cold, the biggest problem was lice. There were no washing facilities and all of the men were 'driven stark raving mad by lice'. Every man was given a rubber bombe of DDT with a nozzle to squirt the poison powder over his body; heads and armpits were shaved and at times even the genitals suffered the same indignity. 'No one knew the slightest thing about the harmful effects of DDT on human beings,' Cashman says. All the diggers inhaled it ('You couldn't avoid it'). Not until the 1980s was it discovered that DDT caused serious liver damage.

Rats and mice, too, fossicked around foodstuffs in the hutchie. After a battle, rats would feast on dead bodies and then come into the bunkers for warmth. Both rats and mice carried a flea that caused Manchurian fever. They were hated more than the enemy.

Lacking the manpower of the American or South Korean units, the Australian force was unable to occupy a continuous line of trenches, broken only by rice paddies, across its entire front. 3RAR's answer to the problem was to construct self-contained positions each consisting of three platoons on hilltops and high ground, which could be defended against attack from all directions.

The Commonwealth Division was ordered to defend two pivotal bastions at the approaches to the Imjin Valley. These were the familiar ridgeline of Little Gibraltar (Hill 355, or Kowang San) and a jagged, J-shaped ridge ten kilometres to the south named The Hook. Over the next twenty months the Australian area of operations ran from Little Gibraltar and its foothills along a narrow strip called the Bowling Alley to the Samichon Valley, where the line tilted south-west to The Hook, just fifteen kilometres north-east of Panmunjom, where the negotiators were deadlocked over the exchange of prisoners of war.

It had been assumed at the beginning of the peace negotiations that POWs would be returned to their respective sides at the end of hostilities. The United Nations had discovered, however, that the NKPA contained many South Koreans who had been forcibly conscripted into its ranks. These men had no desire to be returned to North Korea and the UN agreed with the ROK government that they should be allowed to return to their homes in the South.

Some of the Chinese POWs presented a similar problem. As former Nationalists who had been inducted into the People's Volunteer Army they wished to return to their families in Taiwan rather than to Communist-ruled mainland China.

The Americans favoured a system under which each prisoner would be permitted to make a choice; the Communists, fearing a massive propaganda defeat, disagreed. Their negotiators insisted that every one of their prisoners in UN captivity should be repatriated, regardless of their wishes.

The distance across no-man's-land separating the men of 3RAR and the massed ranks of the Chinese People's Volunteer Army was as wide as two thousand metres and as narrow as two hundred metres. To enable patrols to come and go, narrow zigzag pathways were left in the barbed-wire entanglements at the front and rear of the Australian trenches. Outposts were manned at the outer limit of these paths, which were well covered by fixed-firing light machine guns. Minefields, marked with red triangular signs, were interspersed with the wire as an added deterrent to the Chinese.

After spending four months in Korea, Cashman qualified for five days' rest and recuperation leave (R&R) in Japan. He had written a letter to Keiko-san saying how much he missed her and that he hoped to see her again, but he had received no reply.

The main leave point, however, was Tokyo. Cashman was flown to the Japanese capital and taken to Ebisu barracks, where he disrobed and showered while his clothes were taken away and burned. He was given a new uniform and some occupation currency and let loose on the civilian population. 'Most of the time was spent in beerhalls chatting up Japanese girls,' he says. 'As soon as we walked out of the main entrance of the camp we were swarmed over by Japanese pimps giving us cards advertising their places.' Keiko-san was soon forgotten.

Cashman wrote a censored version of his adventures to his mother in Smith Street, Williamstown. Edna Cashman's letters were full of warmth and concern for him, with rarely a complaint about her husband, but he knew instinctively that she would be suffering the usual ill-treatment in Williamstown; moving homes and new-found prosperity would have changed nothing. Michael Cashman would still be as mean as Scrooge and as violent as ever.

Ron had no idea how much longer the war was going to last, but he swore once it was over he would take care of things at home. As a boy nursing the welts on his body from another beating with the leather strop, he had prayed to be made big and strong enough to take on his father. His prayers had been answered. All he had to do now was to stay alive.

CHAPTER 8
The razor's edge

The Jamestown Line began to resemble the Western Front of 1916. The men of 3RAR turned their rudimentary defences of the previous year into a sophisticated system of trenches, tunnels and sandbagged forts behind barbed-wire barricades, while their artillery and mortars pounded the enemy across no-man's-land.

The Chinese desperately wanted to win back Little Gibraltar, the long, razor-backed mountain with steep frozen slopes that were back-breaking to climb and difficult to dig into for defence. At any hour of the day or night the Chinese on neighbouring Hill 227 would open up with their mortars. 'They were so expert they could drop a mortar into a fighting pit,' Cashman says. 'We were literally living on the razor's edge.'

Chinese snipers picked off any digger who showed himself on the skyline. Cashman learned to tell when a mortar bomb would land close by and when an artillery shell would pass over by the different sounds they made. 'When a mortar was landing close there was a sound — *tssssst!* — and you had a split-second warning to hit the ground. If you were still standing when it exploded you were dead. With mountain artillery, you could sometimes hear the gun being fired in the distance, sometimes not. If you heard plenty of noise, it meant the shell was going past. The more noise it made, the further away it was. Everybody's nerves were on edge day and night, and you needed cat-like reflexes to stay alive.'

Ron Cashman and his mates in B Company developed a profound respect for the Chinese soldier. 'The Chinese were an honourable enemy most of the time,' he says.

All shooting stopped whenever stretcher bearers showed a white flag to collect their dead and wounded after a night-long battle. Once a neighbouring UN unit opened fire with a Vickers machine gun on a Chinese stretcher party, causing a number of casualties. This incident caused a great deal of wrath among the men of B Company.

There was one monstrous breach of the rules of war by the Chinese when they captured Private Allan McInnis of Geelong. McInnis had been wounded and was being carried on a stretcher towards the Chinese positions. For some reason the Chinese decided to abandon him, but instead of simply leaving him on the ground they fired a sub-machine gun at him. 'He had twenty-nine bullets pumped into him but miraculously he lived,' Cashman says. McInnis managed to crawl back towards the Australian lines, where he was found by a stretcher party searching no-man's-land for him. It was the most remarkable escape of the war.

For their part, the Chinese hated phosphorous grenades and warned the UN forces that any soldier caught with one would have it used on him. One British soldier paid the price. 'They barbecued him with it in front of Hill 355,' Cashman says. 'It pressed home the point rather dramatically.'

The Chinese attacked either under cover of darkness or, when weather conditions were right, through the morning mist that gathered in the valleys. 'At daybreak I would sit on top of the mountain and look down on a milky white sea of mist,' Cashman says. 'Then the first rays of the rising run would shoot along the valley and gradually the mist would start to rise. It was the most beautiful sight I had ever seen, but terrifying. You knew that there were Chinese soldiers hidden in the mist. The 36 mm grenade came into its element there; you could bowl them down the hill and take care of a lot of people.'

Grenades had an added advantage as a weapon: unlike rifle or machine-gun fire, they did not give away a man's exact position on the hillside.

From 19 January to 18 April 1952, 3RAR was deployed in front of Hills 159, 210 and 227 south-west of Little Gibraltar. The key

Chinese hilltop positions were named Matthew, Mark, Luke and John, known collectively as The Apostles. On the night of 26–27 January the Australians crossed the Bowling Alley and attacked John (Hill 227), which had been in Chinese hands since the previous November. After heavy fighting they were driven off, with seven killed and nine wounded. It was a bitter setback.

The most exposed part of the line were the four hillocks that made up The Hook at the western end of the Bowling Alley over-looking the Samichon Valley. Its first defenders were the men of 1st Battalion, the Welch Regiment, who braced themselves nightly for a Chinese onslaught. The weeks passed and it did not come. Bewildered but delighted at their good fortune, in March 1952 they handed over their positions to the 1st Battalion of the Princess Patricias.

The Canadians set up their Browning machine guns and, like the Welch, they waited. They were not so lucky, though. On the night of 26–27 March a Chinese company attacked a forward platoon after advancing through a minefield. Four Canadians were killed and ten wounded in fierce fighting, but the Chinese were repelled. This was the first battle for the landmark whose name would become synonymous with bloodshed for many thousands of UN fighters and their Chinese opponents.

As the snow melted and the men began to thaw out in the spring sunshine, Ron Cashman's platoon got a new commander. Lieutenant Ludwik Bogdan Zwolanski had been born in Topola, Poland, in 1926. He had been a member of 1 Polish Parachute Bri-gade Group at the Battle of Arnhem in World War II and, bored with civilian life, had volunteered for K Force. After the men had made several clumsy attempts to pronounce his name, he told them, 'Just call me George.'

He called them 'Sixa Platoon'.

'We soon learned that George was no shrinking violet; no man to lead from the rear,' says Cashman, who fought with him for a year. 'Instead, we had a platoon commander who was tougher than most of us, more uncouth in speech and always spoiling for some action.'

119

The war at this time was primarily a series of battles between patrols that were sent out to provide early warning of an enemy attack and to dominate no-man's-land as a sign of strength. There were two types of patrol — the fighting patrol and the reconnaissance patrol. Ron Cashman and 6 Platoon participated in both.

'The fighting patrol went around looking for trouble,' he says. 'It consisted of around sixteen men and it was meant to find the enemy. Sometimes it would have a platoon commander in charge, sometimes a platoon sergeant. Then you'd have a signaller and two sections. After a while there was no need for any great preparation for this type of fighting patrol, because we had been in that area — the Samichon Valley, the Bowling Alley and Hill 355 — for so long there were always enough blokes who knew it intimately. They could take you out and put you right on a particular ants' nest if that's what you wanted. For those patrols you would select your personnel in the morning. The platoon commander and usually the two section leaders would go over the ground on the map and then go over it visually if they could see it from wherever we were. Basically they would tell the blokes where we were going and what we would be doing. Nobody ever left our positions without a clear idea of the objective. A lot of other units didn't do that; they just took the men out and if the blokes leading the show got knocked off the others had no idea what they were up to.

'Our blokes were in the picture all the way. We wouldn't rehearse on any of those patrols but we would rehearse raids if we were going out to snatch a prisoner. We would select an identical piece of ground with either trenches or bunkers and mark out our attack with tape. We'd do two or three dry runs so that everyone knew exactly where they were going. It always worked fine until you got to the target area, and then total chaos reigned. It always happened. Once the first shot was fired, the plans vanished and it was every man for himself.'

The three-man reconnaissance patrol consisted of a section leader, a radio operator and one other soldier. It would head off to investigate a designated area such as a section of a river or hill or a village. If the Chinese had attacked from that direction and were likely to attack again, a three-man recce patrol would go out and lay up out there. With a grandstand view of the locality, they would radio the enemy's movements to base.

'You had to be pretty bloody spot on,' Cashman says. 'These patrols were very demanding and you wouldn't take anyone out who suffered from bad nerves. Even though a war was being fought in the Samichon Valley, it was still full of wildlife. The Poms shot quail and pheasant for the pot, but on patrol pheasants were our worst enemies. They would be hidden in the rice stalks and would wait until you were just about to put your foot on top of them and then they would take off. If you've ever heard a wild pheasant taking off, it sounds like a chaff-cutter. This would frighten the living hell out of you, and of course it would let everyone for a hundred yards around know you were there.'

One night a digger on ambush patrol poked his head over the mud wall of a paddy-field bund or track. To his shock, he found himself looking at a fully grown tiger that was investigating the movement on the other side of the wall. The soldier screamed and let fly with a burst from his Owen gun into the air. The tiger disappeared into the darkness. The ambush, however, had been fatally compromised.

Frogs also gave the game away. After the rains, they would croak happily to one another all night long. But the moment a soldier from either side stepped into a paddy field full of frogs, the croaking would stop. It was the sudden silence that marked the enemy's presence.

Then there were the mosquitoes. 'You might have fifteen or sixteen blokes lying quietly on an ambush patrol and the mosquitoes would be driving you stark raving mad,' Cashman says. 'We had a repellent but the mosquitoes developed a taste for it. They would bite you through your clothing, no beg your pardons. It didn't matter whether you were wearing a shirt and a singlet, they would zap straight through that. Normally you could be very discreet and quiet, just swearing to yourself and brushing the things off. But every now and then some bloke would lose patience and *whack!* — in the dead of night a resounding slap would echo across the fields.'

The tension of constant patrolling led to a rare breach of discipline when Cashman was charged with disobeying a lawful command given by his superior officer, 'in that he, in the field, on 20 March 1952 did not assist in digging a road when ordered to do so'. He was sentenced to seven days' loss of pay.

The incident still raises Ron Cashman's ire fifty years later. 'I was stricken with diarrhoea and vomiting,' he says. 'I could hardly get out of my sleeping bag. A fellow came in to get me for my turn on picket and they took me away in an ambulance to a field hospital for several days until I felt well enough to go back to B Company. I asked to go back and got the okay from the doctor. On the day I was all set to go back into the line it rained like buggery. They had a lot of Korean labourers digging drainage ditches along the side of the road and the staff sergeant in charge had accidentally wounded himself with a very convenient flesh wound just before Operation Commando.

'Accidental flesh wounds before big operations were not unusual, so he wasn't highly regarded in the company. But then out of nowhere when I'm trying to organise myself a lift back to the line, he wants me digging ditches. There was no way he was going to get me in there when I was heading back to my place in the line.

'So I just waved him away. And under normal circumstances I might have got away with it, but when the case came to be heard by the CO, Frank Hassett, it coincided with the next time we were on reserve and almost half the battalion had gone AWOL with the Kiwis and got on the piss on Anzac Day. Hassett had a massive great queue of defaulters on the Anzac Day sins and he was in a foul mood. When it came to me I was just part and parcel of this great multitude of sinners and he wouldn't even listen to my explanation. He was furious, so bang, I copped it.

'I've always been insulted that it was on my record — disobeying a lawful command in the field from an arsehole who'd accidentally shot himself to avoid combat while I'm trying to get back into the line.'

The 28th Commonwealth Infantry Brigade were in reserve from mid April until the end of June 1952. A second Australian battalion, 1RAR, commanded by Colonel Ian Hutchison, arrived during this time in response to a call from the United States for its allies to commit further ground forces to the war. Their arrival doubled the number of Australian troops in Korea to more than two thousand. It also gave their commanders several opportunities to fight in close proximity to one another.

Ron Cashman enjoyed three weeks' R&R in Japan, leaving Korea on 18 May 1952 and returning on 10 June. 3RAR moved into the forward line again on 2 July 1952, and four days later Frank Hassett handed over command of his battalion to Lieutenant Colonel Ronald Hughes and returned to Australia. 'Hassett was well regarded by the diggers and most of the officers,' Cashman says. 'I never heard anything derogatory about him, nothing at all.'

Hassett had been awarded the DSO for his leadership in the Battle of Maryang San. He rose to become General Sir Francis Hassett, Chief of the General Staff and later Chief of Defence Force Staff. He looked back on his Korean experience with great clarity and deep emotion. 'The Koreans had a high regard for the Australian fighting man, and they were not wrong,' he says. 'I fought against the Chinese. They were pretty good when they came into the war and they got better all the time. We got to know them pretty well; they were capable of acts of graciousness. They were tough but they were honourable. It was not unlike the relationship between the diggers and the Turks at Gallipoli.'

Ron Hughes, another Duntroon graduate, was a veteran of the New Guinea and Tarakan campaigns in World War II. Before taking over 3RAR he had spent eighteen months at Puckapunyal commanding 2RAR, which was engaged in training K Force and regulars as reinforcements for Korea. He had travelled to Korea with Brigadier Tom Daly, who had been appointed the first Australian commander of the 28th Brigade.

The monsoon started almost immediately after Colonel Hughes's arrival, and because of a lack of timber supports and other building materials many of the hutchies collapsed in the deluge. Some of the diggers were buried alive and had to be dug out. Luckily there were no fatalities. The torrential rains also stimulated the rapid growth of vines, shrubs and grass on the hillsides and across the abandoned rice paddies, providing cover for the enemy and obscuring minefield fences and warning signs.

Whenever enemy artillery blasted away sections of fencing, the danger to both sides became acute. One night a patrol from A Company, 3RAR, walked into one of its own minefields after following a paddy bund that the patrol commander knew would lead him to the minefield fence. His plan was to follow the bund until he came to the fence, then turn left and follow the fence to the minefield gate. In the dark the leading scout could not see that the fence had been blown away and unwittingly led the men into the minefield. Six members of the patrol were killed by jumping-jack mines.

Every night Colonel Hughes sent out one or two fighting patrols and one or two reconnaissance patrols. He made sure that the routes and timing of these patrols were coordinated so that even with faulty navigation the chances of one Australian patrol accidentally fighting another were reduced to a minimum.

Patrols gave 3RAR eyes in the dark, ensuring that the enemy did not take them by surprise. It was the battalion's proud boast that it never lost a position. Once a potential attack was spotted it would be broken up by artillery fire before it could pose a serious threat. If the Chinese breached the barbed-wire defences and stormed the Australian trenches, the diggers were lethal at hand-to-hand fighting.

Cashman discovered the truth of the axiom that war brings out the best and the worst in men. Most of 3RAR's frontline infantrymen were courageous and loyal. Their bravery emboldened the new arrivals and set an example to young, inexperienced subalterns. There were, however, one or two exceptions.

'We had one fellow,' Cashman recalls. 'I won't mention his name because he might still be alive — but he was at best sixty-five cents in the dollar, and that was his top value. How he ever got past the shrinks I have no idea. We were in a particular position on the Bowling Alley and our feature overlooked a long knoll that ran down into the valley and Charlie used to harass us from there on a regular basis. Night after night we were ordered to stand to and everyone was opening fire and grenades were going off, but nothing was happening: there were no Chinese. The platoon sergeant was pussyfooting through the trench late one night when he spotted this bloke standing in his fighting pit. He was on picket duty and had his hands in his pocket. Then he nonchalantly pulled his hands out of his pocket, grabbed a grenade, pulled the pin and threw it down into the barbed wire. Of course, that started the chain reaction. This sod had been doing the same thing every night, and we were getting no sleep night after night. His term with 3 Battalion was cut off in its prime.

'We didn't get many like that, but one was enough. Admittedly a few blokes found out that it wasn't exactly their cup of tea when they got there — it differed from the comic books they'd been reading back home — so there were just the odd few who were lacking in moral fibre. But most of them were good, honest young diggers. We'd often get four or five arriving together who had all gone through the same recruit platoon back in Puckapunyal or Kapuka. You couldn't find fault with many of them.'

One of Cashman's mates was Private John Kennedy, a self-described 'three-star footslogger' from Goulburn who had chucked in his job at the Bank of New South Wales in April 1952 to join K Force. He says: 'One time in Area 6 — the rest area — Don Wells, another footslogger, got into the Korean whisky and the CSM, Paddy Williams, copped him and said, "Consider yourself under open arrest". Wellsie wouldn't have it. He got hold of a grenade and bowled it down towards the tents. We could see it bouncing down and we went diving in all directions into slit trenches and under floorboards if we could. It exploded and thousands of pieces of shrapnel went through the tents. No one was killed but one Korean was badly hurt. Wellsie was court-martialled and spent five years in Long Bay.'

Morale among the diggers was always at its lowest ebb when boredom set in, and that would occur when absolutely nothing was happening in 3RAR's sector. 'But we never got bored on Hill 355 or The Hook,' Cashman says. 'Down in the Samichon Valley and in the Bowling Alley everyone was alert, bright-eyed and bushy-tailed for the sake of self-preservation. Morale was always good in the most dangerous places.'

CHAPTER 9

Killer buffalo

Lieutenant George's style of taking the fight to the enemy had won the respect and loyalty of 6 Platoon during skirmishes in the Samichon Valley. But disaster struck on the night of 13–14 August 1952, when the Polish officer was ordered to attack Chinese-occupied Hill 75 and bring back prisoners for interrogation. The mission was codenamed Operation Buffalo. It was memorable for one other reason: for the first time in Korea the Australians were fitted with flak jackets, which were on loan from the Canadians.

The enemy's position on Hill 75 was 1200 metres to the west of the battalion's forward defences. It was on the southern tip of a ridge-line and could therefore be attacked from three sides. Colonel Hughes decided to use the whole of B Company, commanded by Captain Peter Richardson, with 6 Platoon as the spearhead.

The attack plan was rehearsed on similar ground to the rear of the battalion's position until every man was familiar with his part in the raid. With covering fire provided mainly by batteries of the New Zealand 16th Field Regiment and the Centurion tanks of the 5th Royal Enniskillen Dragoon Guards, 6 Platoon were to assault the Chinese outpost, while 4 Platoon followed closely on the right flank to provide covering fire. The remaining unit, 5 Platoon, would be held in reserve. It would protect the rear against attack and also provide stretcher bearers to carry out the wounded.

In full battledress, 6 Platoon silently crossed the valley and formed up at the bottom of Hill 75. At zero hour, 11.45 pm on 13 August, Centurion tanks, artillery, mortars and machine guns opened up on the Chinese outpost held by a platoon supported by two machine guns. 6 Platoon picked its way up the hill with two sections forward,

Lieutenant George's HQ in the centre and one section at the rear. Immediately they ran into trouble.

The Chinese had a two-man listening post at the base of the hill and although the lead section on platoon HQ's right killed both enemy soldiers the element of surprise had been lost. After 6 Platoon had advanced, other Chinese rushed out from underground bunkers and attacked them from the rear, causing several casualties.

Lieutenant George was hit by a phosphorous flare and was on fire, but he was so determined to press ahead with the assault that he seemed not to notice. His signaller, Eddie Wright, tackled him to the ground and threw dirt all over him to put the flames out. 'He didn't bother to say thanks,' Wright says, 'and was off to catch up with the lead sections.'

With shells from the Kiwis' 25-pounders and the Guards' 20-pounders landing in front of them, the surviving troops of 6 Platoon reached the main Chinese trenches at the top of Hill 75. 'We were sadly depleted and taking Chinese prisoners was the last thought on anyone's mind,' Cashman says.

The platoon's left forward section, commanded by Corporal Max Wilson, came under intense machine-gun and grenade attack at close range. Wilson was hit by a grenade and most of his men were wounded, but he charged the machine-gun nest single-handed, throwing phosphorous grenades and killing the gunner.

The UN guns had been firing from the Australian side of no-man's-land at right angles to 6 Platoon's line of advance and the exploding shells had forced the enemy to keep their heads down. The fire plan then provided for the guns to lift their trajectory slightly so that the scream of the rounds would terrify the enemy into staying under cover while 6 Platoon closed in for the kill. But Richardson's Company HQ, which had been reporting progress to the gunners from the rear, suddenly lost contact with Lieutenant George.

After an unnerving few minutes, it seemed to Colonel Hughes that 6 Platoon was in trouble so he took the decision to lower the tank guns onto the enemy position again. Within a few seconds of that order, Eddie Wright was back on the radio screaming, 'Cease fire!'

He and Lieutenant George had been too busy to report that they had reached their objective and were engaging the enemy.

The Chinese defenders then dived into deep tunnels and turned the tables on B Company by calling down 81-millimetre mortar fire on their own position. Several more Australians were wounded and at 12.20 am Richardson ordered Lieutenant George to withdraw his badly mauled platoon. With the aid of 4 Platoon, which had joined the fray, they made a fighting retreat down the hill.

Cashman and his mate Johnny Gill rescued Max Wilson, carrying him to the bottom of the hill and handing him over to the stretcher bearers. As other Australian casualties were being brought off the hill, enemy mortars exploded in their midst, but these brave men carried on with their life-saving duties.

After delivering Wilson, Cashman realised that several members of 6 Platoon were missing and were probably still on Hill 75. In the darkness he started searching through the scrub and along the trenches.

The Chinese had withdrawn and the only person he encountered was Sergeant-Major Wing Key, B Company's CSM, who was also looking for wounded men who might have been left behind. Key was of Chinese ancestry and, had he been taken prisoner, would undoubtedly have faced a tough time from his captors.

The two men searched in vain for fallen comrades and then Key said that they would have to go back; daylight was approaching and withdrawal had already been ordered. Moments later a group of Chinese soldiers materialised on the top of the hill near the main trench. Throwing their remaining grenades in that direction, the two Australians bolted. The ground was treacherous, with craters, trenches and low scrub. Cashman was making his way cautiously through a patch of scrub when the ground suddenly gave way and he fell into a Chinese trench.

'There were three occupants in this hole, which may have been six foot long and eighteen inches wide, perhaps smaller. Whatever the case, it became very crowded upon my arrival and by the grace of God I had landed on two of the men, with the third jammed at the end of the slit trench by our combined bodies. The unfortunate man beneath my backside was desperately clawing at me, his comrade in the middle was beneath my legs and the third was jammed hard against the end by the weight of the three of us. Pure reflex action enabled me to point the Owen gun between my legs and shoot a burst into the fellow doing the clawing, then up with it and give the remainder to the fellow in the middle.

'Though it seemed forever at the time, this all happened in a few short moments — time enough anyway for the third fellow to disentangle himself and try to bring his rifle with fixed bayonet towards me. It was fortunate he had the bayonet out, ready to use, because that kept him from easily getting the rifle around to deal with me. It restricted his movements long enough for me to withdraw an American carbine bayonet from my gaiter. I had carried it for quite a time as a weapon of last resort. His momentary delay in bringing his weapon to bear gave me time to lunge at him with my fighting knife and bury it in his chest, whereupon it stuck. He was screaming and struggling, I was trying to pull it out and finish him off and being drenched by his blood all at the same time. He was only a lad, eighteen at the most. He fell back on to the bottom of the slit trench with myself still struggling with the bayonet.

'At that moment Wing Key reached the hole and, putting his hand down, yelled, 'Get out!' He grabbed me by the arm and bodily hoisted me out, leaving the Chinese lad screaming in a most terrible fashion. Together we ran down the hill and joined up with the rest of B Company at the creek. From that point on I have no memory of crossing the valley and reaching our lines. Apparently we were mortared along the way, but all I could clearly recall were the screams of the young Chinese lad.'

Operation Buffalo, like many similar operations directed at attacking a Chinese position to seize a prisoner, had had almost no chance of success. 'The Chinese were no ragtag army; they were pretty good soldiers,' Cashman says. 'They weren't about to surrender to us unless we were lucky enough to get a wounded bloke, and nobody was trying to wound them. It was a matter of self-preservation: if you needed to put ten bullets into a bloke, you put ten bullets into him.

Those sort of actions were doomed before they got off the table in the CO's office.'

Operation Buffalo had virtually finished 6 Platoon as a unit. It had borne the brunt of B Company's losses of one man killed, twenty-four wounded and two missing. The toll would have been higher if the men had not been wearing their borrowed flak jackets. 'The Canadian flak jacket saved my life,' Eddie Wright says. 'It was completely shredded with shrapnel and bullets but all I got was slight bruising and welts around the midsection and back.'

In a letter from hospital, Max Wilson thanked Cashman for cutting down a Chinese soldier who was about to throw another grenade at him as he lay wounded on the ground. During the assault Wilson had taken a burst of bullets in the chest from a burp gun but had also been saved by his flak jacket. For his attack on the machine-gun nest, Wilson was awarded the Military Medal.

Lieutenant George was honoured with the United States Bronze Star for his leadership and bravery in the face of enemy fire. Always one for the personal touch, he took several bottles of rum over to the New Zealand gun emplacements to thank the Kiwis for their accurate supporting fire. Having consumed a fair amount of liquor himself, he spent the night as an involuntary guest in a New Zealand dugout.

But 'Sixa Platoon' did not die. After being reinforced, it was back in action the following month, ordered to hold a tiny knoll on which another platoon had been attacked by a strong Chinese force the previous night. In fading light sixteen members of 6 Platoon set out from their position in the Samichon Valley as a fighting patrol to engage the enemy. There were also a number of three-man reconnaissance patrols scattered about the valley whose job was to report on enemy troop movements.

The platoon had only just taken up its position on the tiny knoll when one of the recce teams reported that a force of about two hundred Chinese was heading in their direction, obviously intent on attacking 3RAR positions. Shortly afterwards another recce team who were shadowing the Chinese reported that they had almost reached the knoll.

'We sat and sweated and then there they were at the bottom of our pimple of a hill,' Cashman says. 'They seemed to be aware of our presence and began to fan out for a rush.'

Suddenly Lieutenant George stood up and, at the top of his voice, shouted at the Chinese: 'Come up and fight, you bastards! I have ze sixateen men here, ze three Bren guns and thirteen Owens. Come up and fight.'

Everyone froze. The Chinese stood stock still. Then Wing Key jumped to his feet and tried to pull George to the ground to shut him up but was shaken off and the challenge was roared out again:

'I have sixateen men here from Sixa Platoon . . .'

Cashman started digging a hole with his combat shovel to prepare a small fighting pit for the inevitable battle. The Chinese, however, seemed undecided. Then a curious thing happened. Instead of overwhelming the tiny group, they melted away into the night.

'It was commonly thought that perhaps their commander believed it was a trap,' Cashman says. 'Whatever the case, George on his own caused about two hundred Chinese troops to break off their planned attack without firing a single bullet. I would love to have listened in to the conversation when George was explaining to our company commander why the Chinese had turned tail.'

CHAPTER 10

A deadly good deed

The failure of Operation Buffalo rankled deeply with the survivors of 6 Platoon. Ron Cashman decided to mount a solo, unauthorised raid. 'I had been more than cheesed off after several fruitless attempts to capture a prisoner,' he says. 'The cost to us had been great in killed, wounded and missing, and we had not one POW to show for it. The Chinese fought as well as we did and had little desire to go "in the bag", so it was stupid to go into their established positions in the hope of grabbing one. I brooded over this problem and decided to go out into the valley and capture one myself.'

Leaving a letter in his hutchie explaining his plan, and armed with an Owen gun and grenades, he set off one clear night across the Samichon Valley until he reached the river. He knew the Chinese sometimes manned an outpost next to an old ford crossing that might be vulnerable to a surprise one-man attack. The valley was 1500 metres wide at this point and he made his way carefully, wary of ending up a prisoner himself.

Late in the night he found himself in country he had not crossed before and was lucky to spot a minefield laid out by the Chinese in a section of rice paddy. 'I sat awhile and gave the matter some thought, then decided it would be best if I returned with this information in case any of our people should blunder into it at a later date,' Cashman says.

On arrival at B Company's outpost, however, he was intercepted by Johnny Gill, who had orders to disarm him and march him before Colonel Hughes. His letter had been found and handed over to his commanding officer. The Chinese had indeed spotted Cashman and had sent a patrol in pursuit to capture him. It was hot on his tail and had to be driven off by Vickers machine-gun fire.

Hughes considered the motive behind Cashman's one-man initiative and decided that, although it had been ill-advised, it was nothing more than a foolish mistake. 'He told me many years later that he declared I would be a fine soldier some day and this opinion kept me in a line platoon,' Cashman says.

Shortly after this incident, in early September 1952, the Chinese stepped up their penetration of the Samichon Valley. It became imperative for 3RAR to learn as much as possible about the enemy's disposition and intentions. Johnny Gill was very close to the end of his tour when he was ordered to take out a three-man reconnaissance patrol following a clash with the enemy the previous night.

Gill's home town was Murwillumbah in the North Rivers district of New South Wales and he was looking forward to drinking some Australian beer, eating oysters and checking out the bathing beauties at Coolangatta. Normally a man so close to going home would not be given hazardous duty, but after Operation Buffalo 6 Platoon was short of experienced soldiers. Gill was six foot two inches and thirteen stone of hard muscle. He was anything but a slacker, but he had no wish to risk his life again unless it was absolutely necessary. He discussed the situation with Ron Cashman.

'Johnny wasn't too thrilled about this,' Cashman says. 'I think Buffalo had been enough for him. As I had decided to stay on for another tour, I swapped jobs and took his recce, while he looked after my section positions.'

It was a decent thing for Cashman to do and Gill appreciated the gesture. As darkness closed in, Cashman and two soldiers set off through B Company's barbed-wire entanglements and minefield and were soon making their way along the valley floor. Cashman had made the trip many times and was familiar with the safest routes, but he immediately became aware that the enemy were out in force that night. 'The Chinese were all over the valley like a heat rash,' Cashman says. 'My two digs and I had a very torrid night of it.'

When the first Chinese patrol crossed their path, the Australians dived down in a paddy field and squirmed into the mud, half burying themselves in the slush and lying still until the danger had passed.

The only advantage of so much enemy patrol activity was that Chinese machine-gunners had to be careful not to rake the valley with indiscriminate fire. But that did not prevent the Chinese artillery from opening up at more distant targets. Cashman and his men were safe in the mud as shellfire screamed overhead towards 3RAR's positions. 'We managed to avoid being chewed up, though it was a bad night one way and another.'

As the first rays of morning light filtered down from the mountains, Cashman pulled his men back towards the Australian line. Dawn was breaking when they approached the safety of B Company's position, and Cashman was relieved that he and his men had made it in one piece. He headed for 6 Platoon's area to tell Johnny Gill that everything was all right.

'I was greeted by the news that Johnny had copped it during the night,' Cashman says. 'He had been manning my pit with a brand-new reo when the Chinese artillery opened up. They were both killed instantly. Johnny copped a shell fair and square and it blew him to pieces. The other poor bloke was cut clean in half.'

Cashman mourned his friend and was grateful when 3RAR was pulled out of the line after fourteen weeks' active service and moved into reserve. The battalion was allotted an area below the bloodied slopes of Gloster Hill south of the Imjin River. The Australians, respectful of the Glosters' sacrifice, built a new camp for themselves in a beautiful, unspoiled area nearby.

Cashman had impressed his superiors with his leadership qualities and was sent down to the NCO battle school at Uijongbu on 15 September 1952.

'The school was run by the Canadians. They had a full brigade in Korea. The course was a little bit of drill and next to no military law; that's why, when we came out of it, we didn't pass with sufficient status to get a confirmed rank. It was 90 per cent a battle school; you concentrated on field tactics.'

Cashman passed the course with a B qualification on 19 October and the following week he elected to serve a further eight months with 3RAR in Korea.

'I'd been there at this stage for twelve months and an officer came to me and said, "Your time's up. You've got to go home." I told them I had already signed up for my second tour but he informed me that it was a bit late. He did some bookwork and found out that I was making up some three weeks or so from my "holiday" in Japan when I was wounded the first time. You had to make up your time if you got knocked, thank you very much. So I made up my time and was officially into my second tour. I finished the battle school and then went back to 6 Platoon and carried on as though nothing had happened.'

3RAR's spell in its Arcadian setting came to an abrupt end when Brigadier Daly agreed to transfer the battalion temporarily from the 28th Commonwealth Infantry Brigade to the 29th British Infantry Brigade. The 1st Battalion of the Welch Regiment was due to return to its camp in Hong Kong and its place was being taken by the 1st Battalion, the Duke of Wellington's Regiment. 'The Dukes', however, needed time to acclimatise and to train in the unfamiliar terrain. So on 25 October 1952 3RAR relieved the Welch Battalion behind the line at Yongdong, a fortified hill on the eastern side of the Samichon River.

Unlike other battalions which were rotated en masse with another unit, 3RAR was reinforced by the 'trickle' system, which meant that men were constantly being replaced by reinforcements when their tour of duty was up, or they were killed or wounded or became sick. For all of those reasons, there had been a heavy intake of new men into the battalion and it suited Colonel Hughes to be transferred to Yongdong while they settled down.

As the Chinese lines were two thousand metres beyond this point, it was considered a quieter part of the front and Hughes wanted to spend the time bringing his new men up to battalion standard, particularly in the arts of patrolling and radio procedures for calling down defensive fire.

The peace and quiet did not last long, however. 3RAR's nearest neighbours across the river were members of the 7th US Marines Regiment, who were defending The Hook. On 3RAR's second night in occupation at Yongdong, 26–27 October, the Chinese staged a heavy assault that dislodged the Marines from several of their positions on the fishhook-shaped spur.

Colonel Hughes grouped his battalion's medium machine guns together on the western slopes of Yongdong and supported the Americans with withering fire across the river into the massed ranks of the Chinese attackers. The Marines counterattacked and succeeded in driving the Chinese into the night. The following morning the Australians returned to their training exercises.

Cashman's B pass had been sufficient to win him promotion to the rank of temporary corporal on 10 November. He was now commanding his own section of ten or twelve diggers, depending on the battalion's available manpower. Conscious of the need to train green, inexperienced troops, he took his responsibilities as section leader seriously. 'My job was to make sure that my diggers were all up to scratch, that there were no malingerers, and that they kept their weapons and themselves clean and tidy,' he says.

He remembered his own arrival at 3RAR on The Hinge. 'I learned from that experience and I used to take my new blokes in hand and introduce them all around,' he says. 'I would put them with a good bloke, someone I knew would be a good buddy to them. There used to be a fair bit of whinging from the old-timers, but they would wear it because the same thing had happened to them. The new men would be broken in as gently as possible. This served two purposes: it kept them alive, and by keeping them alive it also kept us alive. So it worked out pretty well.'

After three weeks, 3RAR handed over the Yongdong position to the Duke of Wellington's Battalion and returned to Tom Daly's 28th Brigade. Since early November the brigade had been holding the easternmost sector of the divisional line, a six-kilometre front that stretched from Hill 187 as far as a creek on the north-eastern flank of Little Gibraltar in the direction of Maryang San.

Fighting had intensified along the MLR after the Chinese launched a major offensive in early October against White Horse Hill (Hill 395), a strategic point in the west-central sector of the Jamestown Line, with the aim of influencing the US presidential campaign.

Mao hoped to persuade the American public that the war was unwinnable and that US negotiators should compromise at the peace talks, particularly on the issue of POW repatriation.

White Horse Hill had been chosen as a target by Mao's strategists because its defenders were units of the 9th ROK Division and the Chinese anticipated little difficulty in dislodging them. In previous encounters during the war's early stages, the South Koreans had been easily put to flight by human-wave attacks of screaming, bugle-blowing troops.

Since those dismal times, however, the ROK Army had been reformed and retrained, and its morale was high. Forewarned of the attack through the interrogation of a Chinese deserter, the division's commander, General Kim Jong Oh, placed two battalions on White Horse Hill and protected their flanks with tanks and Quad-50s, half-track vehicles mounted with four 50 mm machine guns, while a formidable array of American guns, including scores of the 8-inch howitzers known as The Persuaders and 4.2-inch mortars, were positioned behind the hill. The Fifth Air Force was on hand to strafe and bomb the Chinese, not only as they attacked but also as they formed up in their assembly areas before attacking.

As a measure of their intent, the Chinese committed 25 000 troops to the battle and, although they captured the crest of White Horse Hill several times between 6 and 15 October, they were unable to hold it against determined South Korean counterattacks. The Chinese launched a total of twenty-seven full-blooded assaults on the hill before accepting defeat and withdrawing. The 9th ROK Division had lost 3500 men but it was estimated that Chinese losses ran to 10 000, nearly half their attacking force.

Eight days later, on 23 October, the summit and western slopes of Little Gibraltar were the scenes of a ferocious battle between their defenders, the 1st Battalion, Royal Canadian Regiment (1RCR), and fresh hordes of Chinese. After several of their patrols had been ambushed in no-man's-land, the Canadians limited their patrols to their more exposed outposts. Thus they lost control of much of the territory in front of Little Gibraltar and the Chinese, assembling in huge 'rabbit warrens' burrowed into the valley floor, were able to infiltrate up to the Canadians' barbed-wire defences without being detected.

Under a hail of artillery fire, which destroyed the fighting pits and communication trenches of A and B Companies, the Chinese attacked in large numbers and succeeded in driving the Canadians from the summit. The battle raged for two days, at the end of which the Canadians had succeeded in regaining their positions in a brave counterattack supported by intense artillery fire.

After the Chinese had withdrawn, Canadian sappers went out into the valley and blew up the Chinese bunkers, but the damage had been done. The Canadians had lost eighteen killed, forty-three wounded and fourteen missing, and their defences had been severely mauled.

Very little of the damage had been repaired when the men of 1RAR relieved the Canadians on Little Gibraltar on 1 November. The handover certificate signed by the Canadian commander, Lieutenant Colonel P. R. Bingham, and the commander of 1RAR, Lieutenant Colonel M. Austin, reads: 'This is to certify that Kowang-San, Feature 355, otherwise known as Little Gibraltar, and attached real estate, has been handed over complete, slightly worse for wear and tear, but otherwise defendable.'

In fact, the Australians were furious. Many of the trenches were damaged in such a way that they acted as funnels for incoming shells and mortar bombs, and several of the bunkers had completely collapsed. Empty food cans scattered around the fighting pits reflected the sun's rays and gave the Chinese a target to shoot at.

Following the handover there was serious fighting in no-man's-land for ten nights while the men of 1RAR drove the Chinese back to their base at Hill 227, just two hundred metres to the north, and established their dominance over the approaches to Hill 355. The Australian patrols suffered nearly fifty casualties. At the same time 1RAR had to repair badly maintained minefields, which posed a constant threat to their patrols.

Lieutenant William James had his left foot blown off, one man was killed and three others injured when their patrol walked into an unmarked and unrecorded minefield laid by the Canadians. James insisted on being the last man rescued and it was three hours before he received treatment back in the battalion's position.

No one complained when 28th Brigade's front was reduced in early December after all three of the division's brigades were brought into the Jamestown Line at the same time. Brigadier Daly's men could then concentrate on Little Gibraltar, the troublesome Hill 159 and their defences in front of Hill 227.

In mid December the Chinese launched another big offensive. This one fell, not on the 28th Brigade, but on the South Korean 1st Division, which was defending the sector between Maryang San and the Imjin River. After three days of intense fighting, the Chinese had secured a patch of territory no bigger than two football fields at a cost of 2500 men dead and wounded. The plucky South Koreans, who had held their positions once again, had lost 750 men.

3RAR had moved into a reserve position to act as the counterattacking force should 1RAR be driven off Little Gibraltar. This arrangement was the idea of the 1st Commonwealth Division's new commander, Major General Mike West, who had replaced Major General Cassels. West had redeployed his three brigades so that each held a sector of line rather than dividing the front between two brigades, with the third in reserve. The advantage was that each brigade could now have two battalions in the front line while holding the others in reserve and could rotate them as necessary.

At this stage of the war the 28th Brigade consisted of four battalions: the 1st Battalion of the Royal Fusiliers, the 1st Battalion of the Durham Light Infantry and the 1st and 3rd Battalions of the Royal Australian Regiment, plus a variable number of attached South Korean units.

Cashman fought a number of engagements with the Durham Light Infantry. 'All the Australians were volunteers, but at least fifty per cent of British battalions were National Servicemen,' he says. 'The lucky ones got a cushy berth in Germany but the ones who drew the shortest straws finished up in Korea. Not very many of these young blokes were rushing around bubbling with glee; they did not particularly want to be there. A lot of their reservists also had a very good reason for not wanting to be there: they had done their time in World War II and had settled into civilian life when — zap! — they were on their way to Korea, and far from impressed about the whole thing.

'But the Brits fought well; they were fine soldiers. When I was with the DLIs, sixty per cent of them were young conscripts and still wet behind the ears. I got involved in a couple of dicey incidents with them out in front of Hill 355 on Cloncurry — that was my least favourite place; I always got into trouble on Cloncurry. We were out there with 6 Platoon on one occasion and there were about ninety Chinese hunting us. The DLI held up; they held their end of the deal up. They were a good outfit. They were all very badly paid — while I was with them, I learned that my pay as an Australian corporal was equal to the pay of a DLI lieutenant. It was a pathetic sum, almost Third World scale.'

The Korean War was deeply unpopular by the time the American people went to the polls on 5 November 1952. Eisenhower, whom Americans associated with victory, knew that the war was unwinnable and had pledged to 'go to Korea', if he was elected, 'to bring the war to an honourable end'. This astutely ambiguous statement appealed to the peace lobby and the militarists alike: the doves thought it meant a peaceful settlement, while the hawks interpreted it as a call to arms. 'Ike', the headline writers' dream candidate, defeated Adlai Stevenson by 6.5 million votes.

True to his word, the President-elect spent four days in Korea, just sixty minutes of which was in the company of Syngman Rhee, whom he despised as a right-wing fanatic. Eisenhower spent most of his time talking to officers and men in the front line, including members of the 1st Commonwealth Division. These conversations confirmed his view that Korea was a boil that needed to be lanced.

On 28 December the men of 3RAR were back on Little Gibraltar when they relieved 1RAR in the front line. The fieldworks and entrenchments were in tremendous shape. Colonel Hughes described them as 'the best we ever had'. In the previous weeks, engineers had built dugouts using thick timbers for uprights and beams. The roofs were sandbagged and covered with earth two metres thick. Communication trenches were more than two metres deep and the fighting pits had good overhead cover. 1RAR had also repaired the minefields and confronted the enemy in no-man's-land.

The enemy was still very active, however, and 3RAR was instructed to continue the policy of aggressive patrolling to dominate no-man's-land. The Pioneers — the battalion's explosives experts, under the command of Captain John Hutcheson — were ordered to locate and mark the outer perimeter of the minefields.

Hutcheson brought a distinctive sangfroid to his dangerous work: he often ventured out on his own because of the danger to his men of unlocated mines, and on such missions he always carried his toilet kit with him in case he was taken prisoner. One morning he was returning towards A Company's position when a sentry opened fire on him. Major James Norrie, the company commander, apologised for the mistake. Hutcheson's only comment was, 'That man fires high and to the right'. He was later awarded the Military Cross.[37]

President Eisenhower moved into the White House in January 1953 determined not to escalate the war despite the urging of General Mark W. Clark, who had replaced Matthew Ridgway as Supreme Commander.

Ridgway wrote in his memoirs: 'If we had been ordered to fight to the Yalu, we could have done it if our government had been prepared to pay the price in dead and wounded that action could have cost. From the purely military standpoint the effort, to my mind, would not have been worth the cost ... We stopped instead on what I believe to be the strongest line.'[38]

Meanwhile General Clark drew up a secret contingency plan that called for a combined force of UN and Nationalist Chinese troops to drive to the Yalu using tactical nuclear weapons. Fortunately it got no further than the drawing board.

CHAPTER 11

Sydney's Betty Grable

The big news in Australia during 1952 was not the Korean War but the Helsinki Olympic Games. Marjorie Jackson had won gold medals for Australia in the 100 and 200 metres but had dropped the baton in the relay when the team was in a winning position. In a nation of sports fanatics, this was a major tragedy.

Cashman was given a chance to study Australia's indifference to the sacrifice that 3RAR and 1RAR were making in the name of democracy when he was granted 'winter relief' leave. 'By this time I was a real old-timer,' he says. 'I knew everyone in the platoon pretty well.' He was flown to Sydney on 24 November with a year's pay in his pocket, and he was not too fussy about how he spent it.

He was appalled to discover that no one seemed to know anything about what was happening in Korea. Apart from brief reports about the fighting on the evening ABC radio news and small headlines in the newspapers, there was no publicity at all. 'The public perception about the war was non-existent,' he says. Places like the North Korean capital of Pyongyang, or Panmunjom where the peace talks between the Chinese and United Nations delegates were grinding remorselessly on, sounded alien, even comically so, and the events taking place there were too complicated to interest any but the most dedicated listeners.

The problem derived partly from an incident at the beginning of the war. At a crowded news conference, Harry Truman was asked, 'Mr President, would it be correct . . . to call this a police action under the United Nations?'

'Yes,' Truman replied, sensitive to the fact that the US Constitution reserved the right to declare war to Congress, and that no such congressional consent had been sought before US combat forces were committed. 'That is exactly what it amounts to. We are not at war.'[39]

While politically convenient, the term 'police action' robbed the conflict of its essential point of identification in the public mind. So soon after the defeat of Germany and Japan in World War II, people understood the horrors of war, whereas a police action sounded like a bunch of coppers monitoring a political demonstration. 'It really was a most unfortunate misnomer,' Olwyn Green says, 'because it was very much an all-out, brutal, terrible war.'

The point was driven home to Cashman on a train when a young woman passenger, noting his smart uniform, asked him why he was wearing it. He explained he was serving in Korea. 'Oh, I know,' the women replied, her face lighting up. 'You're a policeman!'

At first Cashman stayed with his parents in Williamstown. He downplayed the danger of his frontline experiences to quell his mother's fears, but when he'd had a few beers he would complain about the lack of concern in Australia for the men who were risking their lives to save democracy.

'We'd had our eyes opened to the fact that democracy in South Korea wasn't all that crash-hot,' he says. 'But I had a genuine belief that we were trying to prevent Communism and its evil roots from spreading down through Asia and possibly into Australia. It was literally knocking on our front door and it wasn't a pretty thought. So we had gone to Korea to stop it, but no one seemed to care.'

The only positive thing about his homecoming was that his father's attitude towards him had changed markedly. Michael Cashman, the archetypal bully, was not about to take on a fully grown man trained in unarmed combat. But the younger man didn't tarry too long under his father's roof. His pay packet was burning a hole in his pocket. There were girls in every dance hall and saloon bar in the country, and he was determined to make up for lost time.

He flew to Adelaide. 'I'd been given an introduction to a girl-friend of Peter Cerdapavia,' he says. 'She was an ex-army nursing sister and she had a girlfriend, so I was over there courting her.'

Cashman had turned twenty in September and the sap was rising. His amorous liaison went well and he went into an Adelaide pub frequented by wharfies and merchant seamen to celebrate. 'I was booked to catch a plane back to Melbourne that night,' he remembers. 'I could hear these wharfies talking and they were red-hot commos and one thing led to another. Heated words passed between us and we finished up out on the footpath. There were three of them and we were stoushing on when a hand grabbed me by the shoulder and pulled me around. I spun around swinging and I decked a policeman. He'd come along to intercede, but when you're fighting and a strange hand grabs you on the shoulder you don't turn around and ask for identification. And that's how I happened to deck a copper.'

He was fined £12 with 7/6 costs.

'I was not only going with the Adelaide girl,' he says. 'I was also seeing an ANA air hostess named Carmel White, who was based in Melbourne. I was just having an incredibly good time, waltzing around between Melbourne and Adelaide, and I had another fling with a girl in the Barossa Valley. I remember catching a taxi from Adelaide up to the Barossa Valley and arriving on her doorstep in the wee small hours. Money was no restriction. Actually, money wasn't worth a bumper to me back in Korea, and you didn't know whether you were going to live to spend it or not. So why let it go to waste?'

As his leave drew to an end in January 1953, Cashman moved to Sydney and stayed at the LTD barracks in Charles Street, Marrickville. One night, while drinking at the Henson Park Hotel three blocks away, he started chatting to the barmaid, a comely woman with a friendly face and a good figure. Noticing that the young soldier looked lost and lonely, she invited him home for a cup of tea when the pub shut for the evening. 'She was quite a bit older than me but I'd had a few drinks and I thought I might be on to a good thing,' he says.

The barmaid's name was Ivy Whittle and she lived in a house directly opposite the LTD Depot. Cashman quickly discovered that Ivy was married, so he turned his attention to an attractive redhead who was sitting in the lounge. 'She turned out to be Ivy's niece and I spent all evening chatting her up, only to discover that she too was married and was just waiting for her husband,' he says.

By now Cashman had expended quite a bit of charm without getting anywhere, and then the door opened and a vision appeared before his eyes. Ivy's daughter Betty had come home. 'I had gone out on a date,' Betty says. 'When I got home I found that my mother had brought this young soldier home.' Betty chatted to the soldier for a few minutes and then it was time for him to say goodnight. But he had been smitten by the blond girl with the dancer's legs and the statuesque figure: Sydney's answer to Betty Grable. 'She made a big impression,' he says.

The following evening Betty returned home from her job in a local confectionery factory to find the battle-hardened Korean veteran hanging over the back gate like a lovesick youth. They talked for a while but Betty thought no more about it. Cashman, however, had made the acquaintance of Betty's grandmother and had taken her up on an offer to send books to his platoon. Before he left for Korea he scribbled his name and army address on a piece of paper and gave it to the elderly lady.

Years later he recalled his visit to Australia for a television interviewer: 'I lived a life of sheer debauchery, spent twelve months' accumulated pay in about two or three weeks, which was enough to buy a motor car in those days. Oh, I flew from Sydney to Melbourne to Adelaide, all in the pursuit of love ... I made a lasting impression on the airlines in Sydney, Melbourne and Adelaide. I didn't make a very good impression on my mother and father, however; they weren't at all impressed. I think I was three parts hit most of the time.'

The anticipated showdown with his father had not materialised, and Cashman found himself back with B Company in the Korean hills with little more than a bad hangover and a headful of thoughts about Betty Whittle. Shortly afterwards he heard that a packet of books had arrived at the regimental post. The parcel had not been addressed to him personally but to the platoon as a whole. He grabbed the envelope with the sender's name and address: Betty Whittle, Charles Street, Marrickville.

'I kept the envelope so no one else could write to thank her. I wrote to her myself and pretty soon we were pen pals.' Cashman asked for a photograph and she sent him a pin-up shot of herself with a big smile. After they had corresponded for a while she started to send him bottles of wine inside large loaves of bread. He fell in love with her. They had not even kissed goodnight but he now had another good reason to stay alive. He had found his soulmate.

CHAPTER 12

Korea's unsung heroes

One thousand South Koreans were attached to the 1st Commonwealth Division to fight alongside the British, Australians and Canadians. Called KATCOMs, for Korean Augmentation to the Commonwealth troops, these soldiers were usually very young and barely trained. Some had a slight knowledge of English but most had to learn as they went along.

KATCOMs were deployed all along the line, from Divisional HQ to the infantry sections. Most settled in well, despite living in an unfamiliar environment, speaking a foreign language, eating strange food and putting up with odd Western customs. 'Many of these lads fought alongside the Australians and quite a few were killed or wounded in action,' Cashman says. 'They conducted themselves as worthy soldiers in the face of adversity and discomfort. Their general conduct could not be faulted. Once they learned that their Australian comrades stood and fought, so did they. This suggests that the panic retreats among early Korean divisions were mostly caused by poor leadership and poor training.'

Thousands of other Koreans flocked to 3RAR to become vital cogs in the war machine as porters, house boys and medical orderlies — carrying food, water and ammunition to the frontline troops on A frames strapped to their backs; digging trenches, often under fire; doing housework; or ministering to the needs of the wounded.

None had a longer or more action-packed career than Yung Kil Choi, the schoolboy who had joined the battalion at Pakchon in October 1950. Yung Kil had been born in the North Korean town on 24 December 1934 as the 'first grandson', a respected position in the traditional hierarchical Korean family structure. However, Yung Kil's 'bourgeois' parents were separated. When his mother took Yung Kil and his brother to Seoul to join their father, who had gone there to operate a business, she found that he had taken another woman into his home. Her difficulties increased after the NKPA occupied Seoul in June 1950 and people originally from the North were ordered to return to their homes. She took her sons to an assembly point and put them on a train back to their grandparents in the North.

Pakchon had been freed from the Communists by the UN forces, but when the Chinese entered the war in late October Yung Kil's grand-parents, fearing that he would 'end up in the Red Army', decided that he should go to his father in Seoul. Packing a few belongings, Yung Kil and two friends left their families behind to walk there. It was during this journey that he was picked up by the Australians while searching for food among the North Korean dead. He had a few words of English, and after obtaining an English dictionary he was able to interpret for wounded North Koreans brought to the RAP.

Yung Kil had joined the battalion just before the Battle of Chongju, and soon after it ended he noticed that normally rowdy members of the battalion had suddenly become very quiet. He sensed sadness and learned that the CO, Charlie Green, had been fatally wounded by a shell fragment.

Heading south towards Seoul during the UN withdrawal, Yung Kil one day looked down from a hill and saw US planes bombing a town. At the same time, engineers were building a floating bridge for 3RAR troops to cross a river and take the town. At the RAP was a mortally wounded Australian soldier who was craving a fried egg. Yung Kil and another orderly decided to go down to the town and get some eggs to comfort the soldier. They took a jeep but when the road became too narrow they parked the vehicle and crept into the town on foot. In this way they discovered that a sizable force of North Koreans was hiding in the town, waiting to ambush the Australians. Abandoning the fried egg patrol, the two stole back to Battalion Head-quarters and reported what they had seen to Colonel Ferguson and his intelligence officer, Alf Argent. The attack was called off and many lives were saved.

The battalion reached the outskirts of Seoul in December. Just before Christmas Captain Gandevia, who had looked after Yung Kil from the time he arrived at the unit, told him he was leaving for Japan, where he would be reposted. But before he left he took Yung Kil to visit his father with the intention of leaving him there. The young boy had made a decision to stay with the unit, however; as he explained to Gandevia, 'the battalion felt like a family'. So Yung Kil returned to 3RAR's camp and Gandevia asked his replacement, Captain Edward Manchester, to look after him.

After the Battle of Kapyong, Yung Kil joined B Echelon, where he assisted in all duties involving the Quartermaster's Store. Captain Reg Whalley, commander of B Echelon at the time, impressed him as 'a very fat man who liked whisky and used to scratch himself'. Boxes of gifts from Australia arrived at the QM Store containing Johnson's Baby Powder, toothpaste, 'pudding cake', cigarettes and toothbrushes. Yung Kil says some unscrupulous diggers kept the boxes, packed them with the American rifles and parkas and sent them home.

His saddest duty was to sort and pack the personal belongings of dead soldiers to be returned to their families. During a battle, Yung Kil and his comrades would wait at the end of a valley and watch for a jeep. The driver would signal with his fingers how many dead bodies he was carrying. Yung Kil's squad would then rush to the QM Store to get ponchos and blankets, needles and string, hot water and towels. When they received the bodies in the tent they would put the body on a stretcher, undress it, go through the dead man's belongings and sort them, then wash the body with hot water. The funeral service was conducted by the chaplain or the officer in charge of B Echelon. After the service the bodies were sent for cremation.

Yung Kil's service in 3RAR, like that of his fellow Koreans, was never regularised. He was given a Commonwealth Division certificate to enable him to pass through the lines, but no official documents placed him on the nominal roll. He was fed, of course, but received no pay until halfway through 1952. In his two years and nine months with 3RAR he had only two weeks' leave, including a few days off to bury his father. Yet he had only one complaint: he was proud to wear an Australian uniform like the other diggers, but he hated it when some of them called him by the nickname Rhubarb. 'Captain Gandevia,' he says, 'would not have allowed it.'

Ron Cashman fought closely with two KATCOMs, Lee Min Bang and Kim Heung Koo, and saw to it that they were treated with respect. Lee and Kim came from the same village and had been rounded up in the draft for the South Korean Army. They joined the Australians while they were defending Little Gibraltar in late 1952. Neither man spoke a word of English but they were fast learners.

'Ron Cashman came to our battery and took two of us into his squad. That was my first connection with him,' Lee Min Bang says. 'I couldn't understand what the Australians were saying, but they were kind, so in my case I didn't have too much trouble, even at the beginning. Ron Cashman was a very warm-hearted man and he looked after his men. As soon as we were attached, we went to the front line on Hill 355. The Chinese artillery were shooting at us, and after it stopped he turned around and said, 'Are you all right?', patting my shoulder. This kind of action comforted me a lot. He did a lot of caring for us and did it well.'[40]

Cashman was like a big brother to Lee Min Bang, though he later discovered that the South Korean was two years older than him. He took Lee and Kim Heung Koo out on patrols, listening posts and ambushes but was careful not to expose them to any undue risk of being captured. 'The Chinese would have handed them over to the North Koreans and they would have been executed,' Cashman says. 'They left nothing to be desired as soldiers. I was proud to call them mates.'

'From the start, we went forward on patrol with Ron Cashman,' Lee says. 'We trusted him so we followed him.'

Laughs were in short supply on the Jamestown Line, but the Australians enjoyed getting a rise out of the Americans at every opportunity. An American unit in the Commonwealth Division's sector posted a sign over its camp entrance proclaiming itself 'SECOND TO NONE'. This rankled with the diggers until the Australian radio relay station a few hundred yards away put up a sign of its own, proclaiming itself 'NONE'.

Yung Kil Choi says some members of 3RAR stole an American jeep one night and painted it with a map of Australia, a kangaroo and the battalion's emblem. It was parked out of view and covered with camouflage netting. Three hours later American military police came looking for it, but 'nobody knew anything'. It became 3RAR's jeep.

Despite the near disasters of Operation Buffalo, Brigade Head-quarters remained determined to capture Chinese prisoners to enable them to keep tabs on which divisions were in the line and to ascertain their most likely intentions. On the night of 24–25 January 1953 Colonel Hughes ordered A Company to stage a raid on Chinese trenches in a bid to snatch a prisoner. The plan was that Sergeant Eddie Morrison would lead a five-man snatch squad into one of the trenches on a spur nearly two kilometres to the north-west of 3RAR's westernmost defences on Little Gibraltar. Having grabbed one of the Chinese manning the trench, the snatch squad would then retreat while two groups of thirteen men protected their rear.

At 7 o'clock that night the 3RAR patrol, commanded by Lieu-tenant Francis Smith, slithered down the frozen slopes of Hill 355 and moved silently across the snow-covered valley towards the Chinese positions. As they neared the enemy, Smith and twelve of his men established a base to protect the withdrawal while Corporal Francis Mackay and his twelve men formed a second base on a small spur further on.

The Chinese trenches were 600 metres to the west of Mackay's base and Morrison's squad reached them at 10.20 pm. Leaving his men on the embankment, Morrison jumped into one of the trenches but was spotted by two Chinese sentries who opened fire but missed. Morrison killed both of them.

The gunfire had alerted Chinese soldiers further along the trench and they started to fire at the snatch squad on the embankment. Morrison climbed out of the trench and pulled his men back thirty metres. Over his radio link, he called down artillery fire on the trench.

No sooner had shells started exploding on the target than the Chinese flooded that section of the valley with troops and Lieutenant Smith found himself under attack at his base position. The patrol had earlier devised a plan to cover this eventuality: Morrison's squad would rendezvous with Mackay's group and their combined force would go to Smith's assistance.

Having fought off one attack, Smith found himself attacked again on three sides while the reinforcements were still heading in his direction. Morrison saw that more Chinese were racing to join the attacking force and requested the New Zealand gunners to direct their fire onto the routes that would be used by these Chinese to reach Smith's position.

Morrison then saw twenty Chinese heading in his direction and scrambled his men into cover. They held their fire until the enemy were within two metres of them and then killed all twenty before they could fire a shot. Some of the Chinese were so close to the Australians that the dead fell across the blazing guns.

Smith's base, however, was still in danger of being overrun and he ordered a withdrawal. Some of his men disappeared into the darkness, but before Smith could move he was knocked unconscious by a concussion grenade. He was never seen again.

Morrison's group of eighteen men now found themselves as the hunted rather than the hunters and quickly retraced their steps towards Hill 355. The route led them to a ridge 700 metres from the forward Australian positions. Finding their way blocked by six more Chinese soldiers, Morrison and Mackay attacked all six and killed them in hand-to-hand combat.

The Australians had barely reached the ridge when they were under attack from two new groups of pursuers from the flank and the rear. Morrison led two charges to beat off the attack on his flank, killing a number of them. Then Private Lionel Terry charged at one group of twenty Chinese, hurling grenades and firing bursts from his Owen gun. His one-man action separated him from his comrades and he disappeared from sight. Like Lieutenant Smith, he was never seen again.

The patrol reached the Australian lines at 1.15 am. It had lost thirteen missing and ten wounded. Morrison estimated they had killed eighty Chinese. Brigadier Daly and Colonel Hughes wanted to recommend Terry for the Victoria Cross but there were insufficient witnesses to his brave action, which had undoubtedly saved the patrol at the cost of his own life. Instead he was mentioned in dispatches, the only other award that could be made posthumously.

Five days after this tragic failure the Commonwealth Division, less some artillery units, went into reserve at Camp Casey near Tongduchon, twenty kilometres to the rear of I Corps. For two of the worst winter months, the weather-beaten veterans of 3RAR lived under canvas and were spared the sound of gunfire, although it remained as a ringing echo in their eardrums.

While at Camp Casey, the 2nd Battalion, RAR, commanded by Lieutenant Colonel George Larkin, arrived from Japan to relieve 1RAR. The 3rd Battalion had been in Korea since late September 1950, and it would stay until the bitter end. For the first and only time the three battalions of the Australian regiment were briefly in the same place at the same time. It was too good an opportunity to miss and on 21 March all three battalions formed a hollow square on the parade ground, where they were addressed by Brigadier Daly. He thanked 1RAR for their tremendous contribution and welcomed 2RAR to the war. Then, in acknowledging 3RAR's ongoing role, he announced a nickname worthy of the battalion's outstanding endurance: 'Old Faithful: always there when needed'.

Colonel Hughes returned to Australia with the Distinguished Service Order pinned to his chest but without ever having captured a Chinese prisoner, despite all the efforts of his snatch patrols. 'Hughes was a good commander but he never got the same chance as Frank Hassett to show his skills,' Cashman says.

Hughes' replacement was 34-year-old Lieutenant Colonel Arthur MacDonald, a short man who stood on the bonnet of a jeep so he could be seen while he told the troops what he expected of them. 'He made it quite plain what sort of a terror he was going to be,' Cashman says. 'On his way to take over the battalion his jeep had passed two diggers walking along the road. They didn't know him from a bar of soap and, besides that, saluting wasn't encouraged by most officers. MacDonald had the driver stop and reverse, then put the two digs on a charge for failing to salute him. And that was before he even commanded the unit.'

Colonel MacDonald took his battalion back to the Little Gibraltar sector of the Jamestown Line on 7 April for the final sixteen weeks of the war. 3RAR went onto Little Gibraltar itself, while 2RAR took possession of Hill 159. 'The Chinese had a sense of humour,' Cashman says. 'When our 2nd Battalion went into the line, they played a tune over the loudspeakers called 'It's foolish but it's fun'. They welcomed them to the war and said they trusted they would keep up the standards of 1 and 3 Battalions. There was never any hatred between the Australians and the Chinese, but the Chinese loathed the Americans for ideological reasons.'

The men quickly discovered that their new commanding officer was a stickler for cleanliness, and they were often to be seen sweeping out loose dirt from their trenches with witches' brooms. It was said that in MacDonald's time the Chinese could spot 3RAR's position in the line by the cloud of dust that hovered over it from all the sweeping.

'He had a thing about cleanliness and there is no fault in that,' Cashman says. 'Sweeping the trenches was a joke but it had to be done. However, he often cruised the trenches just on dawn, and woe betide the lads around whose fighting pit he saw so much as a dead match. Seven extra patrols was a common penalty.

'He would check grenades and ammunition in the fighting pits, and once again there was nothing wrong with that, except that a smudge of dust would earn the offender another batch of patrols. He also ordered that trenches that had been blown in during the night had to be dug out in the morning post haste. You can imagine Charlie's reaction upon seeing shovelfuls of dirt flying out of a trench. Whammo! They would let fly with a volley of mortars, and they got a few victims as well.'

The good news was that Stalin had died on 5 March and the new leadership in the Kremlin showed no signs of wanting to increase the Soviets' involvement in the war. When the peace talks resumed at Panmunjom in late April after a six-month suspension, it was a near certainty that the war was coming to an end.

But not yet.

The two sides had failed to agree over Item 4: Arrangements Relating to Prisoners of War. The United States had announced that on humanitarian grounds no prisoner should be repatriated against his will; that also applied to any American or other national fighting for UN Command who wished to stay in North Korea or China. When a survey of Chinese and North Korean prisoners was taken, only 70 000 out of 150 000 opted to return to their homelands. The damage to the Communist cause was enormous. The Communist negotiators immediately rejected the UN plan and insisted on total repatriation.

The deadlock was broken when the North Korean and Chinese negotiators accepted an earlier United Nations proposal for an exchange of sick and wounded prisoners. This went ahead on 20 April 1953 and the truce talks resumed a week later.

'Mao's strategy was to bleed the Americans white, and he didn't mind that the static war went on and on,' Olwyn Green says. 'The Americans showed great ineptitude in negotiating the armistice, and all the delays meant that more and more soldiers died. There was no real intention on the Americans' part to actually win the war after it had become bogged down in trenches. They advanced and retreated and in the end they achieved nothing.'

CHAPTER 13

The lone gunner

In the final phase of the war the 28th Commonwealth Brigade was placed on the right of the Jamestown Line while the 25th Canadian Brigade took up the central position with the 29th British Brigade on the left.

In mid May the Chinese renewed their attacks on I Corps, but instead of attacking the Australians they concentrated on The Hook and a group of small hills a little further west called the Nevada Complex. The strategic importance of all these positions and their proximity to Panmunjom made them the target of a major Chinese offensive.

In the last three months of combat the Chinese would lose 135 000 casualties and the UN forces 65 000. All of it would be senseless, avoidable slaughter. 'So many good men were lost for no good purpose,' Olwyn Green says. 'They went out in patrol after patrol for a few yards of real estate.'

At least the disputed territory was beginning to look a little more appealing. As winter lost its grip on the land, the valleys assumed a quilt of bright yellow wildflowers. The austere brown hills turned green with fresh growth, and soon purple azalea bushes and clumps of rhododendrons would burst into bloom.

On the night of 13 May 1953 Ron Cashman threaded his way down the zigzag pathways through the barbed-wire fortifications to the floor of the Samichon Valley. He was second-in-command of a patrol that had been ordered to investigate Cloncurry, a small hill below Little Gibraltar. The Chinese had made this feature an extremely hot spot, hence its codename.

About halfway between the forward trenches of 3RAR and the Chinese lines, Cloncurry was a key position and a constant source of dispute between the two forces. As they approached their starting line, 6 Platoon were alerted by radio that the Chinese had beaten them to it. They were ordered to attack the enemy and occupy the site themselves. This was no cause for particular concern. The reconnaissance report numbered the Chinese occupiers at fifteen, while their patrol had sixteen members. The odds looked good. In fact, the Chinese force numbered far more than fifteen.

Private John Kennedy had caught a good look at the enemy force in the late afternoon. 'We had seen the Chinese on the skyline above us — between thirty and fifty soldiers silhouetted like a camel train,' he says. 'We pounded them with piss and pick-handles before we went up to Cloncurry and we thought we'd knocked the living daylights out of them. We thought, "This'll be a piece of cake". It was anything but.'[41]

Darkness had fallen as the platoon commander, Lieutenant John Duff, split the patrol into two sections of seven men. Cashman's group took the left wing and his mate Bluey Clark took his men to the right. The commander and his signaller were in the centre and to the rear. Cashman says: 'We began to run up the slope in an extended line when my Bren-gunner, Tom Foot, called to me, "There's two blokes in a hole here — what'll I do?" At the same time five Chinese, who were in a hole right in front of me, began to shoot and lob grenades. I yelled out to my friend, "Shoot the bastards!"'

Fighting was going on all around but he had lost sight of Tom Foot. Cashman shot one of the five Chinese in front of him before a grenade exploded nearby. As soon as it landed, he threw himself behind a pile of large rocks and escaped injury, but every time he moved more grenades were thrown at him. 'Fortunately you have a bit of time to move when a grenade lands near you,' he says. 'It takes a moment before it explodes and that can be time enough to roll out of the way.'

He counted eight grenade explosions before he was hit in the head by shrapnel from the ninth. 'I was quite helpless and totally at the mercy of my four opponents,' he says. 'But at that point John Kennedy appeared on the skyline behind the Chinese and dropped a grenade in their hole. They were all killed.'

Kennedy ran over to Cashman and asked if he could move on his own. 'Foolishly I said yes, and he took off in search of others,' Cashman says. 'Fighting was still going on but not many of our weapons were firing. It was then that I found I couldn't stand up.'

There were no troops of either side in his vicinity, which meant he could leave the protection of the rock pile and, dragging his Owen gun beside him, he began the painful task of crawling down the hillside. At the bottom, he found the remaining members of the patrol with Lieutenant Duff.

Duff, Lance Corporal Fred Roberts and Privates Len Murdock and Fred Prior had been wounded, and four others were missing: John Kennedy and Tom Foot, Corporal John Nicholson of Moonee Ponds and Private John McKandry, a New Zealander.

The patrol had been ordered to withdraw but Cashman could hear the sound of at least one Owen gun still firing somewhere on the slopes of Cloncurry. 'I realised we were leaving someone behind and protested, as did my fellow NCO, Bluey. Together we said we had to go back, and the men were ready to come with us. We were four short, but some at least were alive and fighting back up the hill we had just left.'

Cashman and Bluey started to lead the men back to Cloncurry when Duff ordered them to stop. At that moment they all heard one final burst from an Owen gun, then the sound of two grenades exploding. 'This was followed by the most heart-wrenching silence I have ever experienced,' Cashman says. 'Our mate was fighting alone and it seemed we had left him to die that way.'

Cashman was ordered to lead the way back to Hill 355. At some point on the return journey he collapsed; he had to be carried back to camp on a stretcher. Later examination would reveal seventeen pieces of grenade in shrapnel wounds to his scalp, jaw and right thigh. His next memory was of sitting on the floor of a bunker with a field dressing around his head. The following day he woke up in the Indian Field Ambulance and once again was fed a piping hot curry. After his experiences on Cloncurry, it seemed appropriate.

His head wound brought on severe concussion and he was considered ill enough to be placed in a plastic bubble on the side of a Bell helicopter and airlifted to a Canadian MASH behind the lines at Uijongbu. Over the next three weeks he recovered.

His most vivid memory of that time is of a group of black musicians entertaining the patients. The last song they sang was one of the hits of the period, 'Jambalaya'.

'Racial discrimination was pretty strong in the US forces in those days and after the show they went to their own little compound,' Cashman says. 'They were having a drink around a fire when the hospital was attacked by North Korean guerrillas. They slaughtered these American entertainers, who were unarmed and just sitting there singing. Then they ran down the lanes between the huts shooting into the wards and throwing grenades. Bullets started flying, and near me this Pommy shot out of his bunk onto the floor and this billycan full of boiling tea got hit and he copped it ... most of it on his arse. He'd have been better off staying in his bed and risking the bullets.'

Returning to 6 Platoon on 21 May 1953, Cashman was anxious for news of the men abandoned on Cloncurry. He discovered that John Kennedy had come across the missing Bren gunner Tom Foot, who was seriously wounded and could not walk. Kennedy had stayed with him for some time but had to leave him to get help. When he returned, the Chinese had taken him away. Kennedy was mentioned in dispatches for his bravery. 'We have no idea about the fate of the other two men who had been fighting on,' Cashman says. 'In the night I still hear that lonely Owen firing. Then I hear the two grenades explode and, worst of all, I *hear* that terrible silence.'

It was incidents like this that made the frontline troops yearn for a few days' leave that would remove them from the bloodshed and the anxiety. After eight months' service in Korea, a digger qualified for three weeks' R&R in Japan. They would fly back to Tokyo and live 'rather lecherously' for the first week. 'But by then we'd be tired and the money would be running low, so we'd take in some sightseeing and do civilised things until it was almost time to go back to Korea,' Cashman says. 'Then we'd get drunk for a couple of days and off we'd go. The fellas in the front line always looked forward to their R&R. It saved their sanity on many occasions.'

Shortly after the Cloncurry disaster, the KATCOM Kim Heung Koo was a member of another fighting patrol that ran into serious trouble. 'I saw an Australian soldier hit by an enemy grenade,' he says. 'He was a chubby soldier and I saw him bleeding profusely. Ron Cashman went to help him.'[42] It was the night that Cashman's dedication to the men of B Company would officially make him a hero.

CHAPTER 14
Saving Tubby Ballard

Lieutenant Alfred William 'Slim' Gargate had served in the Royal Artillery and earned a living as a jackeroo before he joined B Company as the new commander of 6 Platoon following George Zwolanski's departure for Australia. In Ron Cashman's estimation, he was a 'terrific bloke — a Pommy, I might add'. Indeed, Slim Gargate was born at Easthowle, County Durham, in the north of England, on New Year's Day 1926.

Cashman was again second-in-command on the night of 24–25 June 1953, when Lieutenant Gargate took out a fighting patrol of fifteen men. They set out at dusk from D Company's outpost at the base of Hill 159 near Little Gibraltar; their destination was an elongated peak to the north known as The Mound, a hotly contested feature adjacent to enemy-held territory around Hill 227.

The Mound protruded from the floor of the valley like a shark's dorsal fin, with its highest point facing to the north. It ran down along a saddle to a slightly lower hill and then disappeared into a tail. The main peak had been hit by artillery so often that the heights were practically bald, but the smaller peak was still heavily wooded.

The Mound itself was too exposed to be held during daylight hours, so almost every night with the last of the light Australian and Chinese patrols raced each other to occupy the high ground. The first to arrive would take possession of the fortifications and wait in ambush for the enemy to arrive. If the Australians got there first, they could face successive waves of attacking Chinese troops and might be driven off. If the Chinese got there first, there was the inevitable ambush.

To reach The Mound, Gargate's patrol had to travel along the Bowling Alley, which was then so dangerous that soldiers on both sides went down like ninepins from artillery, mortar and machine-gun fire if they were caught in the open. 6 Platoon was halfway across the Alley that night when the commander was informed by radio that Chinese troops had been seen moving onto the higher peak of The Mound at last light. He was ordered to attack them.

Lieutenant Gargate discussed with his number two the best way to mount the attack. It was decided that Cashman and four men would make sure the smaller hill — the wooded knoll — was free of Chinese, while Gargate would take the rest of the men as far up the side of The Mound as possible, then spread out in readiness for an assault on the crest. If Cashman's group did not run into trouble, they would make their way across the saddle to The Mound, and at a set time both groups would rush the Chinese positions.

The patrol split into two sections and Cashman took his men onto the wooded hillside. 'It was terrifying,' he says. 'I couldn't see more than a couple of yards in front of me and we were making a lot of noise. The fellows with me broke every branch it was possible to stand on. By the time we got to the top we were nervous wrecks.'

To their immense relief, they discovered that the wooded hill was untenanted. As planned, they made their way across the saddle and met up with the rest of 6 Platoon near the crest of The Mound. At 10 pm they were in position to launch their assault when they were spotted by a Chinese observation post and attacked with rifles, burp guns and grenades. Private Elvin Royce 'Tubby' Ballard, a seventeen-stone Tasmanian, was lifted up and thrown down the hillside 'like a rag doll'.

'I could see showers of grenades coming in all directions,' Cashman says, 'and I could see the bullets, because apart from hearing them being fired you can see all these little fireflies in front of you. And you would swear every one is pointed straight at you.'

Cashman saw Slim Gargate go down, followed by several of his men, and he immediately took over as platoon commander, rallying the men to throw grenades and make another charge. He had no idea how many of 6 Platoon were left standing, but about eight of them hurled grenades at the nearest enemy position before making a rush for the brow of the hill, where they ran into more heavy fire and were forced to withdraw.

Cashman checked Gargate's wound. He had been holding his Owen gun across his stomach when a burst of gunfire traversed both his arms and the Owen gun itself. When Cashman reached him, he was holding a 36 mm grenade under the heel of his boot and trying to pull out the pin with his wounded hands. Cashman took the grenade away and made him lie down. At that moment the Chinese commander and his radio operator suddenly stood up in the scrub no more than ten metres in front of them. The commander was bellowing orders to his men, presumably to go in pursuit of the Australians, when Cashman fired a full magazine from his Owen gun at the two Chinese. 'Blind Freddie couldn't have missed,' he says. 'They went down very rapidly and to make sure I flipped my last two grenades into the bush with them.'

The Chinese had stopped firing and Cashman judged that it was time to make a break for it. With Gargate's right arm around his shoulder, they staggered down the hill. 'Slim was pretty groggy — he had lost a lot of blood.'

Cashman's hearing had saved his life many times in Korea, and when he heard the clunk of something hitting the ground behind them he automatically threw Gargate and himself to the ground. Looking behind, he was just in time to see a bell-shaped anti-tank grenade roll towards them before it exploded. Gargate was screaming in agony as all of his weight had fallen onto his wounded hands.

Neither man seemed to have been hit by the grenade and they were about to get to their feet when three Chinese soldiers with fixed bayonets burst out of the bushes. Cashman's Owen gun was trapped under Gargate's body and he was powerless to fight them off. 'They weren't after prisoners,' he says. 'We were gone for all the money.'

The three Chinese were right on top of the two men when Don Harris emerged from the bushes, dropped to one knee and opened fire with a Bren gun, killing all three of them. 'They nearly fell on top of us,' Cashman says. 'Then Don loaded up, while Slim and I got to our feet.'

Together they made it back across the valley to D Company's out-post to find that the surviving members of the patrol were already there. Cashman learned from them that six wounded men had been evacuated but five others, including his long-time mate Eddie Wright, were unaccounted for.

A Chinese machine gun had started firing along the Bowling Alley, spraying bullets towards D Company's hillside position. During a lull in the shooting, Cashman and Don Harris heard an anguished voice calling for help out in the rice paddies.

After the events at Cloncurry, Cashman had no intention of ever again leaving a wounded man to fend for himself. He was now in charge of the platoon and he called for volunteers to go with him. Don Harris, exchanging his heavy, unwieldy Bren gun for an Owen, volunteered to join him. The two men crawled towards the source of the voice and located a badly wounded man, Private John Kennedy. Wounded the previous month on Cloncurry, Kennedy had already returned to active service.

'On The Mound, I was a forward scout,' he says. 'I went up the mount and found a Chinese listening post — went right up to him, and he probably saw me too. I went back to Slim Gargate and told him. Gargate said, "Go up and shoot him". I had an Owen gun, so I went back and blasted this bloke. Then we were told to spread out and go up The Mound. We got to within about ten yards and were about to move in when suddenly they gave us the full treatment, tossing grenades and firing at us. I pulled out a grenade; I had it in my left hand and was about to pull the pin when I looked up and there was something headed for me; it looked like a cake tin coming down at me.

'Then it exploded and blood came shooting out of my nose like a pump; half my toes were shot off and my body was burning. I don't know how I got out — I crawled or walked or rolled, and then I lost consciousness. When I came to I rolled down the hill to the paddy fields about 100 or 200 yards away and started through the paddy to get back. As I got along, a machine gun opened up and the bullets were flying over me and around me, thumping into the paddy — I don't know for how long, maybe an hour — until I dragged myself back to the place where I could get through the minefield. I was getting quite close to our positions and I had to call out the password — I think it was 'Truck Road' and then I passed out.

'A couple of blokes came from somewhere and carried me in. That might have been Ron Cashman, I'm not sure. All I know is that the bloke said to me, "Please don't die; please don't die".'

Kennedy had passed out, and Cashman and Harris managed to haul him back to the outpost. 'That still left me four short and so I reckoned we had to go back up the hill,' Cashman says. 'I asked for volunteers again and Donny Harris said yes, he'd be in it.'

The Chinese machine gun located among the trees on a small knoll beside The Mound had resumed firing, aiming for the tracks that led up through D Company's barbed-wire defences to the higher ground. Cashman and Harris made it safely to the bottom of The Mound, but it was impossible to go further without being seen and shot.

'I decided to try my luck,' Cashman recalls. 'I stood up in full view of the Chinese with my Owen gun held above my head in fully outstretched arms and shouted 'Skoshi towshong' loudly and often. Towshong was Chinese for surrender and skoshi was Japanese for small or little. The machine gun ceased firing and I then called out in English, in the faint hope that one of them might understand, "I am only coming for my wounded and am unarmed". I hurled the Owen behind me into the paddy field and walked towards them, repeating 'Skoshi towshong' with my hands held very high. I wanted them to know that I was making a 'little surrender', a temporary arrangement, and not actually surrendering.'

The Chinese were not expecting this. They watched Cashman walk up the hill towards them with his hands in the air, while Don Harris covered him with his Owen gun. 'I'd made sure they had seen my Owen gun disappearing back into the paddy fields behind me,' Cashman says. 'And I was calling out skoshi towshong on a regular basis.'

Cashman reached the Chinese position and said again in English, 'I'm looking for my wounded'. Then, to emphasise the point, he shouted: 'Are there any 6 Platoon wounded around here?' There was no answer. Two of the Chinese soldiers came out from the bushes, got behind Cashman and prodded him with fixed bayonets towards the machine-gun nest. There were six men in the group and they started talking among themselves. After some heated discussion about what action to take, they gave Cashman 'a half-hearted kick in the bum to send me on my way'. 'That was probably to tell me off,' he says. 'And away I went, still yelling out for my 6 Platoon wounded.'

Watching Cashman set off towards the Chinese position, Harris had serious misgivings about the wisdom of his actions. But having seen the result, he decided to try the same manoeuvre himself. He stood up, yelled out, threw down his Owen gun and walked up the slope to join Cashman. The Chinese let him pass.

'Looking back on it years later,' Cashman says, 'maybe they weren't being so kind-hearted. They could sit there firing their machine gun into the valley while Donny and I were waltzing around up there without worrying about anyone dropping a 25-pounder or a mortar on them. We were perfect insurance for them. Whether they had that in mind, I'll never know.'

Cashman and Harris found the spot where the earlier clash had taken place. It was bathed in moonlight and they could see it was deserted. 'There were field dressings and pools of blood all over the place, so we'd nailed a few of them apart from the three that Donnie had cut down and the two that I had shot in front of me.'

The Australians moved to the rear slopes of The Mound and found a large number of fighting pits scattered about in the scrub. Finding no sign of life, they then split up to continue the search for the four missing men. Cashman remembered that Tubby Ballard had been the first man to be hit, blown over one of the slopes by a grenade. Cashman retraced his steps to that spot and then climbed down the slope.

After reaching the bottom and crossing a small creek, he found the 22-year-old Ballard lying on the ground. He was badly wounded in the head and appeared to have one knee smashed, as well as other wounds. He was fading in and out of consciousness, shouting or moaning then falling silent.

Cashman called out to Harris for assistance, and after they had patched him up with field dressings they looked around for the materials to make a stretcher. Nothing suitable was available, so it was decided that Harris should go back to the D Company outpost and return with one. Cashman stressed to him that no one else should come back with him because 'the machine-gun crew will let one through but they are not going to let a group through'.

Cashman tried to make Ballard comfortable on the creek bank but hordes of blood-sucking mosquitoes were driving them mad. He took off his shirt and draped it over Ballard to give him some protection. Then he knew they had company.

'I heard the sound of movement coming towards us and, peering through the gloom, I saw a Chinese patrol heading straight towards us. They were not deviating one inch; they were coming directly at us. I realised that Tubby was too badly injured to have crawled down to the creek on his own. The Chinese must have carried him down there but he had proved too heavy for them and this fresh party had been sent to pick him up.'

Cashman could see the faces of the approaching Chinese clearly in the moonlight. At that moment Ballard started to moan from the pain and Cashman stuffed the tail of his shirt in his mouth to muffle the sound. The Chinese were almost on them — 'just a few yards from putting us in the bag' — when one of the Vickers guns from 2RAR at the UN end of the Bowling Alley proceeded to spray the valley. This was a nightly occurrence: gunners would open fire at irregular intervals in the hope of catching the enemy in the open.

With bullets pinging around them, the Chinese squad dived to the ground, and when the firing ceased they ran for the cover of some rice paddies. 'They regrouped, turned around and went back home,' he says. 'So maybe the Vickers gunner had hit some of them.'

Shortly after that incident Don Harris reappeared carrying a stretcher and they manhandled Ballard onto it. Harris was the same height and weight as Cashman — five foot ten and a well-muscled twelve stone – but Ballard was an exceptionally heavy casualty and the ground proved too slippery to carry him back over The Mound. They set off on the longer route around its base. 'Foolishly we had his torso at the front-end of the stretcher, which meant the lead bloke had his hands behind him and was getting his shoulders pulled out of their sockets by the weight,' Cashman says.

'The fellow on the other end only had the feet and legs to carry. It was murder. Tubby was huge and after a while our arms were screaming and our shoulders were burning. We could only carry him for about five minutes, then we'd have a little breather, swap ends and pick him up and carry on again. I know it got to the stage with me where I was hoping Tubby would die so I could leave him with a clear conscience; he didn't, though, so we kept going. Each time we stopped it was difficult to even open our hands, they were so tightly clenched around the stretcher handles to avoid dropping it.

We were pussyfooting along in the paddy fields, up over the next bank, when there was the faintest little tinkle. Field telephones were heavily muffled to make practically no noise whatsoever, but we heard a tinkle coming from a clump of bushes and knew we were heading towards a Chinese position, probably an outpost. We sank to the ground and, of all times, one of the Chinese decided to light a fag. What you used to do in the bottom of your fighting pit was to cover yourself with a poncho, light your fag underneath that and then you smoked it cupped in the palm of your hands. That's why you could always tell a front-line digger: his palms were covered in nicotine. So this Chinese chap was having a puff in the bottom of his pit and we could just see the tiny glimmer of his cigarette end. I said a silent thank you and we changed course.'

Minutes later they reached another creek. It was not more than fifteen metres wide and the water was no more than thigh deep, but in common with every other creek in the region its banks had been gouged out by the rush of water in the monsoon season and were very steep. It was physically impossible for Cashman and Harris to clamber down the bank while holding on to the stretcher.

The solution, they decided, was for Cashman to climb down into the creek bed and work the stretcher forward from the bank until he was bearing the weight on his shoulders. Harris could then slip down into the water and get his shoulders under the rear end. In that position, they would shuffle the short distance across the creek and deposit Ballard on to the other bank.

'We had it all figured out and it was working nicely. I was in the middle of the creek with the stretcher on my shoulders and Don was ready to come in when we heard more movement. Coming along the far bank were nine Chinese soldiers. There had been no other fighting in this area that night and I realised it was the blokes we'd been fighting earlier on The Mound because some of them were wearing bandages. One bloke actually had his arm in a sling. He was the lead man and he had a bloody burp gun too. And here they were coming along the bank.'

Tubby Ballard started to groan again. As Cashman stood stock-still in the middle of the creek with the stretcher on his shoulders, Harris had to edge forward from the bank and place his hand over the wounded man's mouth to silence him. Just as the Chinese were about to reach a spot fifteen metres away where they couldn't help but take in the strange sight of an Australian soldier supporting a stretcher in midstream, they veered off along a paddy bund, one of the cart tracks that ran through the paddy field, and disappeared from view.

Quaking with nervous tension and exhausted from the physical strain, Cashman and Harris carried the stretcher across the creek and dumped Ballard on the other bank, but they were too worn out to carry him any further. Not far away was a stand of bulrushes and Cashman decided to hide in them with Ballard while Harris made his way back to the D Company outpost once more and returned with a fighting patrol.

As Harris slipped away into the night, Cashman made Ballard as comfortable as he could in the bulrushes. While he waited, he had plenty of time to think. If it ended here, so be it. He was in charge of the platoon and had decided to go back for his wounded mates. After Cloncurry, that had been the right thing to do, and if he survived he would do it again. Sitting in the moonlight with the wounded man beside him, he thought about Betty and felt a tinge of regret that he had not even kissed her. She also owed him a letter — she always owed him a letter . . . Then he snapped out of it and took some action to clear his mind.

'I got some water from the creek and gave Tubby a drink. I was pretty shook up. Then I heard the sound of feet crunching through the dry rice stalks. I crossed my fingers and, peering through the bulrushes, saw a beautiful slouch hat approaching. It was the prettiest slouch hat I ever saw in my life. And there was Don with a sixteen-man patrol from D Company and a stretcher party to carry old Tubby. They even had straps to tie him onto the stretcher. I gave a feeble little wave so they could see it was me and not somebody else. Don had even made a detour to retrieve our Owen guns, the cheeky sod, before going back to get the patrol waiting at the outpost.'

With Cashman and Harris leading the way, the party reached the D Company outpost at 3.30 am, five and a half hours after the initial ambush in which Ballard had been wounded. They began the zigzag climb up the hillside and through the barbed-wire defences. Threading their way through rolls of barbed wire with the heavy stretcher was hard work, and they were desperate to get back to their lines, mostly for a mug of hot tea.

The Chinese machine gun in the wooded approaches to The Mound had stopped firing, but at that crucial moment the Chinese opened up with a volley of mortar fire. The soldier carrying the front of the stretcher was hit and killed instantly and Tubby Ballard received further wounds but was still alive. Cashman and Harris bolted the short distance to the company area and hurled themselves into a trench.

Later that day an army doctor removed four more grenade fragments from various parts of Cashman's body, giving him his third 'wounded in action' medical report. It was, he felt, a small price to pay for the pleasure of seeing that every one of the patrol's casualties had made it back to the Australian lines. His mate Eddie Wright, though injured by a grenade, had got back of his own accord, as had two other wounded diggers.

Cashman would never forget the aftermath of that incredible night. 'I got an immediate Military Medal off the Pommies. Major General Mike West, commander of the Commonwealth Division, nominated me in person.'

According to the battalion's official history, 'Corporal R. K. Cashman took command when a burst of rifle and machine-gun fire badly wounded Lieutenant Gargate and several men. After leading a fierce assault against the strongly-positioned enemy, Corporal Cashman ordered a withdrawal but stayed behind with a companion (Private Don Harris) to search for wounded. Finally, he evacuated a badly wounded Tasmanian (Private E. R. "Tubby" Ballard) under fire from within about thirty yards of the Chinese positions. Cashman was awarded the Military Medal for his actions and for taking control of the platoon. The citation praised his "courage and outstanding leadership" during a clash with the Chinese on the hill known as The Mound.'[43]

Don Harris's gallantry earned him a Mention in Dispatches. 'It was totally inadequate that he got an MID,' Cashman says. 'He deserved a higher award. MacDonald had recommended me for the Military Medal but it was granted only because, when the citation got to Division Headquarters, the Pommy general jacked the recommendation up to an immediate award. As far as MacDonald was concerned, my recommendation would have gone into the stewing pot along with a lot of other names and stayed there. So Major General West obviously took the trouble to find out more about what had actually happened.'

It could be that Slim Gargate had passed the word to his British comrades that Cashman had probably saved his life, thus drawing attention to his name on MacDonald's list.

John Kennedy woke up in bed at the Indian Field Ambulance. 'I was sent to an American hospital, and after the operation they had pasted the shrapnel they'd taken out of my thigh, leg and arm onto my chest: pieces as big as matchboxes. 'When I returned to the battalion I worked in HQ as a typist. Ron Cashman should have received the DCM [Distinguished Conduct Medal] and Don Harris should have got the MM. What they did was pretty bloody special.'

Tubby Ballard, who must have thought he would never get off The Mound alive, was repatriated to Australia and discharged from the army that same year.

Corporal Cashman had been acting as platoon sergeant for two months and was now acting platoon commander. It was reasonable to expect that he would shortly be given his third stripe. 'Then we went across to The Hook,' he says. 'The Hook was the final straw.'

CHAPTER 15
The Bloody Hook

The thousands of hours of fear, suspense, discomfort and brutality had come down to a few square metres on the smoking moonscape known as The Hook. Hades must be like this, Ron Cashman thought. This was the Devil's Little Acre.

The Hook was the most dangerous position in the Jamestown Line. So many soldiers had died there that it was known among all the UN forces as 'The Bloody Hook'. The distance from the enemy along the divisional front differed widely. On The Hook it was at its narrowest. United Nations troops actually shared part of the same east–west ridge with the Chinese.

Incessant bombardment over many months had denuded The Hook of any vestige of natural cover such as trees or bushes. Its surface was pockmarked with shell craters and stained with human blood. Twisted coils of barbed wire, lumps of shrapnel, ripped sandbags and empty ammunition cases littered the smouldering junkyard.

The solution to massive bombardment from the Chinese guns had been to construct prefabricated fighting bunkers in the ruined forward trench line using concrete embrasures, heavy timbers and galvanised iron walls. Each bunker was sited in a hole gouged four metres deep in the heavy clay soil then covered with earth and sandbags to a depth of almost two metres. Each of these bunkers could withstand four direct hits by artillery shells or mortar bombs, and they were linked to one another by a network of communication trenches.

The fate of The Hook and the men defending it at any given time depended to a large extent on the goings-on at Panmunjom. Both sides had agreed on the principle of voluntary repatriation of POWs provided they were screened by a commission of neutral states, but the Communists then haggled over the timing.

On 25 May the United Nations Command put forward as its 'final position' that all prisoners should be repatriated within sixty days of the armistice being signed. Prisoners refusing repatriation would then be transferred to the care of the neutral commission and their fate decided within a further ninety days.

Washington backed up this proposal by solemnly informing Mao Tse-tung and Kim Il Sung through diplomatic channels that if this proposal was rejected the United States would escalate the present 'limited war', and possibly use nuclear weapons. The threat infuriated the Chinese. Throughout May and June they intensified their efforts to take The Hook and the neighbouring Nevada Complex, comprising the outposts Detroit, Berlin, East Berlin, Reno, Carson, Elko and Vegas. Reno and Elko had been lost by the Americans, and the Turkish Brigade had surrendered Vegas.

On the night of 28–29 May, 1st Battalion, the Duke of Wellington's Regiment, comprising mainly young national servicemen from Yorkshire, suffered 126 casualties when 10 000 Chinese mortar and artillery rounds pulverised their position on The Hook and they were subjected to repeated human-wave attacks. All the main bunkers were damaged and trenches three metres deep collapsed under the bombardment, but the Dukes held their ground. The Chinese lost an estimated 250 killed and 800 wounded.

After the failure of this attack, on 4 June the Communists agreed to the UN 'final position'. The peace lobby had never been more optimistic. But now Syngman Rhee, who had always opposed a negotiated settlement, took a radical step to sabotage the agreement. On 17 June he released thousands of North Korean prisoners of war into the South Korean community, ordering his people to take them in. The peace talks broke down yet again.

By now the wet season had turned The Hook into a quagmire. Torrential rain was beating down when the 28th Brigade took over its defences on 9 and 10 July. The Australian battalions were placed in the two most precarious forward positions, with 2RAR on the left and

3RAR on the right. If the Chinese broke through in either position, the Commonwealth Division would be forced to withdraw four kilometres, leaving the enemy in control of the lower Samichon Valley and the north bank of the Imjin River.

Proud of his elevation in rank, Cashman led 6 platoon from the Bowling Alley to their new emplacements on The Hook. Lieutenant Colonel MacDonald placed A Company on Hill 146, the highest point of the position near the southern end of the ridge, while B Company was ordered to defend the south-eastern tip of the ridge on its right. C and D Companies were kept in reserve.

Cashman's platoon carried out reconnaissance patrols to determine the enemy's whereabouts and intentions. He made sure his men were efficient in their patrol work and in a state of battle readiness when they were in the trenches. For the first time he donned his steel helmet and was glad of the extra protection when shells from the enemy's relentless bombardment exploded close to his position.

The pouring rain had swamped the trenches and some of the bunkers had collapsed. The men slogged around ankle deep in mud among the detritus of war. When the rain eased they sweltered in the trenches during the day while at night their hutchies were like sweatboxes.

Danger was ever present. Australian sharpshooters were constantly on the lookout for Chinese snipers who crept close to the barbed wire to pick off any unwary digger. Whenever a sniper was detected he was subjected to a sustained burst of accurate fire that either killed him or forced him to move back out of range. A man in A Company who failed to stay off the skyline on Hill 146 was cut in half by a Chinese 76 mm shell.

The most exposed positions on The Hook had been given to three companies of 2RAR. Lieutenant Colonel Larkin deployed B Company in the central position on The Hook itself, with C Company on its left on Hill 121 and A Company on its right on a hill called Sausage, because of its shape.

The US 1st Marines Division held the remaining Nevada positions on 2RAR's south-western flank, and it was these positions that received the lion's share of the enemy's attention. The three main Chinese positions in the Samichon Valley were named Pheasant, Seattle and Ronson.

On the night of 19–20 July the Marines were driven off two of their Nevada outposts, Berlin and East Berlin, close to 2RAR's adjoining positions. This led to a general withdrawal across the Nevada sector, which left The Hook jutting out as a salient into enemy territory.

2RAR's obvious vulnerability made it imperative that the Australians continue to dominate no-man's-land by aggressive patrolling. There were frequent clashes as the enemy probed forward, looking for weak points in the barbed-wire entanglements and minefields before a major attack. The battalion was losing several casualties a day to Chinese artillery and mortar fire. On 22 July B Company, 2RAR, was relieved on the point of The Hook and sent into reserve to recover from the hammering it had received. D Company took over the position and on its first night sent a four-man reconnaissance patrol along an approach ridge named Green Finger, the easiest route of attack for the forces on Pheasant. The Chinese ambushed the patrol, killing Private Francis McDonnell of Brisbane.

With no sign of any slackening in activity around The Hook, Cashman was taken to a forward observation point by the B Company CO, Major Newton, and shown the location of his next patrol into the Samichon Valley. He was to take two soldiers and infiltrate the Chinese feature on The Hook to investigate the enemy's preparations for the impending attack. He would leave a firm base group of thirteen men in an ambush situation roughly halfway between the Chinese and Australian positions. Their purpose was to protect the rear of the returning recce patrol. If Cashman was forced to flee, the idea was to lead their pursuers into an ambush.

Cashman returned to his platoon and picked the two men who would accompany him. 'It was very hot weather and I was getting around in a pair of shorts,' he says. 'Just after lunch I had a blinding headache and started vomiting. I was in a hell of a state. They got the medical fellows over to me and it was decided that I had sunstroke; that's the best they could come up with. The headache was just something out of this world and then the vomiting. As a result, I couldn't take that patrol and Paddy Williams, the CSM, was told to take it. The next day I was as fit as a fiddle and I had no trouble.'

Cashman's fighting qualities were too well known to the men of B Company for any of them to suggest that he had lost his nerve. The sudden illness was put down to sunstroke and that was the end of it. He searched his conscience for another reason and, not finding one, shrugged it off. Sunstroke. It could have happened to any of them. With his third stripe on the way, he got on with the job in hand.

On 23 July Brigadier (later Sir) John Wilton, the senior Australian officer who had replaced the admirable Tom Daly as CO of 28 Brigade, had the pleasing duty to inform his battalion commanders that a signature was imminent on the armistice agreement at Panmunjom. The United States had leaned on Syngman Rhee to support the peace proposals or face the future without American economic aid or military assistance. The old man had caved in and agreed to adhere to the terms of the armistice.

To avoid unnecessary bloodshed among the Australians, Brigadier Wilton ordered that only patrols essential to the security of the position should be sent out. Any last-minute advances would be pointless, because once the agreement was signed the armies would each have to move back two kilometres from the final demarcation line. Battalion commanders were asked to remain silent about the truce to avoid premature rejoicing and carelessness, but the cancellation of several patrols increased speculation among the men that the war might be almost over.

The Chinese, however, made no such life-saving gestures. On the night of 24–25 July they fired 2000 artillery and mortar rounds — one of their heaviest artillery barrages — at the Australians on The Hook, killing two men and wounding fourteen. They also made frenzied attacks both on the Marines outpost on Hill 111 on 2RAR's left flank and on C Company on Hill 121. In anticipation of this attack, a section of 2RAR's medium machine-gun platoon, commanded by Sergeant Brian Cooper of Perth, had been stationed within the perimeter of the Marines position on Hill 111 to provide covering fire across the 500-metre stretch between the Marines and the Australians.

By 8.50 pm a Chinese company had surged through a gap between C Company and the Marines outpost but were driven off. When they pressed forward again at midnight effective artillery fire kept them at bay on Hill 121. But the Marines' position on Hill 111 was under heavy attack, and the Australian gunners radioed in vain for flares to expose the enemy. The Australians fired their own illuminants using two-inch mortars, and the brief artificial moonlight revealed the figure of a Marines sergeant coming down the communication trench. He informed them he was the last man out of Hill 111 and they should shoot anyone else who came from that direction.

The gunners opened fire at enemy activity on the skyline near the Marines' bunkers and at Chinese troops trying to penetrate the barbed wire in front of their own position. Throughout the night they used grenades and machine guns to fight off repeated attacks. One Chinese shell scored a direct hit on the ammunition bay, which exploded, wounding one of the gunners. Sergeant Cooper warned his men that he had called down an artillery stonk on his own position. At first light the Marines stormed back onto Hill 111 to reclaim their positions. It took them until 2.30 pm to dislodge all the Chinese occupiers.

The following night the Chinese resumed their artillery barrage on the Australians on Hill 121, but the main targets once again were the Marines on Hill 111 and Boulder City. Cooper's machine-gun section inside their perimeter on Hill 111 suffered five wounded; the Marine casualties were much higher.

To prevent a build-up of Chinese troops in front of their positions, the Australians maintained a tight grip on no-man's-land in the immediate vicinity of their trenches, and although they engaged some enemy troops there was no direct assault on either 2RAR or 3RAR. The firing petered out around 3 am and the Marines hunted down the remaining Chinese in their area.

In the morning more than 300 Chinese bodies were counted around Hill 111. 2RAR had suffered five killed and twenty-four wounded in fighting over the two nights. The battalion's final toll in battles on The Hook was seventeen killed and thirty-one wounded.

With peace now a certainty, Ron Cashman took a gamble. 'I stupidly allowed three diggers to go back to Battalion Headquarters,' he says, 'though they all apparently had legitimate reasons to go.

'They got on the grog back there and failed to return before dark in time for stand-to. Thus I was three men short in the trenches and I had a very angry battalion commander on my back. It was goodbye to my sergeant's stripes and farewell to my own platoon. The bastards who had let me down got twenty-eight days each in the Canadian slammer in Seoul, which was no picnic spot, but I was back to corporal/acting sergeant again.'

Colonel MacDonald ordered Lieutenant Alex Weaver, a German born Kurt Aleksander Teitelbaum, to take charge of 6 Platoon. Cashman's fall from grace affected him deeply. 'It cost me my army career,' he says. 'I gave up the ghost after that.'

There were small clashes on the night of 26–27 July near Hill 111, but no further Australian lives were lost before the armistice agreement was signed on 27 July by the military commanders of both sides. Thirty minutes before the ceasefire began at 10 pm that night, eight Chinese soldiers advanced towards a 3RAR outpost. The diggers readied themselves for a last attack, but the men were unarmed and had simply come to have a look at the Australians.

Brigadier Wilton visited the Australian battalions at dawn on 28 July. He estimated that between 2000 and 3000 Chinese dead lay in front of The Hook. He wrote: 'The floor of the valley between The Hook and the Chinese position was almost covered with dead Chinese who had been caught in our deadly defensive-fire artillery concentration. On the immediate approaches to 2RAR the bodies literally carpeted the ground sometimes two deep. They were obviously caused by mortar fire and machine-guns of 2RAR in addition to the artillery concentration ... It was a terrible sight which I will never forget.'[44]

'The Chinese were never going to take our positions on The Hook in those final days,' Cashman says. 'We were too well dug in, yet they sacrificed thousands of lives. It was a killing ground for nothing.'

Elsewhere along the demarcation line, thousands of Chinese emerged from their caves like troglodytes and covered the hillsides. It was an awesome demonstration of the unlimited resources of manpower that would have been unleashed against the UN forces had the war continued.

Cashman celebrated the ceasefire in some style. 'Betty had sent me a bottle of wine inside a loaf of bread and I had kept it for a special occasion,' he says. 'I bumped into an Australian war correspondent who had a bottle of Scotch, so we had a few drinks together.'

Cashman's two favourite KATCOMs, Lee Min Bang and Kim Heung Koo, were overcome with joy. Kim was on sentry duty on the evening of 27 July. 'I was told that at 10 o'clock that evening the fighting would cease and if I survived until then I would live. I wanted that 10 o'clock so badly and, sure enough, it came and everything went silent — there was no gunfire at all and suddenly I could hear the mosquitoes buzzing.'

Under the terms of the armistice, the belligerents were given three days to pack up and leave their forward positions. Both Australian battalions retired from The Hook and set up camp outside the Demilitarised Zone. Cashman could see no good reason to delay his departure from Korea. 'Once they began painting the rocks white to mark the parade ground I reckoned I had to get out of it,' he says. 'They wanted a volunteer from the battalion to come back to Australia to do the army's Airborne course. I had my hand up for that quick smart and I got it. I think I got it because MacDonald wanted to get rid of me as much as I wanted to get out.'

Lee was heartbroken. 'Ron Cashman was leaving for his own country and I felt deep sadness in my heart, as if I was separating from my own blood brother,' he says. 'I felt that I could never see him again.'

Australia had sent 11 600 army personnel to Korea in all roles, 6000 members of the RAN and 1115 of the RAAF. The final toll among the Australians was 339 killed and 1216 wounded. The total British and Commonwealth losses amounted to 1263 killed and

4817 wounded. America had sent 1.3 million men into action and 33 629 were killed, while a further 105 785 were wounded. The South Korean Army suffered 415 000 killed and 429 000 wounded. American estimates put Chinese and North Korean military losses at more than 1.5 million dead.

The civilian dead in South Korea numbered one million out of a population of twenty million. North Korea claimed that its losses from all causes were two million, one-fifth of its population of ten million.

Mao Tse-tung wrote: 'The important reason that we could not win a decisive victory in Korea was our lack of naval strength. Without naval support we have had to confine our offensives to frontal attacks along a line limited by sea. Such actions always entail great losses and we are seldom capable of destroying the enemy. In March 1951 I suggested to Comrade Stalin that the Soviet Union would not be apparently involved in the war. Comrade Stalin preferred to be cautious lest it might give the capitalist imperialists the pretext of expanding the war to the continent. I agreed with his point of view. Until we are better equipped for victory it is to our advantage to accept agreeable terms for an armistice.'

Cashman met up with Slim Gargate in Japan and they reminisced over a few beers about that fateful night on The Mound. 'He was fairly pleased that I had extracted him,' Cashman says. Then he flew home to Australia. He had fought a good war but it had ended in the bitterest of disappointments.

In seventeen days he would be twenty-one years old.

CHAPTER 16

Love and marriage

Betty Whittle, the statuesque blonde of Ron Cashman's dreams, stood on tiptoes to scan the hundreds of beaming male faces at Mascot Airport. She hardly recognised her ardent penfriend when he came striding through the arrivals lounge with the other Korean veterans in September 1953.

Although they had corresponded frequently, she had seen Ron Cashman in the flesh only a handful of times during his leave the previous January, and apart from the small photograph he had sent her from the trenches she had very little idea of his appearance. The young man who presented himself to her was blue-eyed, tanned and handsome.

Cashman had sent Betty a telegram from Kure giving his flight details and he was delighted that she had turned up to greet him. It was the homecoming of his dreams; she might not be madly in love with him, but at least she cared. Cashman had two objectives firmly in mind: the first was to persuade Betty to marry him; the second was to do whatever he could to rescue his mother from his father.

Dressing her in a slouch hat and an army greatcoat, he smuggled Betty on board the diggers' coach that was taking them to the LTD at Marrickville. He did not intend to let her out of his sight until he had expressed his feelings. 'The bus driver was stopped for speeding and the police got on to check the passengers,' Cashman says. 'I guess we were fairly rowdy but fortunately they didn't spot Betty hiding in our midst.' After his experiences in the lawless wastes of Korea, it felt strange to be home.

To facilitate unauthorised visits to the pub, the diggers removed two palings in the fence surrounding the LTD depot. Cashman was soon slipping out through the gap to court Betty at her home with the blessing of her mother and father, Ivy and Herb Whittle. 'It started as a casual relationship,' Betty says, 'and then it got better and better.'

There was a problem, however. Cashman was romancing Betty on the couch in front of an open fire in her living room when some gas escaping from the wood made a hissing sound — *tsssst!* — and the next thing she knew Cashman had detached himself from her arms and flung himself under the couch, convinced he had heard an incoming mortar shell. 'He was shivering and shaking and it frightened me,' she says. 'I was dubious about him and nearly broke off the relationship.'

Cashman's letters to Betty had been full of chat about how much he was missing Australia and reminiscences about the past. He had told her very little about the actual fighting or how he had seen his friends blown apart by shellfire and exploding mortar bombs. For the first time they discussed the war. 'I had no idea about Korea at all,' she says. 'Not many people did. Ron told me what had happened to him and his mates. We talked for hours and hours. I discovered that he was a very nice, very kind-hearted man.'[45]

The Australia that Ron Cashman had returned to could hardly have cared less about the 'police action' in Korea. If his compatriots thought about it at all, it was as the cause of the wool boom that saw graziers suddenly driving Rolls-Royces around their back paddocks, unable to believe the figures: a pound a pound — 240 pence for a pound of wool that might, if they were lucky, have returned them twenty pence before the war.

They were more interested in the coronation of the young Queen Elizabeth, a grand spectacle that captivated 20 million television viewers around the world and took place just four days after the celebrated conquest of Everest by Edmund Hillary of New Zealand and Sherpa Tenzing Norgay of Nepal; and the new Australian tennis star Ken Rosewell — at eighteen the youngest champion ever — who, with his pal Lew Hoad, was taking the tennis world by storm.

On the radio 'The Ampol Show' and 'Pick a Box' competed for listeners, with Jack Davy and Bob Dyer outdoing each other hauling in huge sharks from their game fishing boats. Davy joined the famous

Redex Round-Australia car trials, with 'Gelignite Jack' Murray adding a little spice to his competitors' journeys by tossing sticks of dynamite out his car windows as he passed.

The pop song stations played all-American music, old favourites like Bing Crosby sometimes teamed with newcomers like Doris Day or Rosemary Clooney. At the pictures the new craze was 3D, with ticket holders given a pair of cardboard glasses as they entered, and the girls squealing as the monsters seemed to leap from the screen. Marilyn Monroe's nude calendar had made her the world's top pin-up girl.

Ron Cashman had gone away to the folksy theme song from *Dad and Dave* and had returned to 'Rock Around the Clock'. Pushing all the horrors of war out of his mind, he was determined that nothing be allowed to spoil his chances of happiness with Betty. He enrolled in the Airborne course at the School of Land Air Warfare at Williamtown airbase, near Newcastle. Parachute jumping was a thrilling, sometimes breathtaking experience.

'On one occasion I was the last man out on a stick of five,' he says. 'You used to lay back and watch your canopy develop behind you. This time it didn't develop. It stayed in a long ribbon. This can be caused by you twisting as you leave the aircraft, causing the rigging lines to foul. The procedure was to bang hard on the lift webs — the harness — and bring the twist out of the bottom of the line near your head and then spin yourself out of it and your canopy would open. So all right, I've got a big ribbon up behind me. I adopt the bang, bang procedure — and nothing happens. Then I put in my own innovations of spinning to the left and spinning to the right; still nothing's happening and I'm descending at a fairly rapid rate of knots. I decide I've got to use my own initiative and at this stage of the game I've got hold of the lift wings in my hand and I'm literally forcing them apart with sheer brute strength.

'Well, the canopy opened and I had a kitbag attached to my leg; you kept a weapon in it and before you landed you were supposed to let it slide down through a sleeve so it was well clear of you when you landed. So I pulled the pin and let the bag drop and then I hit the ground. It was a particularly soft landing and the four fellows who'd left before me were still drifting merrily up above and there was much

189

commotion going on. An air force photographer came rushing up to me and his exact words were, "I had the shot of a lifetime. Then the fuckin' chute opened!" '

Ron was delighted to discover that he was once more under the command of his old B Company CO, Wings Nicholls. He passed the course with flying colours: Discipline: very good. Nervous reaction: nervous but controlled. Parachuting ability: average. Disposition: cheerful.

Nicholls tried to get him to stay in the Airborne Platoon. In fact, he wrote a commendation that still makes Cashman laugh. 'He commended my calmness and ability under pressure to have averted a serious prang!' But while he was pleased to be among friends, he was 'madly in love' with Betty and wanted a posting in Sydney to be with her. So he opted out of the unit.

'I got posted to the national service training battalion at Pucka-punyal,' he says. 'When I learned about it, it was too late to do anything. The last place in the world I wanted to be was a national service unit in Victoria and they probably knew that when they sent me there, because they were dirty on me for not staying in the airborne.

'I had a pretty cushy job there. In the beginning I was tangled up with the university platoon of national servicemen, none of whom wished to be there, and I certainly didn't want to be running up and down hills with them. I started to go AWOL. I was going into Sey-mour, hitch-hiking up to Sydney and spending a bit of time with Betty. And then when I felt like it I'd hitch-hike back again. I must have done this three or four times and not a word was said. And then finally I took two weeks and of course they had to do something then. The truth is I'd had a gutful and I wanted out.'

There was, however, no escape from the illness that had been stalking him. He began to experience violent headaches similar to the one that had struck him down in his last days on The Hook. 'I spent time in and out of Heidelberg Hospital,' he says. 'They decided that I had post-concussion shock because I had been wounded in the head in mid 1953. They did lumbar punctures and made other tests, but they couldn't find out the cause of all these headaches.'

In fact, shell shock was an illness in its own right. The emotional and psychological devastation wrought on the frontline soldier had first come to notice during the Russo-Japanese War of 1904–05, when weapons of mass destruction had first been used against the Russians during the Siege of Port Arthur. The Russians had written medical papers about the strange condition suffered by many of their troops subjected to prolonged artillery barrages, and similar symptoms had been noted after the massive bombardments on all combatants in World War I.

Korea had seen two years of static trench warfare during which the soldiers experienced a varying combination of cold, boredom, bad food, fear, endless bombardment and hand-to-hand fighting. Army doctors only hinted at the morale problem they faced. 'The modern young man,' two American psychiatrists wrote, 'has only vicarious experience in the stern business of sacrifice for the sake of duty and little call to live dangerously. He has been pretty well-conditioned to regard aggressiveness as an unwonted, dangerous thing. It is very difficult to raise an army where almost everyone feels he should contribute in some other way than by functioning as a rifleman.'

No such difficulty applied to Ron Cashman, an eager recruit and a willing fighter. In 3RAR the code of the mythic Aussie Digger — laconic, uncomplaining (except about the food) and unyielding — was raised to an article of faith. Add to that the power of mateship and little room remained for the individual to reveal his terror in the face of a deadly and unrelenting enemy. And the more he buried and denied it, the more it ate away at the man inside.

'Looking back, I think that day on The Hook was the time when my nerve snapped,' he says. 'I think that was when I'd had it. It was just one too many.'

Compared with many of the physically wounded and the amputees, Cashman looked fit and healthy. He was twenty-one years old and had his whole life in front of him. The official attitude shamed him into silence. Besides, Betty Whittle had just made him a very happy young man. She had fallen in love with him and had accepted his proposal of marriage.

Ron Cashman and Betty Patricia Whittle were to be married in Betty's local church on 12 February 1954. The reception was to be held at Homebush RSL Club and the newlyweds planned to honeymoon at Nambucca Heads. Betty, however, was starting to have second thoughts. 'I had a last-minute attack of nerves and wanted to call the whole thing off. Then I remembered that I had ordered 150 bread-rolls and I couldn't think of what to do with them. I married Ron for 150 bread rolls!'

Michael and Edna Cashman had driven up from Melbourne for the wedding. His mother saw her son in his dress uniform with the gold braid and his Military Medal. 'He looked tremendous,' Betty says. But Cashman's army days were drawing to a close. After his honeymoon the newlyweds moved to Melbourne.

His father astonished him by making him a business proposition: he would buy a semi-trailer and go into business with his son as a haulage contractor. Cashman considered the offer and, after discussing it with Betty, decided to accept. He applied for a discharge.

'I was taken up before the Brigadier and they were going to give me a discharge all right — they had it written out as "unfit for the service of the corps". That's when I appealed and they changed it to "discharge at own request".'

At Royal Park he was asked, 'Do you want to apply for a pension?' He inquired what that entailed and was told, 'You'd have to spend another week here.' Cashman said, 'Forget the pension. Just give me the paper and let me out.'

He was discharged from the army on 30 April 1954. He had served three years and 113 days, including active service of one year and 287 days. He had gone in a boy and come out a man. He had achieved the vital goal that underlay his enlistment — freedom from fear of his father or any man. But what he carried away from the experience was much more burdensome than what he had taken into it. Like so many soldiers before and after him, he quickly learned that the war does not stop when the guns fall silent. The end of combat is often just the beginning of a more terrible struggle, one that affects every part of the soldier's life and those he loves.

With no pension, Cashman had no money to buy a house and Edna insisted that they come and live at the family home in Williamstown. But the haulage venture was doomed from the start. When Michael Cashman reverted to his bullying ways, arguments broke out between father and son. After two years in Korea, Cashman was having none of it; he stood up to him and for the first time in his life the older man backed down. 'But he was still mean with money and wouldn't invest in the business,' Cashman says. 'The partnership went broke. It was another magnificent blunder.'

Tensions in the house in Smith Street reached breaking point. Cashman decided they had to get away. Betty was pregnant with their first child. He took her back to Sydney to make a fresh start. The young couple moved to Leichhardt, where their son was born in 1955. 'He only lived for a day and then died,' Betty says. 'We were heartbroken.'

As his headaches returned with greater frequency, Cashman's behaviour became more erratic. 'I was nervous, jumpy, unstable — a shell-shocked nervous wreck.' It was clear he needed professional help. 'He wasn't bad tempered,' Betty says, 'but he was moody. In his mind he was still fighting the war.'

He revealed to Betty the recurring nightmare in which he was in his fighting pit on top of a Korean mountain looking down into a mist-covered valley. 'Ron was frightened of the mist,' Betty says. 'It was beautiful, but he knew that it was hiding hundreds of Chinese soldiers. His happiest time was when the mist lifted.'

He was admitted to Concord Hospital, where he was treated by a psychiatrist. When he said that he was terrified of going to sleep because of the nightmares, the doctor prescribed medication. He was soon addicted to sleeping pills.

To test his nerve, he joined No. 1 Commando Company in the part-time volunteer Citizen Military Forces and did a stint with them. 'I tried to re-enlist for Malaya but for some reason or other they wouldn't have me,' he says. This is when his convictions for assault and indecent language in the Adelaide pub brawl were uncovered. In his letter to the Minister for the Army, J. O. Cramer, Cashman explained that when returning to Australia from Korea, 'I had the mis-fortune to be posted to the national service, which damn near broke my heart so I applied for a discharge, which was eventually granted after I had gone to great pains to prove that I was not cut out for a shiny shoes base-wallah at that stage of the game.'

It was to no avail. In July 1957 he was informed by the recruiting officer Eastern Command that he had been rejected for re-enlistment.

The couple's first and second daughters, Julie and Vicky, were born in Sydney but work was hard to find. When he was offered a war service house at Seaford, Melbourne, the young family moved south again. Two more daughters, Michelle and Lyndie, were born.

Things looked up briefly when Cashman bought a prime mover and trailer on time payment and started a trucking business on his own. 'But I managed to put the rig over the side of a hill near Gund-agai on a trip from Adelaide to Sydney with a load of washing machines and refrigerators,' he says. 'The insurance would only cover the cost of the wrecked vehicle. It wiped me out financially.'

His headaches were getting worse and he was drinking more heavily to stay on top of them, then knocking himself out at night with sleeping pills. 'I went into Heidelberg Hospital for three weeks and they did a number of tests and said there was nothing physically wrong with me,' he says. 'Another psychiatrist saw me and said the headaches would probably go in a couple of years. I was discharged with a huge jar of aspirin. But things got worse instead of better.'

For nearly two years he lived on his nerves, constantly expecting a grenade to come in and blow him to pieces or someone to shoot him. It would not have taken a great deal of imagination to diagnose combat stress. Instead, he was left to battle on. 'We brazened it out,' Cashman says, 'and some of us paid a pretty high penalty.'

On 28 May 1964, at the height of his troubles, his mother com-mitted suicide. He was stricken with grief over the loss and anger that he had been unable to prevent it. He spent many more weeks in repatri-ation hospitals, where he was pacified with sedatives and tranquillisers for anywhere between two weeks and two months and then released. 'I would go home and terrorise my family until the next bout.'

One night in 1965 while asleep he tried to strangle Betty, believing she was a Chinese soldier. It was his ultimate nightmare — to kill the woman he worshipped. In an act of desperation, he again tried to re-enlist in the army, this time for Vietnam. If accepted, it would provide an escape not just for himself but for the loved ones whose lives he was destroying. 'I knew I had to get away,' he said. 'If I got killed, well . . .'

But even that was denied him. The army psychologists wrote, 'Physically fit but unlikely to withstand the stresses imposed by conditions of living and training in the Army — Reject on medical grounds.'

CHAPTER 17

War without end

There could be only one possible response from Betty to the madness that had seized her husband: it didn't matter that she loved him, she simply couldn't live with the drinking, the ranting, the uncontrolled rage and the violence that welled up in the man.

Their youngest daughter, Lyndie, suffered badly from asthma and in 1966 Betty persuaded her husband that the child would benefit from the sunny climate at Maroochydore, Queensland, where her parents were now living. For a while things went well. Cashman found work skippering a trawler but ran into a gale and the boat almost sank. He and his crewman were rescued by a Liberian freighter and taken to Sydney. The trawler went down as far as the wheelhouse but stayed afloat and was salvaged by another trawlerman. Cashman was sacked for having abandoned it, despite the life-threatening danger he had been in.

One night in 1972 he went berserk in the family home after discovering that Betty was being unfaithful to him. Ambulancemen were called to the house and Cashman was overpowered and led away in a straitjacket.

Such was Betty's circle of acquaintance that almost inevitably she had turned for consolation to an equally flawed character. Dirk was a South African who himself had a drinking problem, but Betty found solace in the companionship he offered.

Cashman was admitted to Greenslopes Repatriation Hospital and briefly placed in a padded cell. At one point he was tied to his bed with leather straps and knocked out with sedatives. When he checked out of hospital and returned to Maroochydore, it was to discover that his wife had moved out and was living with Dirk.

Cashman confronted his rival and challenged him to a duel — bayonets were his weapon of choice, but since none was available they used big kitchen knives. 'If you want to break up my family bad enough you've got to fight for it,' he told him. But though he bested his rival, the age of duelling was long past. The police were called and Cashman was arrested the following day while playing a game of pennant bowls at Coolum. He was charged with attempted murder and remanded to Boggo Road Gaol, Brisbane. 'I now knew for sure I was mentally ill,' he says. 'Normal, sane men do not go round challenging people to duels.'

Refused bail, Cashman languished in prison until his trial, at which he was convicted of unlawful wounding and given a suspended sentence. No one had asked to see his medical record, and he had no money to mount a proper defence. By then, however, Dirk had persuaded Betty to leave with him; they took the two youngest children and went to Moree. Eldest daughter Julie was already fending for herself on the Sunshine Coast. While he was in Greenslopes hospital Vicky had forged her father's signature to get a passport and had fled to Afghanistan, where she joined the Children of God cult. Cashman's whole family — and his dreams — had fallen apart.

He moved to St George in the Queensland outback and found work as a caretaker at the Beardmore Dam on the Balonne River. After they had lived apart for a year he approached Betty, whose relationship with Dirk had ended in tragedy when his rival had committed suicide. Soon they were back together again. Cashman told her — and he believed it — that the worst was over. The nightmares and the rages were receding. It was going to be all right.

The next blow was like a Chinese grenade landing in his trench. It came in February 1977 in the form of a telephone call from a Salvation Army officer: Julie had been arrested on a drugs charge. She was in jail in Sydney and she desperately needed her father's help.

Ron Cashman was 'bowled over'. For his eldest daughter, the 'apple of his eye', to be arrested was bad enough, but drugs! He couldn't believe it. Julie was twenty years old and, to his knowledge, had never been involved in that caper. She prided herself on her mental abilities. Taking drugs was completely foreign to her nature. 'She had a good job as a hotel receptionist,' he says. 'I thought she was doing well despite the family break-up.'

Along with the shock and bewilderment came a crushing sense of powerlessness. St George, far away beyond the NSW–Queensland border, seemed a million miles from his little girl. As usual there was nothing in the bank, and the prospects for change in that department looked slim. As caretaker of the Beardmore Dam, Cashman was never going to make his fortune. 'It was a real hand-to-mouth existence,' he says. Betty, Michelle and little Lyndie had to be provided for, but right now Julie was the priority.

He went to see his boss. 'You owe me a week's holiday. I'm taking it now,' he said. 'It's a family matter.' No further explanation was offered or sought. He had to wait two days to collect his pay, but then he said goodbye to Betty and the kids and took off in his old Standard station wagon for the 800-kilometre trip to Sydney, mostly over indifferent roads. He drove non-stop, cursing himself every mile of the way for not being a better father. In the end, as old Harry Truman would have said, the buck stops here. It was a father's job to keep his kids out of trouble, and he had failed to do so. 'I don't remember too much about that trip, but I called myself every kind of idiot there was,' he says.

Cashman should not have been surprised that his daughter had found herself in deep trouble. Julie had been fending for herself since the age of fourteen, and the lure of easy money had been too much of a temptation for her to resist. She had always been headstrong. He remembered taking her to school on her first day. 'I told her when she got out to turn left and come straight home. Three hours after she should have been home I went looking for her. She'd turned right.'

Drugs flooded into Australia from South-East Asia during the Vietnam War, when thousands of American soldiers came to Sydney on R&R. Heroin and cocaine were prevalent but the favourite drugs among young people were marijuana and its close relative hashish (cannabis resin). Drug importers used 'mules' — mostly innocent-looking tourists and holidaymakers — to smuggle the contraband through Customs.

Julie had indeed been working as head receptionist at Surfair International Hotel–Motel at Coolum but, unknown to her father, she had been through a rough time. Finding herself pregnant, she had gone to Sydney for an abortion and had returned to the Sunshine Coast to discover that her job was no longer available.

She needed money and, through a local man called Michael, she had agreed to become a mule on a round trip to Bangkok. Oddly, she had received two phone calls from Michael while she was in the Thai capital checking on the details of her return flight.

When Cashman reached the home of Betty's Aunt Bertha and Uncle Jack near Sydney, he collapsed for a couple of hours, then began the process of intelligence gathering before making his move. He needed to know the lay of the land before he could decide what best to do. Jack told him Julie was being held in Mulawa prison at Silverwater on the outskirts of the city near Parramatta. She had been arrested at Sydney airport on her return from Bangkok after Customs found about $50 000 worth of buddha sticks — compressed marijuana — packed into the linings of her two suitcases. Dope was bad enough but at least it wasn't hard drugs. Thank God for that.

Jack mentioned that Julie had a boyfriend, Vaughan, and he had his phone number. Cashman called the man and arranged a meeting. He found himself looking at a smooth, handsome young man with shifty eyes — a bit of a pretty boy who would not be worth a pinch of the proverbial in a firefight. He questioned Vaughan closely, and once he'd cut through the bullshit one thing seemed crystal clear — Julie had been nothing more than a courier for the big boys, an expendable pawn.

The court had set Julie's bail at $5000 and Vaughan mentioned 'promises' of help from Michael, evidently one of the organisers of the drug-smuggling operation. Cashman took that with a grain of salt; it would be intended to stop Julie from informing on the gang in order to save herself. They obviously did not know his daughter very well. She would tell the police absolutely nothing.

Cashman's first priority was to get Julie out of prison so she could tell him the truth and to prepare her defence. The only way that was going to happen was if he himself took out a loan for $5000. Then he had to see his daughter, talk to her and let her know the family was behind her.

Having spent time behind bars himself, Cashman knew the procedure for prison visits. He drove out to Mulawa and after the usual form-filling and a long wait Julie was escorted into the interview room. She was tired and pale but her blue eyes lit up when she saw him. His strength and quiet determination contrasted with Vaughan's transparent weakness.

Cashman told Julie that he had already had a meeting with her solicitor and had taken out a loan to pay for her bail. He tried to persuade her that Vaughan's indecisiveness about raising bail himself suggested either a weak character or that he was working for Michael or someone higher up, but he saw she was too infatuated to accept this view.

He had achieved the first step, however: Julie was to be brought before the court the following Monday morning for technical adjustments to her bail conditions and then released to stay with her grandmother Ivy Whittle in Maroochydore.

'I was elated,' Julie said later. 'My battler father had solved all the problems in just a few hours.'

That week Cashman visited his daughter every day to keep her spirits up. Once he took Vaughan with him, and Julie sensed the tension between them. It was clear her father did not respect Vaughan; his idea of a man was someone he could go to war with, someone he could trust his own life with. 'I wouldn't like to have him at my back,' he had told her.

At the Monday hearing Ron Cashman sat in the body of the court and smiled his encouragement. Afterwards he presented the bank cheque made out to Mulawa Women's Prison. This was a mistake; it should have been assigned to the Receiver of Public Monies, and the magistrate refused to accept it. 'I felt like a right dingbat,' Cashman said. Julie had to spend a further night in the cells at Central Court, but next day he was on hand for her release.

About 10 o'clock the prison officers brought Julie up from the cells to meet her father. 'He was beaming with delight,' she said. 'He was so proud to have got me out.' They walked out into the street together hand in hand, laughing like a couple of kids.

Cashman had been staying with relatives, but that night he took a double motel room with his daughter. When they were settled in he gave her 'the third degree' about her association with drugs and running the buddha sticks in from Thailand. Then he listened patiently as Julie told him the true story and then repeated the bogus one she had told to the police — that she had been given the suitcases in Bangkok by a man named Chuck and had no idea they contained drugs. To secure a conviction, the police would have to prove she had known the drugs were there and, Julie naively believed, there was no way they could do that. Cashman looked at her sceptically.

'Will this Michael come good with the bail money and pay for your legal costs?'

'Oh yes. He's selling a block of land to raise the funds.'

Cashman held his tongue.

She also told him about the two phone calls she had received from Michael while she was in Bangkok, although this had been in breach of the rules he had set down himself that they should not contact each other until after the job was done. It was obvious to Cashman that Customs had been tipped off about Julie's arrival and the fact that she was carrying drugs in her luggage. Michael had probably been picked up by the police and had set his daughter up to save his own skin.

Once again he said nothing to upset or frighten her. Instead he asked about the committal proceedings. Julie was sure she would not have to stand trial because the police had no evidence against her and the case would surely lapse. She promised her father that she would put the drugs scene behind her, make a new start and settle down to a decent life.

It sounded convincing. But then Vaughan arrived. He was highly excited. He was sure the police were following him; Michael too.

They were tapping their phones, opening their mail. Cashman could see Julie's excitement at the drama of it all. When he could take it no longer he left them and bought a bottle of rum. When he returned with it Julie and Vaughan took off. They wanted to be alone.

As he checked out the following morning to ride that endless dragon highway back to St George he tossed the empty bottle into the metal waste bin. The clatter bounced around the inside of his skull.

That was the start of it.

Ron Cashman returned to Sydney for the committal proceedings. The day before the hearing he attended a conference with Julie's legal team. One of her two suitcases containing the buddha sticks had 'disappeared' while in police custody. The barrister was hopeful the case would be thrown out; Julie was supremely confident. The magistrate took a more hard-headed view, however, and set a trial date for four months' time.

Once again Cashman travelled back to St George while Julie and Vaughan returned to her stamping grounds on the Sunshine Coast. But the family gathered in Sydney for the trial, Ron and Betty and the girls staying with Bertha and Jack while Julie and Vaughan stayed at Bertha's holiday cottage in Gosford.

On the first day Julie's bail was withdrawn and she spent the rest of the trial at Mulawa. It took only three days. The jury retired for less than an hour before reaching a verdict: Guilty.

In the dock, Julie heard a gasp from her family at the back of the courtroom and her mother begin to sob. The judge sentenced her to two years and six months' imprisonment, with a non-parole period of fifteen months. Julie had just turned twenty-one, and the sentence seemed like forever. She heard the judge say, 'Take the prisoner away', and as she turned to go she saw her father's stricken face and the tears in her mother's eyes. She was led down the stairs.

Ron Cashman took Betty out to Mulawa to see Julie the following day. The single hour permitted passed swiftly. Cashman's bewilderment and rage were mixed with a deep sense of failure. *The buck stops here.* There was nowhere to hide from that; not even the rum bottle would provide the release he sought.

By her own admission, Julie developed a fascination for some of the hardened male criminals she met through the wire while serving her sentence. Initially she was frightened of them, but she came to believe the myth that they took no nonsense from anybody and lived by the criminal code of silence: Don't tell. No matter what, you never told anybody in authority — cops or screws, beaks or briefs — anything about the criminal business. That code appealed to her.

'I picked it up quickly,' she said. 'It wasn't hard.'

'Don't tell' had always been one of her father's guiding principles too. When they were children, it was always the informer who got into trouble with him, not the guilty party. Julie claimed that she learned 'the complexities that lay behind this simple principle', but she was never able to articulate them. In fact, the instinct of silence went all the way back to her father's own horrific childhood. He could never tell anyone of the thrashings meted out to him by his father, never mention the shocking violence against his mother, because the shame would be too painful. If it ever came out, he was certain the man would make it worse for him and for his mother. So he made a virtue of it. 'Don't dob' became one of his moral precepts.

The army reinforced it. Part of the camaraderie of private soldiers was that you 'sorted out' acts of bastardry among yourselves. You kept the officers out of it. They represented the 'authority' that had it in for the lot of you.

Back in St George, Cashman and Betty could do little to support Julie while she was in prison other than write letters, and this became something of a family project — one that would eventually have the most terrible consequences. At the time, however, it seemed like an ideal way to stay in touch, and everyone could contribute to the letters. 'There wasn't a hell of a lot else to do out there,' Ron Cashman says.

On weekends he often went bush, hunting wild pigs around the dams on nearby properties. Little Lyndie was his offsider. 'She was a little ripper,' he says, 'not afraid of a thing, and those big black boars can be pretty scary.' He took up lawn bowls again, but thoughts of Julie in prison were never far from his mind.

Julie was released in 1978, but instead of keeping her promise to resume a law-abiding life, she had become defiant and rebellious. Far from being rehabilitated, she had started on a wild ride that would culminate in the violent deaths of her lover, Bruce Kennedy, and her husband, Ray Wright — both armed robbers with long records — and in Julie becoming known nationwide as the 'Angel of Death', Australia's most notorious woman criminal.

Cashman was drawn into her orbit of crime, partly through a fierce pride in his own, partly through the guilty knowledge that his madness had contributed to her running off the rails, and partly through his and Betty's determination to care for the little girl, Jade, to whom Julie had given birth in jail. While he took no part in the crimes that made her notorious, he could never ignore her cries for help. She knew this and took every advantage of it. Julie's criminal career came to an end on 14 November 1984 after a final chase and gun battle through the Dandenong Mountains. By then all members of the Cashman family — apart from Vicky, who was still living overseas under the assumed name of Mary — were in total chaos.

Julie was extradited to Queensland to stand trial for earlier crimes, and suddenly the spotlight turned on Ron and Betty. Julie had sent them $29 000, the proceeds of a robbery, to have a cottage built on a block of land she had bought at Tuggerah on the Central Coast of New South Wales as an inheritance for Jade. Her parents were charged with accepting stolen money. Julie drew a long sentence; Betty and Ron received a minimum of three months and twelve months respectively. It was the culmination of the nightmare. Ron was offered early release but on such stringent conditions that he would not have been able to hold down a job. Despite the appalling and violent conditions of Boggo Road at the time, he chose to serve his full term. 'I wanted to pay my debt,' he said. 'I did so, in full.'

For the first two months he was in Boggo Road's notorious 2 Wing, built in 1908. His cell measured ten by six feet and the only light filtered through a filthy barred window. Lockdown lasted sixteen hours a day from 4 pm until 8 am. He was allowed out of his cell to exercise in the yard with other prisoners. 'There was nothing to do except play cards or handball against the inside of the prison wall,' he says.

'When he went to jail I'd send him pictures I'd drawn,' Lyndie says. 'One time I sent him a little girl in a dressing gown, I don't know why.'

When he was released he made himself a promise that he would never offend again. But if Ron Cashman thought the world of criminality was forever behind him he was mistaken. Fate had one more grenade to toss at him. 'It was a never-ending run of grief,' he says.

At Julie's urging, Lyndie had begun writing to a male prisoner — a friend of Ray Wright's named Fred Many — when she was only fourteen. Many was a cunning, violent sociopath and he played the little girl like a harp, writing poems to her and gradually drawing her into his web. When she visited him he was totally charming and she was swept away. She agreed to marry him but her father intervened and prevented the marriage taking place in Goulburn Gaol. 'I wrote to the governor pointing out that Lyndie was under age,' he says.

However, when Many left prison in 1986 Lyndie was waiting at the gate for him and, with Cashman still in Boggo Road, took him back with her to her parents' house at Saratoga on the Central Coast. Almost immediately he involved her in his criminal activities; she was caught and remanded in prison.

'When I went inside, Julie had been before me and she was really well liked, and that made it better for me,' she says. 'She wasn't a druggie or anything, and I wasn't into drugs either. I just wanted to do my time and get out. They put me into solitary for three months. They thought someone was going to break me out. I read a lot of books, stories about growing up.'

Soon after her release Many committed a terrible rape and murder attempt on a fifteen-year-old girl. But the victim had not only escaped, she had left her false fingernails in the tail light of his car. Many was picked up, charged and convicted. 'I never met Many in my life but I was going to kill him,' Cashman says. 'He was a Svengali, the bastard.'

Lyndie and the family were sickened and outraged. Lyndie found she was pregnant and terminated it immediately. She and her father gave evidence against the man and in doing so formed a bond with his victim.

Vicky, aka Mary, had escaped from the Children of God cult in Kabul and made her way to London. 'I was ten years overseas, with Britain as my base,' she says. 'I went to Spain and in Barcelona I met Raphael Lopez, who had cleared out from military training. I stayed there with him and stayed when he went back to the military and did the training, and the detention for absconding. Then we went to Britain and we got married in England.

'When we came back to Australia we stayed in a tent in Mum and Dad's yard at Saratoga. Then we moved to a caravan park, then got a mortgage. I went back to school and had to start from scratch. I'd never *seen* an essay, let alone written one. I started in the open plan and went on to get my degree in nursing about five years ago. Raphael and I divorced; we never really had much in common — when we first met we could only communicate through a dictionary — and I now have a relationship with a very nice man.

'When I was young, Dad was really screwed up. Drinking, mostly beer, but attempting suicide regularly by taking sleeping pills. Once when I was about twelve I came home and he had taken pills and was going to die. He gave me his watch. I'd never had a watch before and I was thrilled. Then Julie came home and called the ambulance. I remember I cried because I'd have to give the watch back.

'He always had another get-rich-quick scheme. At one stage he and my uncle went up north hunting crocodiles; that was going to make their fortune. Then he was a security man in the area and then he worked on the trawlers and as a garbo and a nightman. He did everything. But we were always moving and he was always clearing out. ·

'Dad talked about the war; he lived the war. It never ended. When he shouted at Mum, he often didn't know it was her; he thought he was back in the war and it was the enemy. He became a different person. I couldn't communicate with him. There were only two times when he seemed proud of me. Once I got 99 per cent for a maths exam. The other time I bent a bone in my arm and it was very painful. When the doctor looked at it he said I was a very brave girl.

'I don't think he remembers most of the things he did at that time. Dad had a lot of trouble with his father. In his eyes he could never do anything right. People do the best with what they've got. We can't blame our parents for everything.'

But now the transformation was complete — the Cashmans were on the side of the law. Even Julie, still serving out her time, was running classes designed to help her fellow inmates go straight when released.

CHAPTER 18

Above the morning mist

One terrible repercussion of the war remained, the one that had plagued Ron Cashman almost from the day he set foot on Australian soil again — it was the nightmare of the rising mist. It came to him at all hours, that vision of the morning cloud in the Korean valleys rising ominously towards the mountaintop.

Within that mist were all the fears of a violent childhood, all the terror of war, all the rage and guilt of killing or being killed, all the frustration of finding no release except in screams and blows to himself and to the woman he loved. The chain reaction it set off had many times sent him back to Greenslopes and other institutions that offered brief remission. But no cure.

'I had dealt with a lot of shrinks at Veterans Affairs over the years,' he says. 'They all had suede jackets with leather elbow patches, and they were all collecting their money under false pretences.'

He had virtually given up hope of ever getting well when he met Dr Peter Manzie, a former army doctor turned psychiatrist who specialised in hypnosis. Manzie had retired to Wyong, NSW, but agreed to treat Cashman as a private patient. 'I was very lucky to run into Peter Manzie,' he says. 'He was absolutely incredible. He dug me out of the pit. He delved into me as best he could by question and answer and then he decided I might be worth a shot at hypnosis, and as it turned out I was quite receptive to this type of treatment.

'He asked me to visualise the most beautiful place I had ever seen. As it happened, it was on the top of a mountain in the autumn in Korea. It was dawn and the valley was just one giant white ocean of thick, heavy fog and the only thing showing through were the peaks of the mountains. It looked absolutely incredible. I was fascinated. As the sun rose, rays of sunlight shot across the top of this white ocean and started to warm it. The mist slowly lifted. Dr Manzie took me up there under hypnosis and got me to walk down the side of the mountain. But I only got a certain part of the way before I went into a hell of a panic. Apparently I was aware in my subconscious mind that there were Chinese down there and I was walking into serious danger. He had to whip me back up to the top. But it had given him something to work on.'

Over the next three months Manzie hypnotised Cashman many times. He took him back to that mountain top, stilled his terrible fears and showed him, step by step, how to use the mist and make it work for him, to take away the anger and let it drift into the ether. Then he told Cashman to pack all his troubles into his knapsack and, when he was ready, to throw it over the mountainside and watch it disappear.

Cashman did as he was told. It was a revelation. All his fears, and the anger and guilt that accompanied them, seemed to vanish like the rising mist. And with it came an emotional stability he had never known before. 'Peter Manzie trained me to hypnotise myself at home and do this exercise whenever I was stressed,' Cashman says. 'Forty years late, my life changed completely. I started to live an almost normal life. We had all come home nervous wrecks. Several of B Company, including our platoon commander Polish George Zwolanski, committed suicide. I tried to kill myself several times, but thank God I failed.'

Many years later during an appeals process to get a war pension, Cashman received a thick sheaf of paper under the Freedom of Information Act, which included the psychiatrist's report of his interview for the Vietnam posting in 1965. The army's uncompromising medical view was contained in a minute paper prepared for the Acting Minister for the Army, Fred Chaney, by Colonel A. J. Affleck, director of psychology, AHQ. Today it reads more like a moral judgment:

> Cashman's earlier service was terminated in an unsatisfactory way when he found himself employed in a position that did not meet his personal idea of suitable employment. His subsequent life history has shown considerable evidence of poor adjustment and an inability to build a satisfying life as a civilian. His purpose in seeking re-enlistment is to

serve in Vietnam and he has stated that if frustrated in this regard he would once again make a nuisance of himself until someone weakened and let him go to Vietnam. It is the opinion of the examining psychologist, supported by the examining medical officer, that re-enlistment is a regressive attempt to cope with life that is most unlikely to work out. It is also felt that his slim chance of adjusting would depend on his immediate posting to active service but that eventually the Army would have to return him to the scenes of his earlier delinquency. Under these circumstances he would be likely to return to his earlier modes of behaviour or develop the psychosomatic symptoms that have plagued him since his discharge.

After a monumental struggle with the authorities Cashman's 'earlier modes of behaviour' and his 'psychosomatic symptoms' were finally recognised as full-blown combat neurosis. He was granted a Totally and Permanently Incapacitated pension, which gave him a measure of financial independence and, coupled with the tools of recovery provided by Peter Manzie, completely revolutionised his life.

He was living at Saratoga in May 1989 when he heard that his widowed father had suffered a heart attack and was in hospital at Maryborough, Victoria. 'He was a tough old bastard right to the end,' Cashman says. 'He was staying at the local caravan park and had the attack in the early hours of the morning. He managed to get outside and into his car but couldn't drive. So he stayed there and suffered until someone found him when it was daylight. When asked why he hadn't blown the horn to attract attention, he said, "I didn't want to disturb anyone at that hour".'

Cashman was called to his father's bedside. Seeing the old man's frailty and knowing he was close to death, he made his peace with him, but it was difficult to forgive the years of physical abuse he and his mother had suffered. Michael Cashman died a few days later without ever saying he was sorry.

Cashman travelled with Lyndie back to Korea and to China, where he found fellowship and honour among his former allies and enemies. He was reunited with Lee Min Bang and discovered a true friend who had been through a similar journey to hell and back.

'I tracked down Lee and Kim again after many years of trying,' Cashman says. 'I had gone through the Korean military attaché in Canberra, through the Korean veterans' organisation in Seoul, through Korean vets living in Sydney, all to no avail.' He then contacted a public relations officer at the United Nations cemetery in Pusan who placed a story about Cashman's search for Lee and Kim with the Korean media. One of the newspapers traced their whereabouts, and their reunion was widely covered in the press. 'We wrote a few letters back and forth and I learned that Lee's grandnephew and niece lived at Strathfield, just ten minutes from my house in Homebush. I invited them and their visiting parents to a veterans' barbecue. After that we got the chance to meet up at Suwon when my revisit group stayed overnight. I had a marvellous time with them and their families. I only found out when we met at Suwon that Lee is two years older than me. I thought he was "the kid" at the time.'

Lee says: 'I never have ceased thinking about Ron Cashman. Whenever I heard the word "Australia", my thoughts immediately went to him.'

Kim felt the same way. 'I received a phone call from the manager of the national cemetery in Pusan,' he says. 'I asked him why he was looking for me and he said that Ron Cashman from Australia was looking for me. I hadn't forgotten the name "Ron Cashman". For the last fifty years that name had been in my head.'

Despite the Army's censure of his 'poor adjustment and an inability to build a satisfying life as a civilian', here was positive proof of his worth as a human being. No one could take that away from him.

In 2003 Cashman travelled back to Korea with the documentary film-makers Alice Ford and Peter Talbot and recorded a remarkable series of interviews with Lee and Kim.

He had tutored himself in computers and collaborated with an American mate to set up a Korean War website. He sponsored a young Chinese woman, Zhu Sha, whom he met as a guide during one of his trips to Beijing and who subsequently boarded with him and Betty until she found her feet in Australia. Now settled in Sydney, she and her husband are part of a web of respected friends who make his world a positive place.

Julie died of a liver complaint in 2003, and Michelle suffers from epilepsy. The other girls have made good lives for themselves.

'We had some tough times as kids,' Mary says. 'It was no picnic for any of us, and Dad went through a special hell. But now I have a good life. Things are better with Dad now, though we still don't really speak. He gave me a car. I always recognised that he had a good intellect and there was a strength of character that I admire.'

Lyndie lived with her partner, Mick Fotheringham, in a house they built for themselves — complete with swimming pool — in the hills outside Cessnock. She worked in the nearby mining industry. She grew close to her father. 'He was pretty violent and wild but he never touched us kids,' she says.

'It's no fairyland,' Cashman says of his life now, 'but it's so much better than it was.' And he still has Betty's love, the thing that matters most to him in the world. 'We can't bear to be apart,' she says.

John Kennedy, now living in retirement in Canberra, says of the man who got him back to safety that terrible night in June 1953: 'Ron Cashman is an amazing bloke. More things have happened to him than anyone I know. He's had some amazing experiences, and Betty is such a wonderful person. The best thing he ever did was marrying her. I didn't see him for about forty years after the war, and when I did we got together quite a bit and he stayed with me in Canberra. But we didn't talk about The Mound.'

Cashman was also reunited with Bob 'Doc' Simpson, who had been a member of his section of 6 Platoon and had gone on many patrols with him in the latter stages of the war. When it was over, Simpson says, he was 'very restless' and couldn't settle down, so he travelled to England, Canada and the United States, working it out of his system. Then at twenty-nine, after he met his future wife, he joined the police force. He stayed in uniform until he retired at the age of fifty-seven, never rising above the rank of sergeant second class. As a policeman he never crossed paths with Julie, although he might have met her once or twice before she died. 'I only knew what I read in the papers,' he says.

On a warm Saturday afternoon in 2003 thirty Korean War veterans and their families are gathered in Centenary Park to celebrate the 50th anniversary of the ceasefire that ended their war. Ron Cashman arrives with Betty and his visitors and parks at the entrance near the start of the path that winds through the Kokoda Track Memorial Park towards the barbecue area where Doc Simpson and the others are ensconced.

'Ron carried the Olympic torch along here,' Betty says. 'There was only one other soldier chosen to carry it through the park.' Cashman acknowledged the honour, but it was tinged with irony. 'Kokoda, not Korea,' he said. 'There's no memorial park for Korea.'

When they reach the barbecue area, they shake Doc's hand and move on among old friends, men and women, and old greetings before settling at a table beneath the solid roof. There was a time when they would bring their own food to the barbecue and everyone would stand around, prodding the meat with long forks while sipping their wine and gulping their beer. These days the Korean vets engage a catering firm to set up the fare: boiled rice, boiled potatoes, rice salad, cold beans and half a roast lamb.

On the bench behind the barbecue, at the very edge of the cement floor, are three styrofoam boxes containing ice and cans of soft drink — cola, lemonade and lemon squash. Beside them stand two big cardboard casks of cheap wine. The rule is 'bring your own beer', and some do but, with one or two exceptions, it isn't really a day for drinking. It's a get-together.

After so long you wonder what they have left to say to each other, these old men — average age about seventy-two. But for many of them that 'police action' squeezed between the more celebrated World War II and the much-televised Vietnam conflict, has never really ended. Some still wake at night covered in sweat, reliving the horrors. They still resent the fact that their sacrifice is largely unacknowledged, though they took more casualties man-for-man than in any conflict since World War I.

The huge Concord Repatriation Hospital towers above the entrance to the park above Homebush Bay. In the days after their war ended some Korean veterans suffered there. Cashman says: 'After World War II they went down to the water at night. They couldn't take it any more. They said, "I'm going for a moonlight swim", and they never came back.' Korean vets had followed a well-worn path.

Doc Simpson still goes to the hospital most days as a visitor. 'Some of them did some terrible damage to themselves after they got back — the drinking and all that,' he says. 'I just like to give them a bit of company, listen to what they have to say.'

Cashman moves easily among the veterans and their guests, shaking hands, exchanging banter, until he reaches Olwyn Green. They hug companionably. Olwyn is in her eightieth year but her enthusiasm and dedication to 'the cause' remain undiminished.

Olwyn's happiness had died with Charlie Green that terrible day when he 'bought it' in the freak incident after the Battle of Chongju. 'In a fit of trying to blot out the past, I burned hundreds of letters one mad day in about 1951,' she says. 'Somehow or other it was a replay of a weird scene I had seen as a mere girl — of a man who went off and lit this huge fire and circled around it throwing all his possessions on it. Sometimes we replay such events without any realisation of the possible trigger. I have regretted it ever since. I did keep about six letters, which are in the Australian War Memorial.'

Olwyn met Cashman through the Korean War website and has come to know him well. 'He always presents himself well and is above reproach. He is very natural, very intelligent and intellectually honest. He could have been a good officer,' she says.

One of the men she interviewed for her archive was the amazing Yung Kil Choi, 3RAR's youngest recruit. After the war, she says, he went back to the family house in Seoul and rented a couple of rooms from which he received some income. Later he sold the house to finance his education, which he finished at Yonsei University when he graduated with a Bachelor of Commerce.

Yung Kil found employment with the Korean Iron and Steel Makers Association, where he was in charge of administration, but he yearned to be reunited with his Australian 'family' — the men of 3RAR. He applied to go to Australia to do a postgraduate course, but time passed and this proved impossible. Eventually the Korean ambassador helped him to arrange immigration, and he arrived in Australia in June 1968. Although he was sponsored by the Korea and South East Asia Forces Association of Australia, this was a formality and he paid his own passage and supported himself in Australia. The following year he was made an honorary member of 3RAR at an officers' meeting presided over by Lieutenant Colonel Peter Scott, IO 3RAR Korea and CO 3RAR in Vietnam. In 1989 he was awarded the OAM.

'I've been good mates with him for years in Australia,' Cashman says, 'though we didn't have much to do with each other in Korea. But that's just the luck of the draw.'

When the Korea War started in June 1950, Olwyn Green and Ron Cashman were living at opposite ends of Port Phillip Bay. The war brought their lives together. Both had suffered greatly, but it isn't over yet; there is still more work to do. 'Olwyn has fought tooth and nail to have the Korean War recognised and remembered,' Cashman says, 'not just for Charlie Green but for the thousands of baggy-arsed diggers who served there.'

Cashman has some unfinished business of his own with the army. When his mother died in 1964 she had his Military Medal in her care and his remorseful father had placed it in her coffin. It was buried with her. Cashman's application to the army bureaucrats for a replacement was turned down on the grounds that the medal had been given away. 'Awards may only be replaced when they have been lost,' a letter from the Central Army Records Office informed him in October 1967. 'As the location of this award is known, it is regretted that no action can be taken regarding its replacement.'

Ron Cashman still lives in hope that the army will relent and grant an old digger his last wish.

ENDNOTES

AUTHORS' NOTE

1. All Maurie Pears' quotes are drawn from interviews with the authors.

CHAPTER 1

2. All Ron Cashman's quotes are drawn from interviews with the authors.

3. Another explanation of the Swans' nickname is that many of the club's best players in the 1930s were recruited from Western Australia, home of the Swan River.

CHAPTER 2

4. All Olwyn Green's quotes are drawn from interviews with the authors.

5. MacDonald, C. A. 1990, *Britain and the Korean War*, Blackwell, London.

6. All of Tim Holt's quotes are drawn from an interview with the authors.

7. General Semyon Konstantinovich Timoshenko (1895–1970) joined the Tsarist army in 1915 and during the Russian Revolution took part in the defence of Tsaritsyn. In 1940 he smashed Finnish resistance during the Russo-Finnish War, but he failed to stop the German advance in the Ukraine. After the war he improved the system of training used by the Red Army.

8. Private J. H. 'Hughie' Bridger was killed in the Battle of Chongju on 5 October 1950.

9. All Clem Kealy's quotes are drawn from an interview with the authors.

10. All William Ryan's quotes are drawn from an interview with the authors.

11. Allison, John 1973, *Ambassador from the Prairie*, Houghton Mifflin, Boston, p. 136.

12. Perret, Geoffrey 1996, *Old Soldiers Never Die*, Andre Deutsch, p. 545.

13. MacArthur in conversation with Truman's special envoy, Averell Harriman.

14. Cameron, James 1967, *Point of Departure*, Panther, London.

15. Echelon is a term used by infantry establishments to define the support groups that generally make up a battalion's disposition for a battle engagement. There is no fixed establishment for the echelons; their command and composition is changed to suit the circumstances.

CHAPTER 3

16. Quoted in Peter Dennis and Jeffrey Grey (eds) 2000, *The Korean War: A 50 Year Retrospective*, Australian History Unit, Canberra, p. 87.

17. Quoted in Norman Bartlett 1954, *With the Australians in Korea*, Australian War Memorial, Canberra, p. 31.

18. Korean War Archives, Australian War Memorial, Canberra.

19. All Yung Kil Choi's quotes are drawn from an interview with Olwyn Green, held in the Korean War Archives, Australian War Memorial, Canberra.

20. Quoted in Perrett, op. cit., p. 562.

21. Quoted in Perrett, op. cit., p. 563.

CHAPTER 4

22. Quoted in Max Hastings 1987, *The Korean War*, Pan Books, London.

23. Quoted in Perrett, op. cit., p. 571.

24. Extracted from 3RAR's war diary in author's possession.

25. Farrar-Hockley, General Sir Anthony 1995, *The British Part in the Korean War*, Her Majesty's Stationery Office, London, p. 141.

26. Butler, D., Argent, A. and Shelton, J. 2002, *The Fight Leaders*, Australian Military History Publications, Canberra, p. 105.

27. Farrar-Hockley, op. cit., p. 146.

28. Butler et al., op. cit., p. 111.

29. Ibid., p. 112.

30. Breen, Bob, *The Battle of Kapyong* (Headquarters Training Command), quoted in Maurie Pears and Fred Kirkland (eds) 2002, *Korea Remembered*, Doctrine Wing, Georges Heights, NSW, p. 256.

CHAPTER 5

31. Sir Frank Hassett in conversation with the authors.

32. McGibbon, Ian 1992, *New Zealand and the Korean War*, Oxford University Press, Auckland, p. 210.

33. Dennis, Peter, and Grey, Geoffrey (eds) 2000, *The Korean War: A 50-year Perspective*, Australian History Unit, Canberra.

34. McGibbon, op. cit., p. 211.

35. Butler et al., op. cit.

CHAPTER 7

36. Sir Josiah Francis (1890–1964) enlisted in the 1st AIF in April 1916 and saw service in France in April 1917 as a second lieutenant in 15 Australian Infantry Battalion. He was wounded in the shoulder in March 1918; he was RTV 15 Battalion in September 1918 and was promoted temporary then substantial captain in 1918, before being discharged in September 1919. He was Minister for the Army from 1949 to 1955. Knighted in 1957, he retired from politics in 1961.

CHAPTER 10

37. Quoted by Major General Ron Hughes in Pears and Kirkland (eds), op. cit., p. 194.

38. Ridgway, Matthew B. 1956, *Soldier*, Harper, New York, pp. 219–20.

Chapter 11

39. The term 'police action' had first been used by Senator William Knowland of California. On the Senate floor, Knowland had announced his support for Syngman Rhee: 'The action this government is taking is a police action against a violator of the law of nations and the charter of the United Nations.' No declaration of war would ever be formalised. It would become the precedent for other US-led shooting wars by executive order.

Chapter 12

40. Interview with Lee Min Bang.

Chapter 13

41. All John Kennedy's quotes come from an interview with the authors.

42. Interview with Kim Heung Koo.

Chapter 14

43. Drawn from the battalion's official history.

Chapter 15

44. O'Neill, Robert 1953, *Australia in the Korean War*, Australian War Memorial, Canberra.

Chapter 16

45. Interview with Betty Cashman.

INDEX